Facilitating Treatment Adherence

Facilitating Treatment Adherence

A Practitioner's Guidebook

Donald Meichenbaum
University of Waterloo
Waterloo, Ontario, Canada

and

Dennis C. Turk
University of Pittsburgh School of Medicine
Pittsburgh, Pennsylvania

PLENUM PRESS • NEW YORK AND LONDON

Library of Congress Cataloging in Publication Data

Meichenbaum, Donald.
　Facilitating treatment adherence.

　Bibliography: p.
　Includes index.
　1. Patient compliance. 2. Medical personnel and patient. 3. Sick—Psychology. I.
Turk, Dennis C. II. Title. [DNLM: 1. Patient Compliance. 2. Patient Education. 3.
Physician—Patient Relations. W 85 M499f]
R726.5.M45　1987　　　　　　　　　610′.7′1　　　　　　　　　　87-15397
ISBN 0-306-42638-2

© 1987 Plenum Press, New York
A Division of Plenum Publishing Corporation
233 Spring Street, New York, N.Y. 10013

Printed in the United States of America

Dedication

As clinicians and researchers, we have benefited greatly from the pioneering efforts of many investigators in the area of adherence. We pay homage to them throughout the book by reviewing and quoting their notable contributions. Without their efforts, a book on clinical guidelines could not have been written. To these "pioneers" we dedicate this book. One such person we would especially like to single out and pay personal tribute to is Irving Janis, whose personal friendship, collegiality, and distinguished career have been a model to us both. His work finds a prominent place throughout this book.

Contents

Part II Adherence Enhancement Procedures

Part III Integration of Adherence Procedures and Impediments to Their Use

Prologue

A slow accumulation of piecemeal evidence on treatment adherence can now be systematized in practical terms so health care profesionals can more effectively use it.

I. L. JANIS (1982)

Ever since Hippocrates noted that patients often lie when they say they have taken their medicine, health care providers[1] (HCPs) have been concerned with the issues of patient compliance and nonadherence to treatment. Our interest in adherence enhancement methods stems from our clinical and research experience. Over the past 20 years we have worked with a variety of clinical populations with medical, psychological, and behavioral problems (e.g., pain patients, diabetics, schizophrenics, hyperactive children and their families, smokers). One common problem shared by all of these groups is treatment nonadherence.

The incidence of adherence to therapeutic recommendations varies; however, incidence rates are often as low as 20%

---

[1]The term *health.care provider* (HCP) will be used throughout the text to cover the wide array of personnel who confront the challenge of treatment nonadherence. We will consider populations and techniques that are relevant to many professional groups such as physicians, psychiatrists, psychologists, dentists, public health workers, nurses, social workers, nutritional counselors, diabetes educators, physiotherapists, and the like. Few issues can be thought of as having such wide urgency.

with the more typical rate estimated around 50%. The sheer magnitude of the problem suggests that adherence cannot be expected to occur on its own or because we wish it, and it is too important to leave to chance. Instead of bemoaning the fact that nonadherence is prevalent, we must plan measures to reduce its frequency. The efficacy of all of our efforts with our patients is predicated on the assumption that they follow our proscriptions and prescriptions. Lack of adherence is likely to be a major cause of therapeutic failure, and therefore it interferes with our ability to determine the effectiveness of our treatments.

Most recently, we have been involved in a project for diabetes educators to instruct them in ways by which to increase their patients' adherence to the complex treatment regimen required for people who must live with diabetes mellitus. As a first step in our attempt to help them, we assisted in the surveying of a national sample of physicians to determine ways in which they try to secure adherence to treatment.[2] The results of this survey and the materials that we developed on facilitating treatment adherence for diabetes educators clearly had much broader applications and served as an impetus to the writing of the present volume.

Becker and Rosenstock (1984) have observed that "the number of reviews of the compliance literature now exceeds the number of original studies conducted on this topic; and the number of original studies is considerable" (p. 201). Our goal in writing this book, then, is not to provide yet another review but instead to bridge the gap between what patients are asked to do by HCPs and what patients actually do. Although much of the research on treatment nonadherence lacks both methodological sophistication and a well-validated, integrative theory, there is a vast literature from a number of areas (e.g., social psychology, decision making, behavior modification, medical sociology) that converges on the topic of adherence and has important implications for increasing the likelihood of patients' compliance with therapeutic recommendations.

---

[2]We are grateful to Boehringer-Mannheim Diagnostics, Inc., of Indianapolis, Indiana, for their support and especially to Ms Donna Whipple, Director of Professional Services, for her encouragement and assistance.

Given the centrality of the problem of treatment nonadherence, in this book we decided to undertake the task of providing *practical* clinical guidelines and techniques for HCPs. This is especially important since there is a heightened concern in the health care field with patients who have to live with chronic conditions, resulting in a shift in emphasis from direct medical care to continuous patient self-management. In formulating intervention guidelines we came to appreciate the sheer complexity and innumerable determinants of patient noncompliance. We also realize that different forms of compliance behavior may depend upon quite different processes and factors. In fact, numerous variables may interact differently for diverse illnesses and patient populations. This complexity emphasizes the point that there are not likely to be any quick panaceas. In short, there is no single theoretical formulation or technique, no magical formula to increase treatment adherence, no universally effective solution. Instead, we espouse a multicause, multieffect, and multifaceted approach to treatment nonadherence.

Our goal is to alert HCPs to the factors that are important in understanding the process of adherence, to make them aware of the options available to faciliate adherence, and to describe specific ways in which they can customize the combination of adherence enhancement techniques to meet the particular needs of their patients. In short, our goal is to influence what HCPs say to themselves and how they behave the next time they see one of their patients.

In order to accomplish our purpose, we have organized this volume into three parts. Part I consists of two chapters. In Chapter 1 we will consider what the literature tells us about the incidence and nature of treatment nonadherence and consider the difficulties in assessing adherence. In Chapter 2 we will examine the variety of factors that have been implicated in nonadherence. As there are so many scholarly reviews of this literature,[3] our coverage will be selective. Although we recognize

---

[3]For example, reviews of the treatment adherence literature have been offered by Barofsky, 1977; Blackwell, 1972, 1973; Cohen, 1979; Davidson, 1976; Davis, 1966; DiMatteo and DiNicola, 1982a, 1982b; Dunbar and Agras, 1980; Dunbar and Stunkard, 1979; Friedman and Litt, 1986; Gerber and Nehemkis, 1986; Gillum and Barskey, 1974;

the preliminary (often correlational) nature of much of the evidence on treatment adherence and the need for further research, practical suggestions can be extracted and employed by HCPs even at this early stage of knowledge.

In Part II (Chapter 3–7) we provide an in-depth examination of specific factors and procedures most likely to facilitate adherence. In Chapter 3 we focus on the important role of the relationship between the HCP and the patient. We consider what factors must be incorporated within effective patient education programs in Chapter 4. Chapters 5–7 describe a number of specific techniques that can be used to enhance adherence. Throughout these chapters, examples are offered as to how the procedures have been employed with diverse populations.

Part III begins with an integrated application of the suggestions already covered to facilitate and enhance adherence. Like our patients, we rarely comply with, adhere to, or otherwise follow the advice that we are offered. In Chapter 9 we explore the reasons why the reader may be unlikely to adhere to the guidelines and suggestions that we have presented in the previous chapters. We will examine the variety of explanations (reasons, excuses, rationalizations) readers may give themselves (and each other), for not following the suggestions offered herein. It is proposed that if we can better understand our own instances of nonadherence we can then be more empathic with and of greater help to our patients.

We have taken as our task the description of the current state of knowledge on treatment adherence. We have tried to

---

Hare and Wilcox, 1967; Haynes, Taylor, and Sackett, 1979; Henderson, Hall, and Lipton, 1979; Hussar, 1975; Jay, Litt, and Durant, 1984; Kasl, 1975; Kirscht and Rosenstock, 1979; Marston, 1970; Masek, 1982; Mitchell, 1974; Olson, Zimmerman, and Reyes de la Rocha, 1985; Peck and King, 1982; Porter, 1969; Rapoff and Christophersen, 1982; Sackett and Haynes, 1976; Stimson, 1974; Southam and Dunbar, 1986; Stewart, Cuff, and Leighton, 1972; Stone, 1979; Stuart, 1982; Varni and Babani, 1986; Zisook and Gammon, 1981. See also Sackett and Snow (1979), who have reviewed the results of 537 compliance studies. The publication of the recent *Journal of Compliance in Health Care* (Raymond Ulmer, Editor, Noncompliance Institute of Los Angeles, 1888 Century Park East, Suite 800, Los Angeles, California 90067) further attests to the popularity of the subject.

be as practical as possible and have used summary tables to a great extent in order to condense material into a manageable form as well as to provide a set of what we hope will be useful clinical guidelines. Furthermore, we hope that the availability of these tables will serve as a ready source of review and reminder of the important points covered. It has been our intention to point the reader in the right direction rather than to offer definitive or rigid prescriptions. We encourage readers to pay attention to their own thinking as they examine the material and to relate the information to their own clinical experience. It is our hope and expectation that the material we present will provide direction for further research, improve clinical practice, and contribute to higher rates of adherence.

The Nature of Adherence

I

Treatment Adherence:
Terminology, Incidence, and
Conceptualization

> *In an area where efficacious therapies exist or are being developed at a rapid rate, it is truly discouraging that one-half of patients for whom appropriate therapy is prescribed fail to receive full benefit through inadequate adherence to treatment.*

> R. B. HAYNES (1976)

Few issues in the medical and mental health establishments so unify these fields as does that of noncompliance with treatment. Surveys of health care providers (HCPs) indicate that one of the most distressing features of their clinical practice is that of patient nonadherence (Haynes, 1979a). Whether it is in the form of failure to keep appointments, premature dropping out of treatment, insistence on discharge against medical advice, 'drug defaulting, failure to eschew proscribed behavior, or failure to comply with prescribed treatment regimens, nonadherence to medical or health advice is often viewed as the patient's way of thwarting the best intentions of the HCP and inhibiting treatment efficacy.

Before we consider the magnitude of the problem, we must discuss two terms that we have used interchangeably up to this point: *compliance* and *adherence*. In recent years there has been some discussion of the implications and connotations of these two terms. *Compliance* usually refers to the extent to which patients are obedient and follow the instructions, proscriptions, and prescriptions of HCPs. From this definition, compliance refers to the extent to which the patient's behavior coincides with the HCP's medical or health advice (e.g., in terms of taking medication, following changes in life-style, and engaging in health-protective behavior). A number of authors[4] have argued that the term *compliance* connotes a passive role with the patient faithfully following the advice and directions of the HCP. The term *noncompliance* incorporates an evaluative concept that may imply a negative or prejudicial attitude toward the patient and often presumes that failure to comply is the patient's fault.

In contrast, the term *adherence* is used to imply a more active, voluntary collaborative involvement of the patient in a mutually acceptable course of behavior to produce a desired preventative or therapeutic result. Adherence conveys the implication of choice and mutuality in treatment planning and implementation. Patients who are adherent are viewed as acting on a consensually agreed-upon plan that they may have had a part in designing, or at least as accepting the importance of performing the specific actions. As DiMatteo and DiNicola (1982a) note in their very thoughtful text, the object of care is for the patient to internalize the medical recommendations that he or she has had an active part in formulating. Since our perspective is consistent with the emphasis on active patient participation as an enhancer and facilitator of the performance of appropriate and recommended behavior, we will use the term *adherence* throughout this text.

Adherence covers a variety of diverse behaviors including:

1. Entering into and continuing a treatment program
2. Keeping referral and follow-up appointments

---

[4]Eisenthal, Emery, Lazare, and Udin, 1979; Kasl, 1975; Kristeller and Rodin, 1984; Varni and Wallender, 1984.

3. Correct consumption of prescribed medication
4. Following appropriate life-style changes (e.g., in the areas of diet, exercise, stress management)
5. Correct performance of home-based therapeutic regimens
6. Avoidance of health risk behaviors (e.g., smoking, alcohol, drug abuse)

This list indicates the range of behaviors that are encompassed under treatment adherence. As we shall consider, different factors and interventions may be implicated for adherence to each of these diverse forms of behavior.

A word also about our use of the term *patient*. We will use the term generically and we intend it to include people who are being encouraged to protect and promote their health, as well as those who are actively undergoing treatment or individuals who must live with chronic diseases. It is important to acknowledge that proscriptions to engage in health-protective behavior such as monthly breast self-examinations, elimination of smoking, regular exercise, and so forth are provided to the general public and not just to "patients." We will therefore consider the issue of treatment adherence across the full spectrum, from prevention through acute and chronic care to the need for self-management. But first a word about the seriousness of the problem.

Incidence of Nonadherence

Although the precise level of treatment nonadherence is difficult to determine, most estimates range from a low of 4% to a high of 92%, with the most typical range from 30% to 60% (Masek, 1982). Marston (1970) has reported that the incidence of adherence with prophylactic medication is even lower, with an average of 30 to 35%. As Masek noted, "convincing pregnant women or anemic individuals to take iron supplements, atherosclerotic patients to take cholestyramine, epileptics to take anticonvulsants, alcoholics to take Antabuse, hypertensives to take diuretics, or psychiatric patients to take psychopharmacological drugs, to name a few, has proved to be a difficult task" (p. 528).

From 20% to 50% of patients fail even to appear for scheduled appointments, although the rate of appointment keeping is somewhat higher (75%) when patients initiate the appointments themselves (Sackett & Snow, 1979). When they do appear, 20–60% of patients who are prescribed medication will discontinue their use prior to being instructed to do so, 19–74% will not follow instructions, 25–60% will make errors in self-administration and 35% of such errors are sufficient to endanger the patient's health (Stimson, 1974)! Podell and Gary (1976) have provided a general rule of thumb that one-third of all patients always seem to take their medication as prescribed, one-third sometimes adhere, and the remaining third almost never follow the treatment regimen.

A striking example of the seriousness of treatment non-adherence was offered by Vincent (1971), who studied patients being treated for glaucoma. Those patients were told that "they must use eye drops three times a day or *they would go blind.*" Vincent reported that 58% of the patients did not adhere often enough to produce the desired outcome. When patients were at the point of becoming legally blind in one eye, adherence improved by only 16%, from 42% to 58%! Faberow (1986) has even gone so far as to suggest that in some instances nonadherence should be viewed as indirect self-destructive behavior.

The level of treatment nonadherence varies depending upon the form of treatment, with the highest rates of adherence occurring for treatment with direct medication (injections, chemotherapy), high levels of supervision and monitoring, and acute onset. For example, Taylor, Lichtman, and Wood (1984) reported a rate of 92% for adherence to chemotherapy for cancer patients. In contrast, the lowest adherence rates occur with patients who have chronic disorders, when no immediate discomfort or risk is evident, when life-style changes are required, and when prevention instead of symptom palliation or cure is the desired outcome. For example, nonadherence has been reported to be a highly serious problem for psychiatric patients who live alone (e.g., Boczkowski, Zeichner, & DeSanto, 1985; Cochran, 1984), or for the chronically ill who require long-term treatment but who do not see any immediate beneficial results from adhering to the treatment regimen (e.g., Cummings, Becker, Kirscht, & Levin, 1981; Kirscht, Kirscht, & Rosenstock, 1981).

In surveying the data on nonadherence to taking medication it is important to recognize that these impressive statistics do not reflect a general aversion to health-related activities. As Rosenstock (1985) notes, enormous sums of money are spent on over-the-counter medications and on all types of health-related activities (diets, purchasing medical appliances, etc.). Rosenstock even reminds us of the observation of Sir William Osler who commented, "The desire to take medicine is perhaps the greatest feature which distinguishes man from animals."

> Clearly, the difficulty does not lie in any lack of interest in health matters nor with any public reluctance to attempt cures of illness, but rather in people's unwillingness or inability to adopt those specific regimens prescribed by health professionals. (Rosenstock, 1985, p. 611)

Treatment nonadherence is not limited to medication. Problems of adherence have been noted for performance of protective health behavior such as wearing seat belts, reducing weight, increased exercise, as well as in regard to the performance of homework assignments during behavior therapy and dropping out of psychotherapy prematurely. Relapse following successful interventions for substance abuse (alcohol, illicit drugs, food, cigarettes) has become a major concern (e.g., see Brownell, Marlatt, Lichtenstein, & Wilson, 1986). Jennings and Ball (1982) have reported the same degree of nonadherence (50%) for psychotherapy referrals as that reported for patients who will not take prescribed medication.

As one example of nonadherence in the mental health area, Phillips (1986) has recently reviewed the data on attrition from various forms of psychotherapeutic intervention. He identified a similar negatively accelerating, declining curve across delivery systems (e.g., health maintenance organizations [HMOs], comprehensive mental health centers, private clinics) and across therapeutic orientations (e.g., psychodynamic, behavioral, eclectic). Figure 1 illustrates the losses across sessions extracted from various studies. It dramatically depicts the number of patients applying for treatment followed by the number returning for each subsequent visit to the end of the projected treatment (10, 25, or 100 sessions). If one examines the projected curve for 10 treatment sessions, by the third session 70% of the patients have dropped out of treatment. Although one should not view dropping out of psychotherapy as always being negative, these data underscore the scope of the drop-out phenomenon in psychotherapy (see also Baekeland & Lundwall, 1975).

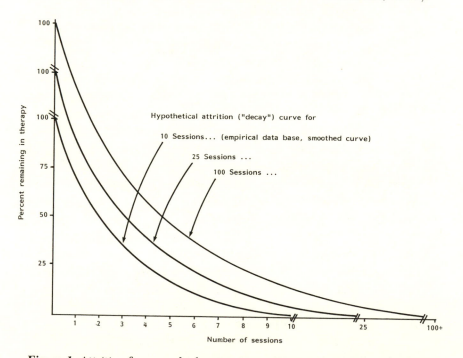

Figure 1. Attrition from psychotherapy. From *Psychotherapy Revisited: New Frontiers in Research and Practice* by E. Lakin Phillips, 1985, p. 415, Fig. 1. Copyright 1985 by Lawrence Erlbaum Associates. Reprinted by permission.

As outlined in Table 1, the scope and magnitude of treatment nonadherence is substantial indeed. Even though there is much agreement and concern about nonadherence, several studies indicate that HCPs systematically overestimate the rate to which their patients adhere to their recommendations (see DiMatteo & DNicola, 1982a). Often HCPs are the last to know about patient nonadherence since patients frequently withold such information and HCPs often use unreliable procedures to assess adherence and avoid or simply fail to ask about it.

Even these high rates of nonadherence may be underestimates since adherence research is based largely on patients who volunteer to participate in such studies. These volunteers may be unrepresentative of the typical patient population because volunteers may be either more committed to the treatment or more compliant in general with requests (Ramsay, 1982).

The reported level of adherence is difficult to ascertain because (a) adherence may be conceptualized in several ways; (b) the criteria for defining adherence may vary; (c) adherence varies widely from one situation to another, depending upon the context; and (d) adherence may be assessed by very different methods, each method with its own inherent problems. To illustrate the problem, we can note that when we suggest that the most typical range of nonadherence is 30–60%, we are including patients who (a) never adhered to any aspect of the recommended regimen, (b) adhered to some but not all of the recommended behavior, (c) initially adhered to the recommendations but after a time relapsed, or (d) performed the recommended behaviors but in an inappropriate manner.

As noted in Table 2, patient nonadherence may take many different forms including both intentional and unintentional behavior. Such treatment nonadherence can lead not only to personal injury but also to recurrent infections, increased patient visits, unnecessary diganostic tests, emergency care, alternative treatments, increased or additional medications, eventual hospitalization, failure to obtain the therapeutic outcome, short-term and long-term degenerative changes, and inability to establish the efficacy of a therapeutic regimen.

Table 1 Data on the Incidence of Nonadherence

It has been estimated that out of the 750 million new prescriptions written each year in the United States and England, there are over *520 million* cases of partial or total nonadherence expected in a *single* year. Annually, between 230 or 250 million prescribed medications will not be taken and a similar number will result in only partial adherence (Buckalew & Sallis, 1986).

Of all patients, 30–40% fail to follow preventative regimens and 20–30% fail to follow curative (relief of symptoms) medication regimes. Moreover, when long-term medication is prescribed 50% fail to adhere (Haynes *et al.*, 1979).

Nonadherence rate for long-time or life-term medication regimens and for lifestyle changes is 50%. The incidence of nonadherence increases over the course of therapy (Haynes *et al.*, 1979).

Fifty to sixty percent of patients fail to keep appointments for preventative programs and 30–40% fail to keep appointments for curative regimens (DiMatteo & DiNicola, 1982a). Approximately 50% of appointments are kept if the provider makes the appointment; 80% are kept if the patient makes the appointment (Dunbar & Agras, 1980).

Among the *elderly* (65+) there is an average adherence rate of 45% (range, 38–57%). The most common form of nonadherence is underuse of prescribed medication, mostly intentional. These results are especially troublesome when we learn that at least 15 million elderly in the United States, or 85% of those who live outside institution, have at least one chronic condition requiring medication. Moreover, although they comprise only 10% of the population in the United States, they receive 25% of all prescription medication, much of which they do not take (Amaral, 1986; Brand & Smith, 1974).

Of *adolescent cancer* patients, 40–60% fail to take prescribed medication as directed (Smith, Rosen, & Trueworthy, 1979; Tebbi *et al.*, 1986).

Nonadherence with *epilespy* drug regimens is between 30% and 40% with the range from 20% to 75% (Conrad, 1985; Penry, 1978).

Only 7% of *diabetic* patients adhere to all steps considered necessary for good control (Cerkoney & Hart, 1980). Of diabetic patients in a study by Watkins, Roberts, Williams, Martin, and Coyle (1967), 80% administered insulin in an unacceptable manner, 73% did not follow their diets, 50% exhibited poor foot care, and 45% did not test urine correctly.

Table 1   (continued)

Aftercare adherence by *schizophrenic* patients:

- Dropout rate is as high as 75%.
- 24–63% schizophrenic of outpatients take less than the prescribed dosage of antipsychotic medication (Van Putten, 1974), and 15–55% of schizophrenic patients do not even take minimal amounts of the neuroleptics prescribed for them (Boczkowski *et al.*, 1985).
- 15–33% psychiatric inpatients take less medication than the amount administered (Van Putten, 1974).
- Failure to adhere to prescribed drug schedule is the most common reason for hospital readmission (Caton, 1984).

Among *bipolar affect disorder* patients, 9% to 57% terminate lithium carbonate medication at some point against medical advice, but this is probably an underestimate of the true extent of the problem (Cochran, 1986).

In *pediatric* populations nonadherence by parents to medication regimens prescribed for their children is 50% with range from 34–82% (Olson *et al.*, 1985).

Among parents of *hyperactive* children only only one-fourth adhere to prescribed stimulant medication (Brown, Borden, & Clingerman, 1985).

- 20% of parents discontinue stimulant medication by fourth month, 50% by tenth month. Only 10% sought consultation prior to terminating treatment (Firestone, 1982).

Up to one-half of parents discontinue behavior modification procedures for their children against therapeutic advice (Pelham & Murphy, 1986).

Among *hypertensives* up to 50% of patients fail to follow referral advice, over 50% drop out of care within one year, and only two-thirds of those who remain under care consume enough medication to control blood pressure adequately (Eraker *et al.*, 1984; Vetter, Ramsey, Luscher, Schrey, & Vetter, 1985). One-third of detected cases fail to seek treatment, one-third dropout, and one-third are uncontrolled. This means that 70% of those who are at risk are uncontrolled (Leventhal *et al.*, 1984). When trained in home relaxation only 40% actually adhere to the daily practice regime (Taylor *et al.*, 1983).

Nonadherence with instructional procedures of *childbirth education* ranged from 59% to 94%. Importantly, however, nonadherence did not interfere with the normal delivery process or cause complications (Lindell & Rossi, 1986).

(continued)

Table 1   (continued)

52% of *headache* patients were found to be non-adherent to medication. Also, there is a danger of some headache patients heavily using over-the-counter analgesics which they combine with prescription medication (Packard and O'Connell, 1986).

In *renal dialysis* treatment only 50% (range 5–92%) of patients adhere to the complex treatment regimen of medication, fluid, protein, sodium, potassium restriction and punctuality in returning for treatment (Blackburn, 1977; Finn & Alcorn, 1986; Kaplan De-Nour & Czaczkas, 1974; Nehemkis & Gerber, 1986). Nonadherence in dialysis patients has been called a contributing factor in an increase in suicide rate by 400 percent (Abram, Moore, & Westervelt, 1971).

Attrition for general medical treatments can be as high as 80%, and the drop-out rate from self-help and commercial groups is in the range of 50%–80% (Brownell & Foreyt, 1985; Stunkard, 1975; Wilson & Brownell, 1980).

- 20–80% drop out of various life-style change programs designed to treat obesity, smoking, and stress management (Dunbar & Agras, 1980; Turk, Salovey, & Litt., 1985). This attrition rate is even more disheartening when we learn, for instance, that only 33% of current smokers who want to quit are willing to attend formal treatment programs (Stunkard & Mahoney, 1976; Wynder & Hoffman, 1979).
- Among individuals who begin an exercise program, 30% to 70% drop out, with the majority of dropouts and relapses occurring within the initial three months, followed by continued deterioration, and eventual leveling off between 50% and 70% after 12 to 24 months (Dishman, 1982; Martin & Dubbert, 1986; Lee & Owen, 1980; Oldridge, 1979, 1982).
- 49% of postmyocardial infarction patients drop out of exercise programs within the first year (Dunbar & Agras, 1980).

In treatment of *alcoholism* there is a 75% attrition rate from treatment programs (Larkin, 1974). Within the first month of commencing treatment between 28% and 80% of alcoholic patients drop out of treatment (Rees, 1985). Of alcoholics placed on lithium carbonate, 48% are nonadherent within six months (Powell *et al.*, 1986).

In the treatment of *addictive behaviors* such as smoking, heroin, and alcohol, 60% of those successfully treated revert to their prior behavior patterns within 3 months after therapy, increasing to 70% at 6 months, and 75% at 12 months (Hunt & Bespalec, 1974). Relapse rates for addictions are in the range of 50–90%, with relapse rates for various addictions (heroin, smoking, alcoholism) stabilizing within the first three months (Brownell *et al.*, 1986).

Table 1   (continued)

One-third or more of the individuals coming to a clinic and judged to be in need of psychotherapy refused the treatment after it was offered to them (Garfield, 1980). Of patients initially referred for outpatient group therapy, 41% never attended a session and of those who attended 25–57% droppped out prematurely (Klein & Carroll, 1986).

Attrition for patients seen in mental health clinics is 20% to 57% after the first visit, and 31% to 56% of patients attend no more than four sessions (Baekeland & Lundwall, 1975). The dropout rate of patients being treated for posttraumatic stress disorder was 81% (Burstein, 1986).

In terms of prevention, only 16% to 59% of persons use seat belts (Dunbar & Agras, 1980). Two-thirds of Americans do not exercise regularly, and 45% may not exercise at all (Martin & Dubbert, 1986).

Nonadherence rates by health care professionals with advised health care practices range from 12% to 100%, with a median of 80%. The profesionals involved included psychologists, physicians, pharmacists, nurses, and dentists (Ley, 1986).

The simple term *nonadherence* may be too broad. Should patients who fall within each of the categories listed above be viewed and treated in the same way? To illustrate the problem consider the results of studies with diabetic patients. Should the 40% of diabetic patients who admitted that they never intended to comply with the HCP's recommendations be viewed in the same way as the 80% of diabetic patients who administered insulin regularly but in an unhygenic manner and the 77% who tested urine glucose levels inaccurately or interpreted results incorrectly (Davis, 1968; Watkins, Williams, Martin, Hogan, & Anderson, 1967)? What about the patients who augment their treatment by taking more medication than prescribed ("If one pill is good then two should be twice as good?" "Taking two pills will bring about improvement twice as fast as one.") Is the nonadherence of these patients comparable to that of those diabetics who regularly inject insulin but who fail to attend to their diet? It would appear important to examine these different types of

Table 2   Different Forms of Treatment Nonadherence

Drug errors

    Failure to fill the prescription

    Filling the prescription but failing to take the medication or taking only a portion of it

    Not following the frequency or dose instructions of the prescription

    Taking medication not prescribed

Treatment attendance

    Delay in seeking care

    Failure to enter treatment programs

    Not keeping appointments

    Premature termination

Behavioral changes

    Not taking recommended preventive measures

    Incomplete implementation of instructions

    Sabotaging of treatment regimen

    Nonparticipation in prescribed health programs

    Creating one's own treatment regimens to "fill in the gaps" of what one believes one's health care provider is overlooking

    Substituting one's own program for the recommended treatment regimens

---

nonadherence more carefully before recommending the same adherence enhancement strategies for all.

As we shall continually observe, the patient adhering to one aspect of a treatment program often behaves quite differently *vis à vis* other aspects of it. Moreover, adherence should be viewed as a complex, dynamic phenomenon that can change over time. The patient's adherence to one feature of the regimen does not ensure adherence to other features or even to the same feature at a later time. Therefore there is a need to analyze carefully each occasion of the patient's failure to perform the recommended behavior appropriately. In the next chapter we will consider some of the important factors that have been related to nonadherence, but first we must consider how adherence is assessed.

Assessment of Adherence

When it is reported that a substantial number of patients are nonadherent, it is important to ask what are the criteria being used to make this determination. Again, because of the breadth of the topic and the multiple behaviors subsumed under the rubric of adherence, many different measures have been developed and the criteria employed have varied (see Dunbar, 1979; Goldsmith, 1976). This variability is evident not only between different behaviors recommended for different problems but even in studies that have measured adherence with the same health problem (e.g., hypertension, weight control).

In some studies investigators have found that less than 100% adherence was adequate to bring about the desired health effects. For example, Luscher, Vetter, Siegenthaler, and Vetter (1985) reported that 80% adherence to a medication regimen for hypertensives resulted in normalization of blood pressure, whereas 50% or less of adherence proved ineffective. Olson, Zimmerman, and Reyes de la Rocha (1985) reported that children diagnosed as having streptococcal pharyngitis required an adherence rate of only 80% to achieve therapeutic results, whereas children taking oral penicillin as a prophylactic for rheumatic fever required only 33% of the medication to reduce the rate of contracting streptococcus infections. One reasonable way, then, to conceptualize adherence is to adopt the criterion proposed by Gordis (1976): "the point below which the desired preventive or desired therapeutic result is unlikely to be achieved" (p. 52). For instance, if on the basis of a count of the number of pills taken by a patient to control hypertension it is determined that the patient has taken 80% of his medication and if 80% of the medication is required to produce reduction in blood pressure, then this patient would be viewed as being adherent. If, on the other hand, a woman performs breast self-examinations every three months, and if to produce the desired result breast self-examination should be performed monthly, then this woman would be viewed as being nonadherent. Performing the recommended behavior in a maladaptive manner such as augmenting the regimen inappropriately or performing the behavior in an ineffective or unsatisfactory manner would also be viewed as indicants of nonadherence.

One problem with the use of the Gordis (1976) criterion is that it assumes that it is known what percentage of the performance of the recommended behavior is necessary to achieve the desired effect. In an area such as psychotherapy, it is unclear how many sessions are required to produce the desired effect. There are many health-related problems for which there is little agreement as to what level of adherence is required to achieve the desired effect. As a result, HCPs should work toward the most functional adequate level of adherence that provides a therapeutic result rather than the some "ideal" level. As Epstein and Cluss (1982) observe, in most instances the recommended prescribed regimen functionally should act more as a guideline than as a prescription for total action.

A number of different forms of assessment have been used to measure adherence including self-report; behavioral, and physiological, and biochemical techniques; and clinical outcome. Table 3 provides a summary list of some of the alternative measures that have been employed. A number of reviewers (e.g., Caron, 1985; Epstein & Cluss, 1982; Gordis, 1976; Masek, 1982) have noted, however, that each of these measures has its own unique set of problems.

Self-Report

Perhaps the most frequently employed measure used to assess adherence is self-report (e.g., asking the patient directly, did you take your medication, how often did you perform the prescribed behavior). Alternatively, patients may be asked to

Table 3   Means of Measuring Adherence

Interview

Self-report

Self-monitoring

Pill counts of unused tablets

Tallies of refills of medications

Behavioral measures

Clinical rating

Marked-sign techniques (inactive or false markers embedded in treatment package)

Biochemical indicators

Record of broken appointments

Clinical outcome improvement or stability in medical condition or symptoms

---

record the frequency, duration, and number of behaviors performed and to bring in, or send in, the self-monitoring forms. Subjective self-report estimates of adherence have been challenged because they may be inaccurate and are likely to be biased. The patient may want to be viewed positively by the HCP and thus overestimate the performance of specific behaviors and the level of adherence with homework directions (Worthington, 1986). Moreover, the simple act of self-monitoring may serve as a cue and thus alter behavior. As we will note later, self-monitoring may be a powerful adherence enhancement strategy.

There is some evidence that the accuracy of self-report can be increased by informing patients that physiological or pharmacological measures are going to be used for verification (Eraker, Kirscht, & Becker, 1984). An interesting verification procedure recommended by Epstein and Cluss (1982) is the *marked-sign technique*. This technique involves checking on the accuracy of the patient's self-report by embedding an inactive or a false marker into the treatment package. A number of different procedures have been used, such as:

1. Dummy hemoglobin assessment strips to measure glucose levels
2. Placebo Clinitest tablets for testing urine
3. Some flavored pills in medication dispenser
4. Urine discoloration agents added to medication

In each instance, the patient is asked to record how often the hemoglobin strips or Clinitest tablets produced a designated result, when the pills of a different flavor were taken, and when urine discoloration occurred. Since the actual sequence is only known to the HCP and the pharmacist, the number and schedule of correct responses offered by the patient is taken as an indicant of adherence.

Another clever, surreptitious measure of adherence was used with hypertensives to determine how often they used a home practice relaxation tape. A hidden micro-electronic system in the tape recorder indicated the degree of adherence by recording the amount of time the tape had been played (Hoelscher, Lichstein, & Rosenthal, 1986). Taylor, Agras, Schneider, and Allen (1983) found that although 70% of hypertensives reported that they had practiced relaxation daily, the mechanical measure revealed only a 40% adherence rate. Similarly, Hoelscher *et al.* (1984), employing a tape recorder with an embedded mechanical timer, reported an overestimate of 126% for self-reported adherence to home relaxation by anxious patients. Martin, Collins, Hillenberg, Zabin, and Katell (1981) have developed a similar marking procedure to assess the degree of adherence to home practice with a tape recorder. The use of such surreptitious measures reveals that self-reports of adherence may be overestimates. There is an obvious need to obtain multiple assessments.

A caveat must be offered about the use of such "detective" techniques as those described above. Although these techniques may be helpful in research to determine the rates of adherence, in clinical practice such forms of "checking up" may be viewed negatively by the patients and thus interfere with the important therapeutic relationship and actually impede adherence. We will discuss the importance of this relationship and the therapeutic alliance in Chapters 2 and 3.

Although there are clear limitations to patient self-report, Dunbar and Agras (1980) and Morisky, Green, and Levine (1986) report that patients can often predict, with a fair degree of accuracy, their likelihood of adherence. For instance, in one recent study, Tebbi *et al.* (1986) reported that levels of serum corticosteroids measured by bioassay "corroborated in every case" self-reports of medication adherence of pediatric and adolescent cancer patients. In Chapter 3 we will examine some recent advances in self-report assessment.

Behavioral Measures

The most commonly employed behavioral measures of adherence include tablet or bottle counts, noting percentage of medication taken, observation of behavioral performance, and records of keeping appointments. When medication use is being employed as a measure of adherence, patients may be provided with an oversupply of their medication and are asked to return the unused portions at periodic intervals. The quantity returned is subtracted from the recommended dosage to determine the degree of adherence. This procedure assumes that the absent medication was ingested. The patient who desires to make a good impression but who does not like the side effects of the medication may remove pills from the bottle but throw them in the trash. Thus, like self-report, behavioral measures are also subject to distortion.

Another behavioral strategy is to observe the performance of specific self-care behaviors in the presence of the HCP to establish that patients are at least aware of the proper way to perform the behavior (e.g., test blood glucose levels, prepare insulin injection). A potential problem with observational procedures is that they may be cumbersome to employ in the patient's natural environment and the observation of the behaviors (such as insulin injection or urine testing) in the health care setting is artificial and potentially reactive (the patient knows that he or she is being observed). Therefore, what is observed in the clinic may not reflect the performance of the behavior in patients' homes.

The recording of appearance at scheduled appointments as a measure of nonadherence has the disadvantage of not including information as to why appointments were not kept. The failure to appear may occur for a host of different reasons with different implications for the assessment of adherence.

Several investigators have attempted to develop indirect behavioral measures of patient adherence. For example, Mayer and Frederiksen (1986, Mayer 1986), working with women who were taught how to do breast self-examination, monitored adherence by asking them to place a tissue sheet upon their chest in order to absorb the excess oil immediately after palpating the breast. This tissue was then signed, dated, and mailed to the educators, indicating the degree of adherence. For each population, clinicians must be creative in designing behavioral indices to supplement self-report measures.

Biochemical Measures

Biochemical markers are useful in measuring adherence because they are less subject to bias than self-reports and pill counts. Chemical tracers incorporated into medication are not discernible to patients but are readily detected by chemical assay in urine or blood. Some markers that have been used include Phenol red, riboflavin, sodium bromide, ketogenic steroids, and atrophine. An alternative biochemical procedure involves bioassay of medication or its metabolites in urine or blood (i.e., biochemical byproducts of a drug or diet).

Unfortunately, not every drug can be readily detected in blood or urine and some biochemical assays are quite difficult and costly. Additionally, such tests would have to be administered frequently in order to be sensitive to deviations in medication. Biochemical assays also may be misleading if they are not taken on a regular basis for the patient may ingest medication prior to testing and thus not provide an accurate measure of adherence other than at times of testing. Furthermore, interpretation of biochemical markers as indicants of adherence is complicated by potential pharmacokinetic differences between different drugs and different patients. For example, some medications have very rapid rates of degeneration and excretion and some patients may absorb medication poorly from their livers or bowels. And, finally, the feasibility and practicality of using pharmacological markers is often prohibitive in general clincial practice.

Clinical Outcome

One face valid way of assessing treatment adherence is to consider the treatment outcome. That is, if the desired outcome occurs, then it might be assumed that the patient was adherent, and if not, then the patient was nonadherent. However, use of clinical outcome as a measure is based on the assumption that there is a close relationship between the treatment and the desired result. Gordis (1976) has suggested that clinical outcome may actually be an invalid criterion to employ to measure adherence. Patients may improve or deteriorate for a number of reasons other than performing or failing to follow the HCP's recommendations. Adherence to the treatment recommendations is but only one of a number of factors that could influence the outcome. Patients who adhere may be less ill or may engage in better health behavior in general. For example, Epstein and Cluss (1982) reviewed several studies that showed that adherence *per se*, whether to a placebo or an active drug, was associated with the best clinical outcome.

Patients may add appropriate behaviors directed toward the target behavior and not adhere to the prescribed regimen, yet still achieve the desired result. A patient who is being recommended a specific diet to lose weight may decide to increase his exercise but continue eating the same number of calories. In this case, the patient may be nonadherent to the diet yet still achieve the desired reduction in weight. Finally, use of therapeutic outcome assumes that the treatment will be effective for all patients with little variability. In reality, some of those who adhere to an effective regimen will not achieve the desired goal. Individual differences in physiology may lead to an undesirable outcome even though the patient is 100% adherent to the regimen, whereas some who are less punctilious may still achieve the desired goal.

Quite simply put, there is no straightforward relationship between treatment adherence and successful health outcome (e.g., see Liddell and his colleagues, 1986). Sometimes, even if patients do everything the HCP recommends, they may still get sick, their condition may deteriorate, or they may fail to get well because the natural history of a disease and the effectiveness of a treatment regimen is uncertain for any individual patient. Moreover, on some occasions, despite poor treatment adherence or the performance of health risk behavior (e.g., smoking), the patient does not become ill or recovers in timely fashion. This may be due to a wrong diagnosis, the natural abatement of symptoms, or genetic, physiological, or environmental factors, the role of which we do not yet understand.

The search for a "gold standard" for adherence measurement is still in progress (Rudd, 1979). The absence of reliable, valid, clinically sensitive indices of adherence is an important problem because it can compromise clinical trials, lead to the ordering of unnecessary diagnostic tests or use of alternative medications, inhibit the identification of reliable determinants, and consequently hinder attempts to establish appropriate treatment regimens. For example, in only 19% of 768 drug effect studies were objective measurements of patient adherence complete, thus potentially contributing to an underestimation or overestimation of the efficacy of drug effects (Soutter & Kennedy, 1974).

The problems of bias and inaccuracy of self-report must be weighed against the relative ease and cost of alternative sources of information (e.g., urine analysis, saliva tests, blood assays). Moreover, self-monitoring may be the only way to determine the performance of certain prescribed behaviors (e.g., frequency of sexual activity, use of assertive behaviors). Because of the many difficulties with each form of measurement, there is some advantage in using several different types of adherence assessment techniques concurrently. Decisions regarding what measures to use will, of course, depend upon the needs and resources available to the HCP. Those who are conducting research on drug efficacy may have to employ more costly procedures, whereas those in clinical practice with certain limitations will rely on the most practical approach given their facilities.

A Cautionary Note for Health Care Providers

An examination of the history of medicine indicates that it is only recently that active useful treatments have become available. As Shapiro (1960) has noted, patients have received such dubious treatments as "purging, puking, poisoning, puncturing, cutting, cupping, bleeding, blistering, shocking, sweating, freezing, heating and leeching." Nonadherence may even have been a way to survive (Hanson, 1986). Given the dubious track record of medical practice through history, it might reflect good judgment on the part of patients not to adhere to some prescribed treatments (Deaton, 1985).

It is also important for HCPs to keep in mind the fact that adherence as a goal must be balanced against other important patient objectives, such as the quality of life, adjustment, and the patient's own efforts to cope with the illness. Moreover, the incidence of iatrogenic effects and the frequency of adverse drug effects is of considerable magnitude (Cluff, 1980). In one study of 817 patients in a general practice, Martys (1979) found that 41% of them certainly or probably had a negative reaction to prescribed medication. Moreover, there is increasing awareness that HCPs are sometimes wrong and that on occasion their instructions are best ignored (Brody, 1980a; Weintraub, 1976). As Chapin (1915) commented on the state of medical care early this century:

> We might not be surprised that people do not believe all we say, and often fail to take us seriously. If their memories were better, they would trust us even less. (p. 502)

Even today, with often overstated and conflicting claims made by HCPs and advertisers, there is a continuing need for what Chapin called "truth in publicity." There remain tremendous gaps in medical knowledge. HCPs need to be reminded of Pickering's (1979) estimate that in about 90% of medical conditions there is no specific remedy or the effectiveness of the treatment is unknown. Such observations had led Sackett (1979a), a major contributor to the literature on adherence, to encourage HCPs to ask themselves the following questions before offering treatment recommendations:

(1) Have I made the correct diagnosis?
(2) Has the preventive or therapeutic regimen I have prescribed been proven to do more good than harm?
(3) Is the patient a free, informed consenting participant in this intervention? (p. 286)

At a minimum, we must aspire to improve adherence only with those treatments or actions for which we have reasonable evidence of efficacy, and we must maintain constant vigilance for any harmful results of our interventions, however well-intentioned. (p. 121)

If the answer to Sackett's three questions is yes, and if the prescribed treatment programs are both relevant and effective, then and only then should we consider the use of the adherence enhancement strategies described herein.

Factors Affecting Adherence

> *Knowledge about determinants of adherence to medical recommendations is slowly beginning to accumulate, but it still remains at a primitive stage of scientific development. Most of the pertinent studies are correlational; they focus on psychological factors that differentiate those who adhere satisfactorily from those who do not. Only a few studies assess the effects of attempting to increase adherence by changing one or another of the factors assumed to be a determinant of adherence.*
>
> I. L. JANIS (1984a)

A great deal of research has been conducted on the determinants of or factors related to adherence. For example, Haynes (1976) in a comprehensive review identified more than 200 variables that have been examined in relation to adherence. The variables examined can be generally categorized as: (a) characteristics of the patient, (b) characteristics of the treatment regimen, (c) features of the disease, (d) the relationship between the health care provider (HCP) and the patient, and (e) the clinical setting. Despite the fact that we will discuss these variables as if they were discrete classes, it will become obvious that they actually overlap substantially and should not be viewed as totally independent.

Although as noted by Janis (1984a) above, most of the findings regarding the association among the variables examined and adherence are correlational and tentative in nature, an appreciation of these results will provide a useful framework to consider the variety and rationale for adherence enhancement procedures that we will discuss in depth in Part II. Table 4 provides a summary of the factors that have been identified. We will select some of what appear to be the most frequently cited[5] and most important ones to examine in detail in the remainder of this chapter.

Patient Variables

Although many HCPs attribute nonadherence to patient characteristics, the search for stable factors that comprise the nonadherent, uncooperative, or chronic defaulter patient has met with little success. Even though no consistent relation with adherence has been found for such variables as age, sex, social class, marital status, or personality traits, 76% of physicians surveyed attributed nonadherence to patient characteristics (Davis, 1966). Such beliefs may contribute to the finding that HCPs are unable accurately to predict the likelihood of an individual patient's adherence to recommendations (Becker & Rosenstock, 1984; Gordis, 1976; Kasl, 1975). In a related set of findings, Stone (1979) reported that a substantial proportion of physicians reported little sympathy with their patients' adherence difficulties, viewing the nonadherent behavior most often as the result of an attitude problem on the part of the patient. This may account for the pessimism and lack of interest of many HCPs in trying to increase rates of adherence. But, as Seltzer and Hoffman (1980) conclude, even the most unmotivated and uncooperative patients are not necessarily the most nonadherent. Every patient is a potential defaulter. In short, nonadherence can be a problem for any population.

---

[5]Epstein and Masek (1978) note that over 193 factors were examined at least 10 times and four of these factors had positive correlations with adherence level in more than half of the studies, namely, race, complexity of treatment, duration of therapy, and the belief in the efficacy of the therapy.

Table 4   Factors Related to Treatment Nonadherence[a]

Patient variables
    Characteristics of individual
    Type and severity of psychiatric diagnosis (in particular, diagnosis of schiz-
        ophrenia, bipolar affective disorder, paranoia, personality disorder)
    Sensory disabilities
    Forgetfulness
    Lack of understanding
    Inappropriate or conflicting health benefits
    Competing sociocultural and ethnic folk concepts of disease and treatment
    Implicit model of illness
    Apathy and pessimism
    Failure to recognize that one is ill or in need of medication
    Previous or present history of nonadherence with other regimens
    Health beliefs (e.g., misconceptions about disorder, no understanding of
        prophylaxis, belief that medicine is necessary only in actue illness)
    Dissatisfaction with practitioner or treatment
    Characteristics of individual's social situation
    Lack of social supports
    Family instability or disharmony
    Parent's expectations and attitudes toward treatment
    Residential instability
    Environment that supports nonadherent behavior
    Competing or conflicting demands or other pressing demands (poverty,
        unemployment)
    Lack of resources (transportation, money, time)
Disease or disorder variables
    Chronic condition with lack of overt symptomatology
    Stability of symptoms
    Disorder-related characteristics (e.g., confusion, visual distortion, psycho-
        logical reactions)
Treatment variables
    Characteristics of treatment setting
    Absence of continuity of care
    Long waiting time
    Long elapsed time between referral and actual appointment (more than 8
        days)
    Timing of referral
    Absence of individual appointment times
    Lack of cohesiveness of treatment delivery system
    Inconvenience associated with operation of clinics (e.g., inefficiency,
        unfriendly personnel)

(continued)

Table 4 (continued)

Treatment variables (*continued*)
    Poor reputation of treatment facility
    Inadequate supervision by professionals

    Characteristics of treatment recommendations
    Complexity of treatment regimen (e.g., multiple medication)
    Long duration of treatment regimen
    Degree of behavioral change (e.g., interferes with personal behavior and
        depends upon alteration of one's life style)
    Inconvenience (e.g., location of clinic, poor transportation)
    Expense

    Characteristics of treatment
    Characteristics of medicine (e.g., color of pill, drug size, preparation form—
        i.e., capsule or tablet)
    Inadequate labels
    Awkward container design
    Failure of parents to supervise drug administration
    Medication side effects or side effects associated with altered behavior (e.g.,
        sedation, extrapyramidal involvement)

Relationship variables: patient–health care provider interaction
    Inadequate communication
    Poor rapport
    Attitudinal and behavioral (verbal and nonverbal) faults on the part of either
        HCP or patient
    Failure of HCP to elicit negative feedback about problems stemming from
        treatment regimen
    Patient's dissatisfaction
    Inadequate supervision

[a]Table based upon literature reviews offered by Buckalew & Sallis, 1986; Caton, 1984; DiMatteo & DiNicola, 1982a; Eraker *et al.*, 1984; Haynes, 1979b; Kasel, 1975; Kirscht & Rosenstock, 1979; Podell, 1975; Shelton & Levy, 1981; Stone, 1979.

This conclusion, however, does not exclude the possibility that under certain very specific treatment conditions patient and sociodemographic variables may indeed be implicated. For instance, consider the following results cited by Kasl (1975):

> In a study of male NASA employees who were followed up after cardiovascular screening, achieving adequate therapeutic control was more often found in older employees in the case of hypertension and in younger employees in the case of hypercholesteremia.

Among individuals trying to stop smoking, a wife's disapproval of smoking increased chances of success for the husband, but women smokers were unaffected by their husbands' disapproval, and disapproval from friends and relatives actually increased their chances of failure.

A study of tuberculosis patients on home medications showed poor compliance among older men and younger women.

Other studies of tuberculosis patients suggest that poor compliance is especially common among those living alone; however, a study of diabetic patients suggested that poor control of the disease was especially common among members of larger households. (pp. 6–7)

Kasl's observations indicate that specific patient variables may be predictive in specific situations and that we should not expect robust findings that apply across all populations and settings. Such findings have often yielded useful profiles that can identify specific high-risk groups of potential nonadherers. For example, Rees (1985) describes a profile of alcoholic patients who are at high risk of dropping out of treatment as being "highly symptomatic, dependent men who are ambivalent about treatment, socially isolated, show little social stability and are from lower socioeconomic groups" (p. 518). Similarly, Martin and Dubbert (1986) have drawn a composite profile of men who tend to drop out of exercise programs as being an "overweight, blue-collar smoker with an inactive job and few leisure pursuits, with low self-motivation and a spouse who is indifferent towards his exercise participation, who lives or works farther away from the exercise facility and who exercises infrequently, alone and at high intensity" (p. 22). It is worth noting, however, that the factors that influence a person's decision to attempt an exercise regimen, that determine ongoing participation in the exercise program, and that may affect the patient's decision to continue exercise after the completion of the training program may each be quite different (see Fontana, Kerns, Rosenberg, Marcus, & Colonese, 1986).

Although specific patient variables have not proved helpful in predicting adherence, recent attempts to develop profiles combining patient, treatment, and social variables may hold greater promise. For example, consider the advice offered by Gillum and Barsky (1974):

> The doctor's index of suspicion should be raised by any patient who does not regard his medical problem as serious, who will admit if questioned that he has doubts about his ability to comply, and who appears hostile, demanding, aggressive, and overly self-sufficient. Likewise, patients with many other important demands on their time, attention, and finances, and those with poor social support at home should raise the physician's index of suspicion. Any patient on a complex regimen, or one that requires much change of basic life-style or habits, is a likely noncomplier, as is any patient with whom the physician feels his communication or relationship is ambiguous, fettered, or constrained. (p. 1565)

There are, however, two exceptions to the generally negative picture of predicting adherence on the basis of specific patient variables, and these arise from research on patient satisfaction and patient beliefs. A more robust relationship has emerged between the degree of *patient satisfaction* with both the HCP and the treatment regimen and the level of adherence. Dissatisfied patients are more likely to reject recommended actions, miss appointments, turn to nonmedical healers, and sue for malpractice (Whitcher-Alagna, 1983). Satisfaction is closely related to the degree to which the patient's beliefs and expectations have been met. In Chapter 3 we will consider how patient satisfaction can be assessed.

Role of the Patient's Beliefs

Patients hold many beliefs about their health and about the potential efficacy of any proposed treatment action. Sometimes the patient's beliefs are based on misconceptions, faulty information, negative distortions, and cultural myths, as described in Table 5. In addition, patient feelings of fear, guilt, fatalism, shame, and "paralysis of will" can also contribute to treatment nonadherence. These beliefs and feelings may be shared by significant others in the patient's life. It is important to keep in

Table 5 *Illustrative Patient Beliefs That Can Undermine Adherence*[a]

"You only take medicine when you are ill and not when you feel better."

"You need to give your body some rest from medicine once in a while or otherwise your body becomes too dependent on it or immune to it."

"The medicine is so powerful that it should only be used for brief periods of time."

"If you take medicines too often you may become immune to them and when you really need them, they won't work any more."

"When I take medicine I feel like a pill-popper. I will become dependent on the medication."

"When my child's symptoms go away I can stop using the medicine."

"I don't feel the drug is doing anything."

"I resent being controlled by drugs."

"They may be trying to poison me."

"I don't see any use in prophylaxis."

"God will take care of my illness."

"My depression is just biological; there is nothing I can do."

"I miss the highs of my hypomanic life-style."

"My spouse won't like me if I only have 'normal' feelings."

"If I write down what I think, the therapist will think I am crazy and commit me."

"My pain must have an organic cause; doing the exercises won't make any difference."

"It couldn't be happening to me; I don't need to do anything special."

"I do too many preventive things to be susceptible to the illness."

"I want to remain sick."

"How will I know if I still need them if I keep taking pills?"

"What's the use of trying?" "I knew I wouldn't be able to stay in control." "Nothing I do seems to help."

---

[a]Examples offered by Becker & Rosenstock, 1984; Burstein, 1985; Croog, Shapiro, & Levine, 1971; Kasl, 1975; Leventhal *et al.*, 1984; Seltzer *et al.*, 1980; Stimson, 1974; Turk *et al.*, 1983.

mind that the advice offered by HCPs is only one element in
the overall decision to adhere.

But there are instances when the patient's decision not to
adhere to a treatment regimen may reflect a rational and logical
result of an active decision-making process. From the perspective of the HCP, nonadherence may be viewed as arising from
some patient deficiency (i.e., ignorance, laziness, forgetfulness,
willful neglect, or lack of motivation, skill, resources, and social
supports). Instead, a number of authors (Adelman & Taylor,
1986; Conrad, 1985; Deaton, 1985; Gerber & Nehemkis, 1986;
Hayes-Bautista, 1976; Janis, 1984b; Leventhal, Zimmerman, &
Gutmann, 1984; Stimson, 1974; Weintraub, 1984) have argued
that treatment nonadherence may not be invariably maladpative
and in some circumstances (as we noted in the last chapter) may
even be adaptive. Nonadherence may represent the patient's
attempt to gain some control over the illness and the treatment,
whereas in other circumstances the decision not to adhere may
be based on misunderstanding, inadequate information, or an
analysis that the costs of adhering outweigh the potential gains.
A concern, however, about *irrationally motivated* nonadherence
(for example, due to denial of illness) has been voiced by the
American Psychiatric Association. Boehnert and Popkin (1986)
have noted that those in charge of revising the *Diagnostic and
Statistical Manual of Mental Disorders—III* (American Psychiatric Association, 1980) are even considering an additional V-
code diagnostic category of noncompliance.

In almost all instances, patients enter any form of treatment
with certain expectations about their problems and what will
and should take place (Turk & Rudy, in press). They usually
hold an explanatory model about their disorder, its etiology,
course, prognosis, and treatment. Often there are differences in
the explanatory models of illness and health held by patients
and HCPs and this can contribute to nonadherence. According
to Leventhal *et al.* (1984), patients' representations of illness
includes their beliefs about the cause of the illness, expectations
about its duration and course (acute, chronic, cyclical), beliefs
about its consequences, and potential responsiveness to treatment. Even serious, life-threatening disorders do not insure

adherence if the patient does not share this perception and the accompanying intention, ability, and perceived benefit for adherence behavior.

For example, Leventhal and Nerenz (1983) reported that hypertensive patients' beliefs that they could subjectively determine their own blood pressure influenced how they used their medication. Some patients reported that they took their medication only when they knew their blood pressure was high and their estimates of when blood pressure was high were based on the symptoms they experienced (e.g., headache or stress). These statements are particularly important when we consider that hypertension is an asymptomatic disease!

Recently, Turk, Rudy, and Salovey (1986) have reported that in addition to the characteristics identified by Leventhal, people's implicit models of illness also include information about their responsibility for the cause and cure of an illness. These implicit models or illness representations are also likely to have an important impact on adherence. This role of explanatory models is not only relevant to adult patients but also applies to children and adolescents. For instance, Adelman and Taylor (1986) have commented on the role of children's beliefs in contributing to their reluctance regarding treatment. Rather than viewing children's negative attitudes and reactions toward treatment as stemming from patient deficits and deficiencies, one may view the children's nonadherence as representing:

1. A response to the negative features of therapy as too demanding, threatening, not worthwhile ("He asks too many questions." "I feel pressured." "It caused more problems." "It's not helpful ")
2. A self-perception of not having any problems ("I don't need it." "I don't have anything I need to talk about." "I don't have any problems.")
3. The perception of not having a choice about whether to seek treatment ("I had to come or I would have got into trouble." "I didn't feel I had any choice.")

Patients often use their symptoms as barometers to determine when they should discontinue medication. Consider the case of patients taking antibiotic medication for an infection. If the infection is widespread and progressive, large numbers of microorganisms will be killed and the patient will feel better within a brief period. Even though the physician may have prescribed 10 days of treatment, the patient may discontinue taking the antibiotics after three or four days because there are no longer any symptoms. Unknown to the patient, the more virulent bacteria which survive the first couple of days of treatment may start to multiply and eventually cause a full relapse. The initial relief of symptoms may be incorrectly interpreted as a signal that the drug treatment has been successful in eliminating the infection, leading the patient to discontinue the medication. In this case, the patient is basing the decision to discontinue the medication on the mistaken assumption that the degree of improvement in symptoms strongly covaries with degree of recovery (Sharpe & Mikeal, 1975).

Patients often view HCPs as engaging in trial-and-error behavior wherein the quantity and frequency of medication prescribed reflects the extent or seriousness of the disorder. Similarly, patients may take themselves off medication or off a treatment regimen in order to evaluate their progress and the course of their disorder. Consider the following report of an individual who had epilepsy:

> I was having one or two seizures a year on phenobarb . . . so I decided not to take it and to see what would happen . . . so I stopped it and I watched and it seemed that I had the same amount of seizures with it as without it. (Conrad, 1985, p. 34)

In this instance, the decision not to take medication reflected the patient's feelings that nonadherence was the only way to regain a measure of control and to evaluate the efficacy of the medication ("I want to see how long I can go without medication." "I am going to stop taking my medicine to see if I am getting any better or any worse."). Thus, patients may discontinue treatment and stop taking medication as a personal experiment, as a means of determining their own normality, or to evaluate their progress in attaining various goals (Leventhal *et al.*, 1984). Such decisions may arise from the desire of some patients to be active agents who play some part in deciding their own treatment goals and plans (e.g., see Trostle, Hauser, & Susser, 1983).

If one adopts a patient's perspective, then the decision not to adhere may make more sense, even though it may lead to complications. As noted in Table 6, the patients' decisions not to adhere may arise for a variety of reasons.

A factor that is often overlooked in understanding treatment nonadherence is how patients perceive their medication. Buckalew and Sallis (1986) report that a medication's visible properties may have important and specific meaning for patients that may support or detract from adherence. The size, form (pills or tablets), and color of medication have differential effects on outcome and adherence. For instance, capsule colors often elicit expectations of particular drug action (e.g., it has been found that symptoms of anxiety show most improvement when green tablets are used, whereas depressive symptoms respond best to yellow tablets; blue tablets are associated with a depressant tranquilizer

Table 6   Reasons Why Patients May Decide Not to Adhere

Uncertainty about the efficacy of the treatment
Prior experience with illness and changes in patient's health
Expectations about symptoms, illness, health care providers, and treatment
Past experiences with health care providers
Concerns about possible side effects and recognition of possible iatrogenic problems
Determination that the inconvenience (effort, expense, side effects) outweighs potential benefits
Embarrassment about being in treatment (i.e., social stigma that may accompany treatment)
Pessimism or skepticism about the effectiveness of treatment
Desire to maintain control over some domains of life
Impatience with the level of progress or the treatment process
Competing environmental demands that are more salient
Sense of fatalism or paralysis of will
Experience of others with the treatment
View of adherence as interfering with life-long belief system, future plans, family relationship patterns, social roles, self-concept, emotional equilibrium, or daily life patterns

effect, and red and yellow tablets are related to stimulant, anti-depressant effects; white tablets are perceived as neutral; see Buckalew & Coffield, 1982, and Buckalew & Sallis, 1986). More-over, capsules are viewed as significantly stronger than pills and larger preparations are equated with greater strength. Buckalew and Sallis note, however, that such perceptions may vary across race and gender. The implication of these findings is the need to include a consideration of appearance in any consideration of treatment planning since clearly medications may have more than pharmacological impact. How patients view their medication and the treatment regimen has important implications for adherence.

Regardless of the source of beliefs contributing to non-adherence, there is a critical need for the HCP to give patients the opportunity to express their point of view—goals, nature of the problem, and how they feel they should be treated. Only when the HCP has this information can he or she decide how best to intervene to increase the likelihood that the patient will adhere to the treatment regimen.

General concerns about the role of patient beliefs have given rise to a specific health belief model of treatment adherence (see Becker, 1974; Becker & Maiman, 1975, 1980; Kirscht & Rosenstock, 1979; Rosenstock, 1974; Rosenstock & Kirscht, 1979). The model was originally proposed to explain the impact of beliefs and attitudes concerning protective health behavior such as obtaining immunizations and chest x-rays. More recently, the model has been extended to the more general class of adherence behavior. The original model proposed that individuals' adherence behaviors would be determined by (1) their belief that they are *susceptible* or vulnerable to a disease or to its consequences, or that they actually have that disease now; (2) their belief that the disease itself or its consequences could have a *serious* negative impact on their lives; (3) their belief that following a particular set of health recommendations will be *beneficial* or effective in reducing the threat or severity of the condition; and (4) their belief that the psychological *costs* or *barriers* associated with following the health recommendation are outweighed by its benefits (Rosenstock, 1985).

On the basis of the Health Belief Model, patients who perceive themselves as less vulnerable to future complications or who perceive such consequences as minimally disruptive are less likely to perform behaviors designed to avoid them. Moreover, the patients must believe that the benefits of taking health actions outweigh the costs or they will not be performed. For example, Turk, Salovey, and Litt (1985) reported that some women indicated that the reason they did not regularly perform breast self-examinations was the lack of an explicit criterion of what is normal together with the high number of false positives and the accompanying anxiety. In this case, the cost was emotional. Thus, when considering barriers to adherence the HCP should consider not only physical and financial barriers but also the meaning of the prescribed behavior for the patient as well as the impact of adherence within the context of the patient's life.

The research on the health belief model, however, has yielded only modest positive correlations among patients' perceptions, beliefs, and behavior (Taylor, 1979). More recent refinements of the model (Becker & Rosenstock, 1984; Rosenstock, 1985) have implicated the role of several additional variables of importance in addition to those incorporated within the original model. These include:

1. General health motivation (e.g., concern for health)
2. Evaluation of practitioner and medication care
3. HCP–patient relationship
4. Perceived susceptibility to recurrence of the illness
5. Structure of medication regimen
6. Cues (or reminders) to action and cues reinforcing the threat of the illness
7. Belief in one's personal self-efficacy, that is, the conviction that one is capable of carrying out the health recommendation

Although it is acknowledged that patients' beliefs and expectations are important, they are not sufficient to predict adherence behavior in all cases. As DiMatteo and DiNicola (1982a) note, the relationship between health beliefs assessed at the beginning of a course of treatment and subsequent adherence is limited, but there is more evidence for a relationship between health beliefs and concurrent adherence behavior.

Viewing nonadherence as an active decisional process leads to consideration of the desire of a patient to exercise a degree of control and to engage in a shared collaboration with the HCP. Whether it is a physican prescribing medication, or a diabetes educator discussing a demanding treatment regimen of diet, exercise, and insulin monitoring, or a psychologist encouraging the performance of various stress-management procedures, there is an increasing need to reconsider the nature of the relationship between patient and HCP. Rather than the HCP's assuming the role of the "expert" who dispenses information and recommendations, increased levels of adherence may be dependent upon *a more collaborative working relationship*. An obvious implication of these findings is that it will be valuable for HCPs to assess the patient's perceptions, beliefs, and expectations concerning the disorder and its treatment. We will return to this point later in this chapter and in Chapter 3.

The need to consider the patient's perspective is most clearly evident when we consider patients who must adhere to a demanding treatment regimen accompanying a chronic illness. For instance, Nehemkis and Gerber (1986) sympathetically describe the plight of the hemodialysis patient and the concomitant impact of the renal disease process on adherence. Becoming a dialysis patient involves being suddenly removed from the ordinary context of life. Because of the dependence on the dialysis machine for survival, all spheres of the dialysis patient's life are affected: body image, diet, travel, family and vocational relationships. Even though the patient knows that dialysis is imperfect and fraught with medical and technical complications, the patient is required to adhere to a demanding treatment regimen. The patient is asked to exercise extreme self-discipline, but with no possibility of the medical condition's improving and often with the knowledge that neither adherence nor nonadherence to the prescribed regimen offers a certain outcome. A somewhat similar picture can be offered for other chronic illnesses (arthritis, epilepsy, diabetes). Many renal failure patients experience an understandable ambivalence toward living on dialysis and non-adherence may be one way of attempting to continue living a normal life. In understanding and treating nonadherence there is a need to understand the patient's perspective (beliefs, feelings, and values) and to recognize that all aspects of the perspective will change over time (e.g., see Christensen-Szalanski & Northcraft, 1985).

Treatment Variables

An examination of the list of variables in Table 4 indicates that features of the therapeutic regimen play a significant role in influencing adherence. Kasl (1975) has suggested that knowing the characteristics of the treatment regimen (e.g., complexity, duration, side effects) can often tell us more about the likelihood of adherence than do the characteristics of the patient.

Complexity of the Therapeutic Regimen

Perhaps the statement that can be made with the most confidence in the area of adherence is that the more complex the demands of the treatment, the poorer the rates of adherence. For example, in one study (Higbee, Dukes, & Bosso, 1982), the ability of patients to recall even simple information about a single prescription medication regimen was quite low. In this study, following a clinic visit during which a medication was prescribed, patients were asked to respond to seven questions about the medication, namely, the name of the drug prescribed, purpose of the drug, route of administration, frequency of dose, when to take the medication, proper dose, and duration of treatment. Patients were able to recall correctly less than 50% of this information correctly. It is quite easy to imagine what would be the correct rate of response if two different medications with different doses, frequency, and so forth, were prescribed during the same clinic visit. Stone (1979) considered this point and reported that when patients were asked to take one drug the error rate or nonadherence rate was 15%. This increases to 25% when patients are asked to take two or three medications and to 35% if more than five drugs are prescribed. Similarly, it has been found that it is the number of times per day that medication is prescribed rather than the number of pills *per se* that is most often related to the level of nonadherence (Malahey, 1966).

Part of the failure in adherence may be associated with confusion regarding what the patient is specifically supposed to do in response to the treatment demands. Svarstad (1976) has reported that three out of four times physicians fail to give patients explicit instructions about how regularly or how often medications should be taken. Zola (1981) has offered some examples of the types of confusion that may arise when a patient must operationalize the HCP's instructions at home:

- "Take the drug 4 times a day." Does this mean taking it every 6 hours? That is, must the patient wake up in the middle of the night? What if the patient forgets; should he or she take twice the dose when he or she remembers?
- "Keep your leg elevated most of the day." How high is elevated? Is it important that it be elevated above the waist? How long is "most" of the day? What about when the patient is asleep?
- "Take frequent baths." Is once a day frequent or should baths be taken 4 times a day?
- "Only use these pills if you can't stand the pain." What does "can't stand" mean? How long should the patient wait? If the patient takes the pill does that mean he or she is a weak person?
- "Come back if there are any complications." What is a complication? What sensations are related to the disease and what to the treatment? Should the patient feel guilty if he or she develops a complication? Is it something they did or failed to do that caused the complication? What does the complication signify? (pp. 247–248).

If we extrapolate from the potential confusion related to simple recommendation of a single medication to treatment regimens requiring multiple behavioral changes such as the self-care regimen for diabetes, then the low adherence rates are not too difficult to comprehend. Consider what is entailed in the self-care regimen for a Type I, insulin-dependent diabetic (Turk & Speers, 1984). The patient must make multiple independent therapeutic decisions based on assessment of urine or blood glucose levels. These self-monitoring strategies require a complex set of skills. Insulin must be injected several times a day. Insulin dosage may not be standard because diet, exercise, physical health, and emotional factors influence metabolic control and must be taken into consideration by the diabetic when making decisions regarding insulin adjustment. Appropriate skills related to injection are required including decisions related to quantity, location, skin preparation, preparation of the injection, rotation of the injection sites, and the actual injection. In addition to injection of insulin, diabetics must constantly attend to their glucose metabolism as related to their diet by carefully weighing and balancing food groups and spacing food intake. They must remain alert for subjective signs of hyperglycemia and hypoglycemia as assessed by means of multiple blood and urine glucose tests. They must carefully attend to any minor injuries because these can readily become infected and they must engage in physical exercise and follow various safety precautions (e.g., wearing a diabetic identification tag). Further, these activities must be performed in a prescribed temporal relationship to each other (e.g., insulin injections should be taken within an hour before dinner). Glasgow, McCaul, and Schafer (1986) have noted that cognitive, environmental, and life-style variables may impede adherence to diabetic regimens as well. Table 7 lists some of the multitude of reasons why diabetics may not adhere to their demanding treatment regimen.

Thus, when we recognize the complexity of the treatment regimen, an adherence level of 50%, as cited in most studies of diabetics, may in fact not seem low (Watts, 1979). In considering this figure, however, it is important to remember that adherence across the different components of diabetes treatment are quite variable. Although scheduled insulin injections are rarely missed, errors in insulin administration are quite common (Watkins, Williams, *et al.*, 1967). As noted before, adhering to one

Table 7   An Analysis of Adherence Behaviors by Diabetics[a]

Factors involved in self-care.   Patient must:

  have information on the nature of the disease and on the specific self-care required.

  have an understanding of the rationale underlying each aspect of the self-care behaviors.

  remember the information provided.

  acquire the skills necessary to carry out the self-care appropriately (e.g., urine or blood glucose monitoring test, insulin injection, use of diabetes food-exchange lists).

  believe that proper self-care is likely to lead to better control of the disease.

  have the confidence to carry out the necessary self-care.

  believe that the "costs" of carrying out the self-care are outweighed by the benefits.

  retrieve information from memory as required (e.g., remember to take the pills before meals).

  know how to deal with dysphoric affect in situations that are emotionally charged (e.g., reminders of the potentially devastating results of disease).

  self-reinforce and/or be reinforced for carrying out the self-care behavior.

  know how to deal with difficult situations (possess problem-solving capability and flexibility).

  know how to deal with the responses of others toward self-care behavior (e.g., telling someone who invites him or her to dinner that a special meal is required).

  know how to deal with failures to carry out self-care behavior.

  attribute the satisfactory completion of self-care to his or her own efforts (self-attribution) rather than attribute them solely to the efforts of the health care provider (external attribution, which leads to less effective maintenance).

Possible reasons for nonadherence

  Many patients (as in the case of Type II diabetics) do not have symptoms that would motivate them to adhere.

  Young diabetic patients cannot conceive of complications 25 years down the road.

  Patients may view their disorder as less serious or themselves as being less susceptible to complications.

Table 7   (continued)

Some patients may have specific barriers (financial, insurance, social, vocational) that interfere with adherence.

Sometimes nonadherence grows out of the simple but painful fact that patients and their families cannot financially afford the expense of diabetic management. Rather than convey this to the staff, the family may avoid attending sessions.

Serious breaches of the management routine may not be associated with clear or immediate adverse consequences. Some patients will "experiment," for example, not give themselves injections. Such nonadherence is reinforced by the discovery that "nothing happens" and that the patient "doesn't feel any different."

"Adapted from Glasgow *et al.*, 1968, and Turk & Speers, 1984.

component of a self-care program is often independent of adherence to other components. This point again illustrates the problem in deciding on the criteria to use in define adherence that we discussed in Chapter 1.

Informational and behavioral overloads are substantially greater when multiple different adherent behaviors are required. It is not surprising that correlations among adherence rates for different behaviors contained within a complex regimen are quite low. Patients may be adhering at a very high rate to the injection of insulin but at a much lower rate to exercise or diet restrictions. These are very different behaviors requiring skills that are often unrelated.

There are a number of explanations to account for the associations between complexity and nonadherence. Simply put, complex regimens may produce information overload. There is a tendency for people to deal with such informational overload by (1) omission (failure to process the information in the first place), (2) error (processing information incorrectly), (3) delaying (putting things off until later), (4) filtering to fit input within existing beliefs, (5) approximation (taking medication once a day when it is prescribed three times a day, better than not doing it at all), and (6) avoidance (nonadherence).

Intrusiveness

Some prescribed regimens are so intrusive on the lives of patients that the decision not to adhere is based on an assessment of the potential impact of carrying out all the prescribed behaviors. For example, aggressive adherence regimens for children with cystic fibrosis may require up to eight hours a day and may indeed disrupt all normal family activities. The benefits of any self-care regimen must be considered within the context of the patient's unique situation. There is a need for the HCP to consider compromise, flexibility, and negotiation. The ideal therapeutic regimen is not likely to have any beneficial effects if the patient decides not to implement them because the demands are excessive, given the current life situation and resources. We will return to this point later in this chapter and many times throughout this book.

Duration of Treatment

A consistent finding is that adherence rates deteriorate over time. Thus, the rates of adherence for treatment regimens associated with chronic illnesses or with the performance of permanent life-style changes or prolonged preventive behaviors are likely to decrease with time unless they become automatic and habitual. For instance, among diabetics, the incidence of dosage error in the first five years is estimated to be 30%, but it increases to 80% for people who have had diabetes for 20 years or longer. This pattern of decline is true not only for self-care behavior over many years. Porter (1969) reported that adherence to an iron tablet program for pregnant women systematically diminished over the three trimester periods. Moreover, weight loss and substance abuse programs consistently revealed that by three months following intervention 60–80% of individuals have relapsed and ceased to perform the recommended behaviors (Marlatt & Gordon, 1985).

In general, treatment nonadherence is more prevalent when the patient's condition is chronic but not life-threatening or when the treatment is prophylactic. When these treatment programs require complex sets of behaviors the adherence rates are particularly low.

Knowledge of Illness

Interestingly, there appears to be minimal association between the amount of information patients have about their illness and adherence. The problem of nonadherence is rarely one of lack of knowledge. This observation has important implications for how we conduct educational programs. We will discuss this in depth in Chapter 4.

Illness and Symptom Variables

There are a number of features of illnesses and the symptoms that accompany them that appear to be related to nonadherence. For example, if an illness has easily recognizable and unpleasant symptoms that are relieved by following the HCP's recommendation, adherence is more likely. In contrast, adherence is lowest when the treatment recommendations are prophylactic and are to be performed in the absence of distressing symptoms (e.g., using dental floss regularly).

Some symptoms may fail to arouse a perceived need for tratment or adherence behaviors. Elderly residents in Detroit who were interviewed about health defined health as "feeling pretty good for my age" (Caplan, 1979). This suggests that people may adapt to a steady state of symptomatic discomfort. Patients whose symptoms remain constant may develop a belief that they are healthy because they have adapted to the symptoms and they may be unaware that others do not experience the same sensations.

The symptoms associated with certain conditions or diseases can mitigate against the appropriate performance of self-care behavior. For example, many diabetics will develop visual problems that can contribute to errors in reading and interpreting color-coded glucose levels in urine, and schizophrenic patients may suffer from periods of distorted sense of time that can affect their ability to adhere to a medication schedule. When considering nonadherence, the HCP must consider the consequences of the disease for the performance of the recommended treatment behaviors.

Given the role that symptoms play in the adherence process, it may be surprising to learn that the side effects accompanying treatment (e.g., medication) do not usually contribute significantly to nonadherence (Haynes, 1979a). The exception occurs when severe symptoms emerge (e.g., psychiatric patients' concerns about side effects such as sedation and extrapyramidal involvement, mild akathisia, resulting from neuroleptic medication), or in asymptomatic conditions for which medication may produce unpleasant symptoms (e.g., hypertension). When the side effects are extreme this may inhibit adherence, but under most conditions side effects have a minimal impact (we will consider this issue further in Chapter 4).

Up to this point we have discussed person variables, treatment variables, and symptom and disease variables in isolation. Actually, these variables are likely to interact in complex ways. How patients perceive and react to their symptoms can influence how they present themselves to HCPs. The form of treatment offered can in turn influence the patients' perceptions and how they interpret and react to possible side effects; this can in turn influence adherence, and so forth. For research purposes we often attempt to identify and measure the impact of specific variables, when in fact complex, highly interdependent processes are more likely operating. The study of specific individual variables, however, have sometimes yielded useful information. For example, it is worth noting that a number of factors that might be expected to affect adherence have been found to have minimal or no association (DiMatteo & DiNicola, 1982a). These include (a) previous bouts with the disease, (b) recency of the last attack, (c) previous hospitalization and its length, and (d) the objectively measured severity of the disease. With regard to the last point the objective seriousness of the patient's disease does not significantly influence adherence, but the patient's *subjective perception* of the seriousness or the severity of the disorder and its treatment does relate to level of adherence (Masek, 1982). Even serious, painful, life-threatening disorders do not ensure adherence if the patient does not share this perception and the accompanying intention, ability, and perceived payoff for adherence.

Relationship Variables

A survey of physicians by Stone (1979) revealed that only 25% acknowledged that they may in any way contribute to their patients' nonadherence. This impression does not fit with the data indicating that *the behavior of the HCP plays a critical role in the adherence process*. All treatment recommendations are influenced by the nature and the quality of the relationship between the HCP and the patient. Since relationship variables are so critical, we have devoted an entire chapter to them (Chapter 3). At this point we wish merely to reiterate that patient satisfaction resulting from good communcation and rapport and continuity of care increases the likelihood of adherence. It probably goes without saying that a caring attitude and a warm, approachable, personalized treatment approach can significantly enhance patient satisfaction and treatment adherence. One of the most promising observations is that patient satisfaction with the HCP and the treatment regimen is an important correlate of adherence. Insofar as HCPs adopt an open, honest, supportive style, demonstrate respect, praise the patient, and provide clear explanations, treatment adherence will increase. Table 8 lists other important relationship variables associated with adherence.

Once a workable relationship has been established between HCP and patient, a variety of adherence enhancement strategies can be employed. We will examine in detail what we mean by good communication in Chapter 3 and discuss specific relationship enhancement strategies in more detail in Part II of this volume.

Table 8   Relationship Variables Associated with Adherence

The patients' perceptions of the approachability and friendliness of their
   health care provider
The patients' feelings that he or she is held in esteem and treated with
   respect
The degree to which the patient participates and understands the treatment
   regimen
The degree to which the patient feels his or her expectations are being met
The amount of supervision by the health care provider
The degree to which the health care provider is perceived as being
   considerate of the patients' concerns and feelings
The degree to which the health care provider establishes trust, elicits
   medically relevant information that has been provided, explains the
   medical regimen, and motivates the patients to cooperate with the
   treatment regimen

Organizational-Structural Variables

Although most discussions of treatment nonadherence focus
on the quality and nature of the relationship between the patient
and the HCP, a number of factors can significantly influence this
relationship and in turn the degree of adherence. For example,
DiMatteo and DiNicola (1982a) report that the stress and demands
on physicians can significantly affect the rates of adherence.
Other organizational factors that have been implicated are listed
in Table 9.

Cameron (1978) has offered an example of how even the
timing of a referral can affect adherence. As a psychologist working in a pain clinic, he noted that different effects were apparent
when patients were referred to him *after* a full medical examination had been performed and when the referral *accompanied*
the medical examination. In the latter case, the referring physician conveyed to patients that their pain was complex and thus
required a comprehensive multidisciplinary team assessment.
The impact of this referral was quite different from that when
patients arrived at Cameron's office after having seen the medical
staff, with the attitude that the hospital was not taking their pain

Table 9 Organizational Factors That Influence Adherence

Nature of the referral process
Continuity of care
Personalized care
Scheduling of appointments
Length of referral times (less than one week enhances adherence)
Length of waiting time (less than one hour enhances adherence)
On-site treatment
Increased patient supervision
Good links between inpatient and outpatient services
Staff's positive attitude and enthusiasm toward the treatment and adherence
to it

seriously. To see a "shrink" (psychologist) must mean they think the "pain is only in my mind. That it is not real." In this case the timing of the referral (medical, then psychological) inadvertently contributed to patient perceptions that interfered with adherence to the treatment regimen. The organizational routine, the ambience of the treatment setting, the implicit professional attitudes—each has message value that can contribute to nonadherence.

As one might expect, the greater the *continuity of care* whereby patients can see the same HCP upon repeated visits, the greater the likelihood of adherence. For instance, there is greater treatment adherence and better keeping of follow-up appointments for patients seen in private primary care facilities than for patients receiving care in an unfamiliar emergency or walk-in clinic. Similarly, there is greater adherence for requests from one's own physician than for the physician's partner or from an unknown physician. This point is important to consider given the large increase in health maintenance organizations (HMOs), walk-in clinics, and group practices. The importance of the patient's seeing the same health care provider should be emphasized in these varied health contexts. A warm, personalized treatment approach whereby patients are encouraged to develop a positive identification with both the individual HCP and the clinic appears essential.

Another example of the importance of personalized care is reflected in the manner in which appointments are scheduled. When patients have *individualized appointment times* set with a specific HCP, instead of block scheduling, adherence improves. Such block scheduling most often occurs at low-income clinics and some Veterans Administration medical centers, where patients are told to come during a general period of time and often have to wait several hours rather than being given a specific appointment time with a specific HCP and consequently a brief waiting period. At one hospital with which we are familiar, all patients to be treated for the day in the podiatry clinic were scheduled to come in at 8:30 a.m. Some of these patients did not actually see a physician until 4:30 p.m.! Interestingly, not only is the patient's behavior influenced by block scheduling, but so is physician's behavior. Dunbar and Agras (1980) reported that in a block system when patients were not assigned a particular doctor, physicians came to the clinic 35 minutes late. Individualized appointments reduced waiting time.

One innovative way to deal with some of the organizational difficulties has been to extend personalized care to the workplace with *on-site treatment programs*. Although such efforts are still in their infancy, some encouraging data, in terms of increased adherence rates, have been published (e.g., Alderman & Schoenbaum, 1975; Fielding & Breslow, 1983). An interesting extension of this approach has been offered by Brownell and his colleagues (1984), who used group competition between business organizations to promote adherence to treatment regimens. If on-site training is to be conducted, there is a clear need to tap the group's, as well as each individual patient's, expectations about their illness and the needed treatment.

Providing treatment on-site can take advantage of peer support, social and organizational coherence, and the patient's sense of belonging. Enthusiasm for on-site programs should be tempered by the findings of Sackett and his colleagues (1975), who reported than an educational program about hypertension at a foundry work site resulted in more workers' entering the program, but it did not increase the degree of adherence to blood pressure treatment. Leventhal *et al.* (1984), however, have criticized the Sackett *et al.* study for not focusing the educational program on changing the workers' representation of their illness from an acute to a chronic disorder.

In the most difficult cases *increased supervision* in the form of home visits, special nursing care, hospitalization, increased frequency of outpatient visits, and special pharmacy service may be required to enhance the rates of treatment adherence. Although such efforts have proved successful in the short run, when limited interventions are required, their success with patients suffering from chronic disorders has yet to be fully demonstrated. When interventions such as home visits increase patient adherence, it is not clear what factors operate to mediate the effect. As Garrity and Garrity (1985) note, it is not clear if supervision in the form of home visits has its effect because the visits (a) provide patients with social support, (b) convey personal concern about the seriousness of the problem, (c) facilitate better understanding of the content of the treatment program, (d) enhance specific skills such as problem solving, or (e) foster some combination of these factors.

Two other organizational factors that have been implicated in affecting the level of adherence are (a) the quality of the communication between staff members (e.g., inpatient and outpatient staff) in setting up continuity of care and patient followup and (b) the attitude expressed by all staff members toward patient adherence to the treatment regimen. There is a need to view efforts to increase patient adherence as a task for the entire treatment and clinic team, not just the primary HCP. Insofar as one is able to mobilize the array of people who have contact with the patient (HCPs as well as secretaries and ward clerks, pharmacists), the challenging task of improving treatment adherence can be successfully met.

To summarize much of what we have outlined regarding the most important variables, nonadherence might arise for any of the following reasons:

1. The patient does not know what to do.

2. The patient does not have the skills or resources to carry out the treatment regimen.

3. The patient does not believe or feel that he or she has the ability to carry out the treatment regimen.

4. The patient does not believe or feel that carrying out the treatment regimen will make a difference (questions the utility).

5. The treatment regimen is too demanding and the patient does not believe that the potential benefits of adhering will outweigh the costs.

6. Adherence is associated with aversive or nonreinforcing events or sensations.

7. The quality of the relationship between the patient and the HCP is poor.

8. There is no continuity of care.

9. The clinic is not mobilized toward facilitating adherence.

In Part II of this book we will consider how each of these general implications can be translated into specific treatment practices.

Adherence Enhancement
Procedures

II

3

Enhancing the Relationship between the Patient and the Health Care Provider

Four major components are involved in physician behavior that may impact on patient compliance with treatment regimens: compassion, communication, activating patient self-motivation and shared responsibility with the patient. An attitude of concern coupled with hope and interest in the patient's future well-being affect compliance.

V. R. COLEMAN (1985)

The importance of the doctor–patient relationship was noted as early as Hippocrates. In his wisdom, Hippocrates commented on the potential strength of this relationship in facilitating the curative process.

The patient, though conscious that his condition is perilous, may recover his health simply through his contentment with the goodness of the physician.

Since Hippocrates' initial observation, a great deal of research has been conducted on the "art of medicine." In fact, Balint (1968) noted that the effect of the doctor's attitude on the action of drugs is so powerful that the doctor himself or herself should be designated a "drug" in relation to the patient. It is this potency that has highlighted the significance of the patient–HCP relationship for both treatment adherence and clinical outcome. In general, research has indicated that what patients expect and want in a medical encounter is that the HCP be technically competent, that they receive adequate information about their medical problems, and that the atmosphere of the encounter be warm, comfortable, and cooperative.

Interestingly, however, HCPs often hold a somewhat different perspective of their relationship with patients. The sociologist Talcott Parsons (1951), using role theory, described the relationship of the patient fulfilling a "sick role" and the HCP occupying a "professional role." Central to this formulation is the notion that both parties share a set of complementary expectations concerning their obligations and privileges. HCPs are expected to act in the welfare of the patient, applying their knowledge and skills as competently as possible and being guided by the rules of professional behavior. The complement to the dominant professional role is the patient's sick role. Those occupying the sick role are not to be blamed for their unhealthy state and are exempt from having to perform many of the normal social duties. In return for this, they are expected to be motivated to return to the healthy state, are required to seek competent help, and should be completely honest in offering information and of general assistance to the professional treating them. Most importantly, those who occupy the sick role are expected to trust the HCP's opinion, heed the advice they are given, and follow all recommendations. According to Parsons, the acceptance of "doctor's orders" not only makes sense from a rational viewpoint because of the greater technical competence of the physician but also satisfies certain emotional needs in the patient for direction and guidance. The extension of the Parsons model to health maintenance and disease prevention would suggest that patients should follow the advice offered by HCPs in order to achieve the mutually desired goal of health.

The Parsons model, however, fails to give adequate consideration to the patient's attitudes, beliefs, knowledge, and expectations that may differ substantially from those of the HCP.

Patients have a great deal of experience with health care, with as much as 90% of health problems handled at home without medical advice or supervision (Fink, 1976). Furthermore, with increased access to the media, patients are exposed to more conflicting information from HCPs about what is appropriate to maintain health. The statistics on the rates of nonadherence reported in the previous chapters provide little support for the Parsons view of an unquestioning, uncritical adherent patient.

As an alternative to the professional–sick role relationship described by Parsons (1951), Szasz and Hollender (1956) postulated three types of HCP–patient relationships that can be adapted to different forms of illness. These are:

1. The active physician–passive patient relationship, appropriate for situations in which the patient is comatose or otherwise unable to act on his or her own behalf
2. The building HCP cooperating mode, appropriate during the most acute conditions and/or acute exacerbations of a chronic illness
3. The mutual participating mode, an active partnership in which HCPs function most appropriately by assisting patients to help themselves.

It is this latter role of *mutual participation* that is most important in attempting to facilitate adherence. As Hanson (1986) notes,

> What should be avoided is the traditional paternalistic attitude whereby the physician assumes in advance what the patient needs to know and thus makes no attempt to include the patient in the decision-making process out of fear of burdening the patient with too much information or too much responsibility. (p. 194)

Although much has been learned about ways in which to improve the HCP–patient relationship and to facilitate treatment adherence, little change has been evident in how most health care interactions occur (e.g., see Pendelton & Halser, 1983; Svarstad, 1976). Podell (1975) has noted that few medical schools or residency programs pay much heed to the importance of communication. This is unfortunate because the evidence indicates that physicians and other HCPs could benefit from training

in adherence enhancement procedures and in particular in communication skills.

Inui, Yourtee, and Williamson (1976), who provided physicians with special tutorials of one two-hour session on adherence enhancement strategies for hypertensive patients, nicely
illustrate the potential of physician education. The tutorial focused
on the communication process and the importance of the physician as an educator of patients rather than solely as a diagnos-
tician. Emphasis was placed on physicians' identifying and dealing
with patients' attitudes rather than focusing on the search for
complications of hypertension. The tutorial training, relative to
control groups, was significantly more effective in altering physician behavior and patient adherence. In the tutored group
there was an increase of over 30% in the number of hypertensive
patients whose blood pressure was adequately controlled and
who were adherent to the drug regimen. The tutorial sessions
resulted in the physicians' spending less time in both reviewing
patient symptoms and conducting a physical examination and
more time on considering the patients' ideas about adherence,
discussing possible barriers to adherence, and sharing more of
the rationale for the treatment program. These changes in the
way the physicians communicated resulted in improved patient
understanding and contributed to a better adherence record and
clinical outcome, with an actual *reduction in time* spent with
patients during the continued course of their treatment.

The positive results by Inui and his colleagues are consistent with the conclusions drawn by Whitcher-Alagna (1983), who
reported that "studies indicate that patients who receive the
information and caring manner they expect from a physician are
more satisfied with the help they receive, like the practitioner
more, and are more likely to follow through on recommended
actions" (p. 142). Parenthetically, she also notes that the most
common cause for malpractice suits in the United States was
poor communication between physician and patient.

Yet another indicator of the important role of relationship
factors in meeting patient expectations is reflected in the observation that patients usually change physicians not because the

doctor is technically incompetent but rather because of inadequate interpersonal treatment. Krupkat (1983, 1986) reports that several recent surveys of patients indicate that they have little complaint with the competence and expertise of their physicians. Instead, they are dissatisfied with the human element—the quality of the relationship, the opportunity to talk and to be heard, and the amount of information provided. If physicians appear to be too busy to listen or disinterested, then patients tend to switch doctors (DiMatteo & DiNicola, 1982a). In short, poor communication and inadequate relationship enhancement skills have more than adherence implications. With this potential in mind we will consider what the literature tells us about relationship factors and treatment adherence.

The Changing Relationship

Any discussion of relationship variables must underscore the changing atmosphere in the health care system. A number of astute commentators on the art of medicine have noted that patients today are much more demanding, knowledgeable, and litigious than patients in previous generations. The aura of medicine and the authority of the physician have been seriously questioned as people are continually exposed to medical controversies, contradictions, and reversals (Brody 1980b; DiMatteo & DiNicola, 1982b; Eraker *et al.*, 1984). Given the open and educated nature of Western society, such social changes are likely to continue, and this has important implications in affecting what patients expect from their HCPs. Today, patients have a much stronger expectation that they will be active participants in the decision-making process. They also expect their concerns to be heard and addressed. They expect not only competence but also friendliness, warmth, courtesy, compassion, honesty, and integrity. These expectations place additional burdens on HCPs.

Such patient attitudes have been reinforced by the medical and legal establishments' own pronouncements. The American Hospital Association's Patients' Bill of Rights and the American Civil Liberties Union Rights of Hospital Patients both underscore the role of active patient participation and collaborative negotiation in the treatment regimen. A number of recent studies have provided evidence to support the utility of the collaborative-negotiation model and active patient participation (e.g., Barofsky, 1978; Eisenthal, Emery, Lazare, & Udin, 1979; Roter, 1977; Schulman, 1979; Tracy, 1977).

In short, how HCPs relate to their patients is critical in affecting the adherence process. The other adherence enhancement procedures to be discussed in this book will work only in the context of a concerned, compassionate relationship wherein the patient is viewed as a knowledgeable ally who must actively participate in the treatment process (Anderson & Kirk, 1982; Turk, Holzman, & Kerns, 1986).

In order to cover the large literature on the communication process in health care succinctly, the present chapter is divided into three sections. The first examines those factors that have been found to interfere with or hinder communication patterns between HCPs and their patients. The second section will consider clinical guidelines to follow to enhance the communication process and nurture the health care relationship. The final section will consider a series of specific interview procedures that have been used to obtain an adherence-oriented history and to tap the patients' representation of their illness and their expectations about treatment. Such a clinically sensitive inquiry can strengthen the amount of empathy, warmth, openness, approachability, likeability, and satisfaction that have been found to correlate with treatment adherence and clinical outcome.

Behavior That Interferes with Communication and the Development of Relationship

Although we readily recognize that any relationship, including the health care relationship, is a two-way street,[6] a bidirectional process, the extensive literature on communication patterns

---

[6]Pettegrew and Turkat (1986) have demonstrated the bidirectional nature of the health care relationship. They report a series of studies indicating that what patients com-

in health care does provide a "hit list" of behaviors of which HCPs may be guilty that interfere with communication and in turn compromise treatment adherence and clinical outcome. Some of these behaviors, as itemized in Table 10, are what one might expect, but others may come as a surprise.

An examination of Table 10 indicates that those behaviors that interfere with a general approachability will interfere with treatment adherence. Physicians who are viewed as personable effect higher adherence than those viewed as businesslike (Whitcher-Alagna, 1983). Often such brusqueness or preoccupation with time and efficiency can take a form we might overlook. Heath (1984) has studied the verbal and nonverbal behaviors of patients' and physicians' interactions. She found that the nature of the eye contact and gaze behavior of physicians significantly influenced the quality and quantity of what patients self-disclosed. If the physician did not look at the patient when the patient was speaking (for example, the physician perused the patient's records), the patient often refrained from speaking and instead engaged in body movements and other activities to capture the physician's attention. In time, the physician would look up from the records and the patient would in turn begin speaking. This interpersonal "dance," of sorts, resulted in most sessions' being longer than if the physician had merely listened attentively. The goal of being superefficient, doing two things at one time, namely, listening and reading the patient's records, backfired. Not only did it lead to longer sessions and more patient dissatisfaction, but Heath also reported that the physicians who were engaged in reading patient records frequently missed or forgot what the patient had said.

The result of such research is not to require that the HCP continually gaze into the patient's eyes; rather, it underscores the need for a careful appreciation of how to deal with patients' medical records. If one waits for an opportune moment to review

---

municate ("stoic," "assertive," "ideal") about themselves and their illness to physicians influences how they utilize the health care system and how HCPs react. In short, patients influence HCPs as much as the reverse.

Table 10   Health Care Providers' Behavior That Interferes with Effective Patient Communication, or The Art of Being a Facilitator of Nonadherence[a]

Act unfriendly, distant, demonstrate a lack of warmth, concern, interest. Be unapproachable and impersonable. Demonstrate disagreement, formality, and rejection. For example, fail to introduce yourself.

Look and act busy—watch clock, look out at waiting room to see how many more patients there are.

See patients in a chaotic setting where there are many interruptions (e.g., telephone calls, interruptions from nurse or secretary). Read case notes while interviewing patient.

Mumble, use medical jargon when speaking to the patient. Never ask if patient understands.

Ask patients specific close-ended questions requiring "yes" or "no" answers.

Cut off or interrupt patient statements.

Ignore patient's questions. Say you will come back to it, but don't.

Don't allow patients to tell their story in own words.

Don't allow patients to express their ideas and concepts about their illness.

Fail to take into account patients' concerns and expectations.

Treat the disease instead of the patient ("What is the problem?" instead of "How are you?").

Omit clear-cut explanation of diagnosis and causes of illness.

Fail to state precise treatment regimen to be followed or state it in an unclear or too technical a fashion.

Ignore opportunities to give patient feedback.

Fail to solicit feedback from patient.

Adopt a hostile, suspicious, moralizing, low-empathy and high-power-struggle stance. Fail to make eye contact or to sit at the same level as the patient. Keep a desk or some other physical obstacle between you and patient.

Abruptly terminate the interview.

Provide little support.

---

[a]Suggestions offered by Becker & Maiman, 1980; Ben-Sira, 1976, 1980; Coleman, 1985; DiMatteo & DiNicola, 1982a; Dunbar & Agras, 1980; Hays & DiMattio 1984; Korsch *et al.*, 1968; Ley, 1977; Miller, 1985; Podell 1975; Svarstad, 1976; Turk *et al.*, 1983; Whitcher-Alagna, 1983.

the files, this does not lead to longer consultation time. Sometimes our efforts to be efficient can have just the opposite effects.

In the same way that we do not usually attend to how or when we peruse patient records, we rarely pay much attention to how we make requests of our patients. The words we choose are second nature and readily overlooked. But as Levy and Carter

(1976) have reported, the way in which HCPs make requests can affect patients' satisfaction, treatment adherence, and clinical outcome. Consider the following contrasting modes of request.

1. What you are to do is. . . . Do the following. . . . Do this. . . .
2. I would like you to. . . . I want you to. . . . This is what I am asking you to do. . . .
3. So what you have agreed to try is. . . . As I understand it, you will. . . . So you will take responsibility for. . . .

A much greater likelihood of adherence follows from the third mode as compared to the first mode of request. Such observations indicate the need for HCPs to listen more attentively not only to their patients, but also to themselves, so they can monitor and change their communication patterns accordingly. A study published by Waitzkin and Stoeckle (1976) illustrates the importance of HCP self-awareness. They reported that an analysis of 300 patients and their physicians in both their offices and hospitals revealed that during an average 20-minute visit little more than *one minute* was actually spent giving information. Interestingly, however, when asked to estimate the amount of time spent in giving information the physician estimated one-quarter to one-half of the visit. Most physicians also underestimated the amount of information patients want to receive. There is a clear need for HCPs to attend not only to how they communicate but to what they communicate as well.

Yet another variable that has been implicated in interfering with the communication process is the level of self-disclosure requested of patients. Janis (1984a) reported that seeking high self-disclosure or asking patients about material that they would not usually share with other family members or friends had a *detrimental* effect on some adherence behavior, such as following a diet. Asking patients personal questions about current and past sorrows, sex life, guilt feelings, secret longings, and the like resulted in the patients' becoming demoralized despite positive comments and acceptance by the therapist. The discussion of personal weaknesses led to feelings of self-dissatisfaction, shaken self-confidence, and the general feeling of being less certain that one could succeed in adhering.

In contrast, moderate levels of self-disclosure that focused on personal strengths as well as weaknesses enhance the sense of self-efficacy and the level of adherence. For example, DiMatteo and DiNicola (1982a) offer an example of an HCP who could act as a coping model for patients by self-disclosing his own struggle in resisting temptations.

> "Oh, I really have trouble resisting desserts too. It's tough isn't it? But I figure its worth it to resist them and to work toward normal weight." (p. 107)

As DiMatteo and DiNicola note, disclosing experiences similar to those of one's patients helps to establish a basis of similarity and enhances interpersonal influence.

The findings on eye contact, on the nature of communication and the level of self-disclosure, and the other factors listed in Table 10 each in its own way attest to the replicable finding that there is a direct relationship between health care communication and patient satisfaction, and in many instances between communication, treatment adherence, and medical outcome. (See also DiMatteo & DiNicola, 1982a; Janis, 1983; Korsch, Gozzi, & Francis, 1968; and Whitcher-Alagna, 1983, for additional reviews).

Facilitating the Communication Process

In order to facilitate the communication process and strengthen the relationship between patients and HCPs two major factors must be considered. The first part of the challenge is *attitudinal* in nature; the second part involves the need to cultivate specific *communication skills*. The two aspects are highly interrelated.

Attitudinally, there is a need to establish a conducive atmosphere wherein patients feel they are what Brody (1980b) describes as "independent worthy people whose contributions are appreciated and needed" (p. 715). Patients need to be seen as *active participants* in the clinical decision-making process, collaborators and allies who share responsibilities in the treatment regimen. Anderson and Kirk (1982) have referred to the HCP–patient relationship as a "therapeutic partnership." There is a need to help patients verbalize their wants and expectations and allow them to participate in treatment decisions.

A call for such active patient participation does not in any way compromise the expertise of the HCP in the examination and diagnosis of the patient's presenting clinical problems, but instead it underscores the underlying equality between HCP's and patient's responsibilities for the outcome of treatment.

There are a number of things HCPs can do to enhance their approachability and foster such an active collaborative relationship. Body (1980a), Ley (1977), and Peck and King (1982) note that the HCP can:

1. Introduce oneself
2. Explore patient's worries, goals, and expectations
3. Answer all patient questions
4. Avoid unexplained medical jargon (educate without being too technical)
5. Discuss pros and cons of alternative evaluations and treatments
6. Engage in some nonmedical talk—being friendly rather than businesslike
7. Elicit patient's suggestions and preferences and negotiate any disagreements

Schulman (1979) has found that patients who were actively involved in treatment programs (i.e., viewed themselves as partners, were informed of treatment rationale and encouraged to report negative effects of treatment procedure, and helped to operationalize medical advice) demonstrated higher rates of adherence and more favorable treatment outcome. For instance, among more active hypertensive patients the involved individuals had a better understanding of their illness, fewer medication side effects, more persistence in adhering to treatment regimen, greater adoption of health-enhancing behavior, and, most importantly, better blood pressure control. Thus, viewing patients as active participants involved in therapeutic planning had a number of salutary affects on the health care process.

Eisenthal and his colleagues (1979) have also found greater patient satisfaction and treatment adherence for patients who had higher levels of negotiation and participation in the decision-making process. Similarly, Hertz, Bernheim, and Perloff (1976) have developed a problem-oriented health care plan in order to encourage both patient involvement and a "therapeutic alliance" between the HCP and patient. The problem-oriented health care plan includes a description of active problems, potential problems and risks, accompanying treatment, and continuing health maintenance plans. Both the HCP and patient sign the completed health care agreement and a copy is retained by each. The likelihood of treatment adherence is increased because of the emphasis on the *shared responsibility* of HCP and patient.

The potential of nurturing active patient involvement is further underscored by Roter (1977), who successfully taught patients how to request information and involvement from their physicians more actively. They found that active involvement resulted in a significant lowering of the patient dropout rate from clinic attendance. Matthews and Hingson (1977) suggest that teaching patients how to observe and record the impact of the treatment (e.g., medication) on their illness and sharing with them the rationale for various features of the treatment regimen can also foster patient involvement.

HCPs can also indicate to patients how often they will be seen (when asked to come back) and why (e.g., adjust dosage, screen for side effects, or check effect of medication). In this context HCPs must explain explicitly the value of treatment adherence. Some practitioners have even suggested using analogies as a way of conveying the importance of adherence. For example, one practitioner said that he told patients:

> I want you to think about adherence as a type of investment
> in the future. By following the plan now (taking your med-
> icine) you are putting something away for a later date.

Another practitioner told his patients to compare the human body to a piece of machinery, both having to be cared for:

> For example, rust can destroy machinery if the parts are not carefully oiled. In the same way, not taking one's medicine, not following the treatment program, is like not taking care of one's farm machinery or car. Just as you make sure your car has proper fuel, air in the tires, oil, and grease, you must take care of your body. You usually don't neglect your machinery. In the same way you can't neglect your body. You must adhere to the treatment program.

The nature of the analogies and metaphors employed should, of course, be matched to the individual patient rather than employed generally. Such analogies can be followed by the HCP's asking patients to reverse roles for a moment. The HCP can ask patients how, if they were the doctor (diabetes educator, psychotherapist, etc.), they would they go about helping someone who had difficulty adhering to the treatment regimen. Many patients do not reveal their desires and expectations or their disappointments when the treatment approach does not match their preferences. Instead, they fail to adhere. There is a need for the HCP to probe explicitly for such information and to adjust the communication accordingly. Such clinical ploys as analogies, role reversals, encouraging patients to ask questions, and the like can foster more active patient involvement and treatment adherence.

As Podell (1975) notes, such efforts at nurturing patient involvement do not mean that HCPs should not speak with authority when this is appropriate. For example, Podell reminds physicians who treat hypertensive patients to say, "I want you to take the medicine", not "We can try the medicine." The certainty of the former statement and the sense of authority it reflects in terms of expert knowledge and professional competence should not be relinquished when we call for greater patient involvement in the treatment regimen. Once the patient agrees to take the prescribed medicine, however, then involving the patient as an active collaborator in identifying potential obstacles (e.g., forgetfulness, dysphoric emotions) can facilitate adherence.

In short, a number of interpersonal and communication skills must be developed by HCPs if they are to balance, on the one hand, their expertise and authority and, on the other hand, the need for empathy, compassion, and active patient cooperation. In trying to maintain this delicate balance it is useful to recall that the term *doctor* comes from the Latin word *docere* ("to teach"). Providing health care is in many ways a teaching profession.

Cultivating Communication Skills

Before we consider the variety of skills and probes that could enhance the health care process, perhaps we can anticipate a recurrent concern that we have encountered when this material has been shared with HCPs. Simply put, HCPs often find the suggestions offered to be sensible and potentially useful, but it all boils down to a question of *who has the time to do what is being proposed*. Although we will consider this issue in more detail in Chapter 9, at this point it is worth noting that several investigators have found that HCPs, and in particular physicians, who took the few minutes necessary to become acquainted with the patients' ideas and expectations would, in fact, *end up saving time*. Korsch and her colleagues (1968) reported that tapping the patients' beliefs, representation of their illness, and expectations resulted in less misunderstanding, fewer arguments and quarrels, and less need for repetition. By allowing patients to tell their story in their own words at the opening of the interview and by probing for the patients' most urgent needs, major concerns, and expectations, physicians are able to render their patients more attentive and amenable to the physicians' ideas and plans. Lazare, Eisenthal, and Wasserman (1975) have also reported a saving in time as patients were able to verbalize specific requests or desires rather than vague descriptions of their problems. The physician's spending a bit more time initially paid handsome dividends later on, not only in terms of time saved but in the patient's understanding and satisfaction, treatment adherence, and clinical outcome.

Let us now consider some of the more specific skills required to nurture a productive health care relationship. Perhaps the most succinct summary on the topic has been offered by Barnlund (1976):

> Communication skills must be cultivated that respect patients' intelligence, acknowledge their needs, accept their feelings, value their openness and promote collaboration in decision-making. (p. 723)

Dunbar and Agras (1980) call for a positive organized environment wherein the staff are warm, friendly, and receptive and provide adequate time, personalized attention, and empathy. One important skill to accomplish this is *listening*. HCPs must learn to listen not only to what is said but also to what is not said. They must learn to listen to the emotional overtones of patients' statements. Often these overtones are reflected in the nonverbal behavior of the patient (signs of tension, averted eyes, confusion, distress). HCPs must learn to be sensitive to nonverbal cues. As Pickering (1978) has noted, "hearing the patient's message is the *sine qua non* of a great physician" (p. 554). He goes on to add,

> To hear the message requires first the physician's interest, second his understanding of the meaning of language, and third his sympathy toward and his knowledge and understanding of the circumstances of the patient's life; these again he hears best by listening to the patient. (pp. 554–555)

Pickering's observations are supported by the findings of Friedman (1979), who reported that patients were most satisfied with medical practitioners who listened, took enough time to explain the patient's medical condition, were available by phone, and cared about them as persons. Miller (1985) has also noted that such listening and empathy skills increased patients' commitment and improved their clinical outcome.

There are a number of areas in which it is important to listen, beyond acquiring the information one needs to formulate a valid diagnosis. As we have been emphasizing, the literature suggests three critical areas to assess systematically:

   a. Patients' meaning, representation, or explanatory model of their illness
   b. Patients' worries and concerns about illness
   c. Patients' expectations about treatment and about the health care provider

It should be noted that the HCP may wish to address these same issues with significant others in the patient's life as well.

Patients' Explanatory Model of Their Illness

As we noted in Chapter 2, how patients and significant others define or represent aspects of their illness can have a substantial influence on the adherence process, especially when the patients' conceptualizations are incompatible with those held by the HCP. As Leventhal *et al.* (1984) emphasize, there is a need to keep in mind that patients do not enter treatment with a *tabula rasa* view of their illness and the prospective treatment but instead have their own representation of health threats and they plan and act in relation to their representation and accompanying concerns and fears.

These idiosyncratic representations and concerns are built up from many sources including friends, family, the media, and their bodily and mental symptoms, as well as from information offered by the HCP. The HCP must assess not only the patient's representation (views of the illness, its cause and course, expectations about treatment) and fears but also how significant others in the patients' life view the illness and the proposed treatment regimen. In many instances, the representations of all those involved may differ from those held by the HCP. For instance, patients may expect the treatment to eradicate symptoms, and when this does not occur then they may decide not to adhere. Or patients may have worries and irrational fears that interfere with adherence but which they are hesitant to raise with the

HCP because they perceive him or her as being too busy to care.

In one example, Roth (1979) reported that many ulcer patients being treated with antacid therapy believed their ulcers could turn into cancer, even though few of them told their doctors about this fear. Such fears, which interfered with adherence, were particularly likely if the pain became persistent or if the ulcer began to bleed. An open communication that provided education about the disorder and the rules and rationale of the treatment regimen were helpful in alleviating the patients' concerns and in increasing adherence. As Roth notes:

> One explanation for this result may be that we relieved unnecessary fears and replaced them with appropriate fears—for example, about recognition of the risk and nature of complications. *We also told patients what they should do about these complications and when they should see a doctor.* (p. 124, emphasis added)

Thus, before HCPs offer treatment advice they must tap the patients' representation, fears and concerns, and explanatory model. Table 11 which was adapted from Kleinman (1980), provides an interview designed to assess the patients' perceptions of their problems, what brought them to treatment at this time, and their expectations concerning the course of their illness and possible treatment interventions.

A somewhat more detailed interview that we have used in mental health facilities is offered in Table 12. But many of the same questions can be raised with patients suffering from chronic illnesses (e.g., diabetes, hypertension, chronic pain disorders, addictive behavior). The interview described in Table 12 may be conducted over several sessions. The sequence and extensiveness of the questions can vary with particular patients and treatment goals.

In considering these interviews the important point is that they should not be seen as a cross-examination, as in the case of a police officer questioning a suspicious witness (like Sergeant Joe Friday in the old television series "Dragnet"—"Just the facts, nothing but the facts"). Instead, the style to be employed is much closer to the television character of Peter Falk playing the

Table 11   Eliciting Patient's Explanatory Model[a]

Etiology
   What do you call your problem?
   What do you think has caused your problem?
Time and mode of onset of symptoms
   Why do you think it started when it did?
Pathophysiology
   What does your sickness do to you?
   How does it work?
Course of sickness (including severity and type of sick role)
   How severe is your sickness?
   Will it have a long or short course?
   What are the chief problems it has caused for you?
Treatment
   What kind of treatment do you think you should receive?
   What are the most important results you hope to receive from this
      treatment?

[a]Reproduced with permission from Galazka & Eckert, 1984, as adapted from Kleinman, 1980.

detective Columbo. In this instance, the HCP uses befuddle-
ment, bemusement, juxtaposition of facts, "plucking" key words
that the patient uses and referring them back to the patient in
order to obtain more elaboration.

Perhaps the following example illustrates the Columbo style
we are trying to convey. It is highly likely that at some point
the patient will say to the HCP that the treatment does not
work. "It just doesn't work!" When we hear patients express
such frustration, this is the occasion to do two things. First, we
tend to take a slow deep breath, thus lowering our heart rates
by six to ten beats per minute and then we say to ourselves,
"Okay, earn your money!" At this point we bring to bear all the
clinical acumen and skill we can muster, all the knowledge we
have built up over twenty years of clinical experience and we
lean over to the patient and say, "It doesn't work?" Note how
much skill is required in this reflection, since one can highlight
the *it*—"It, it . . . doesn't work?"—allowing one's voice to fade
on the phrase "doesn't work." This probe results in exploration
by both therapist and patient of what is meant by *it*. What did

Table 12   Questions That Can Be Asked in Initial Clinical Interviews[a]

Tell me a bit about yourself.

As you see it, what problem or problems bring you here?

How serious a problem is this as far as you are concerned?

What led you to seek help at this time?

Who is most bothered by your problem?

How does the problem express itself on a daily basis? Can you give me an example?

How does it interfere with or prevent you from doing something you would like to do?

Think back to the last time X occurred?

What was going on at that time?

How did you feel? What were you thinking?

Have you had similar feelings (give example) and similar thoughts (give example) in other situations? In what ways, if any, are the situations similar? What does this mean about you as a person?

How do you know when you are stressed?

What are some of the things you feel? think? do?

What sorts of things seem to make the stress worse? Better?

How long has this been going on?

What sorts of things have you tried to reduce your X (stress, depression, headaches, etc.)?

How long have you been attempting to handle or resolve this problem?

Let me ask you a somewhat different question. What accounts for your *not being more* X (depressed, upset, in greater pain, etc.)?

How would you like to change?

How would life be different if your X (pain, distress, etc.) could be relieved?

At a minimum, what would you hope to have happen as a result of coming to therapy?

What are some ways in which you could attempt to reduce your discomfort?

What do you think prevents you from doing or feeling the way you want?

Have you known anyone in a similar situation? How did it turn out for that person?

What advice would you have for someone else who had this problem?

What would it take to change?

On what would the outcome of therapy depend?

I suspect you have thought a lot about your situation. What do you think might be done to improve it?

What else do you think I should find out about in order to help with this problem?

What do you expect will happen in therapy?

What would you like to have happen?

What problems do you anticipate?

[a]Questions gleaned from Meichenbaum, 1985; Peterson, 1968; Salovey & Litt, 1985.

the patient actually do? What were his thoughts and feelings that preceded, accompanied, and followed what he did or failed to do?

Similarly, the HCP can be a "plucker" and focus on the phrase "doesn't work." This reflection, with an appropriate Columbo-style interrogative at the end, will be the occasion for HCP and patients to explore the criterion that the patient is using to determine whether his or her efforts work. Without using technical jargon, the HCP is asking the patient for an "operational" definition of the criterion he or she used to evaluate his efforts to adhere to the treatment regimen. In fact the HCP may even press on by asking the patients: "Let me ask you something a bit different, a bit unusual. How would you know if your following the treatment program did work?" Or the HCP may continue:

> Are you saying to me, and saying to yourself, that it will never work, it's no use?
>
> Recall that we noted at the outset of treatment that each patient is unique and everyone's situation is different. As a result, there are a number of different things we can try in your case. As we try them, some will work and that will be great. But others may fail, but that, too, can prove helpful and valuable. It is rather like a scientist performing an experiment. Sometimes the experiment works and that's fine. But sometimes the experiment fails. Now, when does the scientist learn most? Often, when the experiment fails.
>
> The same applies in your case. Some of the things we try may work but some may indeed fail. But it is exactly those failures that can prove to be valuable.

This particular clinical ploy of anticipating and subsuming the patient's potential failures has a paradoxical flavor to it. There is, in fact, nothing the patient can do or complain about that cannot be reframed as conveying the patient's showing signs of improvement. In addition, the examples illustrate that the art of counseling (medical or psychological, or both) is to be able to pick out the right metaphor for the client or the patient. For some patients, the example of the scientist may make sense, but for others the notion of a scientist failing may be viewed as foreign and unrelated to their experience.

Whether the analogy is a child learning to ride a two-wheel bicycle or a baseball player who hits the most home runs but also strikes out the most, the general strategy of anticipating, subsuming, and reframing failure is the same. The art of medicine and the art of counseling both require being in tune with the patient's background, experience, and expectation and choosing with surgical precision the right example, metaphor, or analogy in each case. Meichenbaum (1985) and Turk, Meichenbaum, and Genest (1983) provide many other such examples.

The point of this discussion is that adherence counseling will involve a *collaborative approach between the HCP and the patient*. One way to nurture this collaboration is to adopt a phenomenologically oriented approach whereby the HCP tries to see the patient's illness from the patient's perspective. In order to accomplish this task one must tap the patient's major concerns about the illness.

Patients' Worries and Concerns about Illness

Often the concerns that patients have about their illness are not readily expressed or recognized. There are several methods by which one can ascertain such concerns. DiMatteo and DiNicola (1982a) encourage HCPs to probe as to why patients sought help at this particular time. Often what motivates patients to seek help is not their presenting symptoms but other, often obscure and medically less critical sequelae of their illness ("I'm starting to gain weight," "My physical appearance is getting worse," etc.) Since patients often have symptoms for a long period of time prior to seeking help, an examination of the triggering events that led to help-seeking behavior, as well as the failure to seek help, can often reveal the patient's underlying concerns or reasons for coming to treatment. If such concerns are not addressed (at least from the viewpoint of the patient) then such unmet expectations can lead to treatment nonadherence. In many instances, the concerns of the HCP (e.g., symptom relief or biochemical changes) are not the same as the objectives held by the patient. The HCP cannot read the patient's mind. Explicit probing for underlying motives is essential.

Korsch *et al.* (1968) encourage HCPs to probe directly for the patient's concerns. For instance, in their study of mothers who brought their children to an emergency clinic, asking the mother two questions readily tapped their concerns:

> What worried you most about your child's illness?
> Why did that worry you?

Korsch *et al.* (1968) documented that often mothers had unrealistic concerns but that when physicians did not inquire about these concerns the mothers often felt the physicians were missing something critical or else were uninterested. Many mothers also indicated that, in fact, their concerns were rarely addressed. They did not have an opportunity to express the fears they really had about their children or they were not given a clear explanation of what was wrong with the children. Many mothers left the physician's office unsure of what had caused their children's illness (see also Turk, Litt, Salovey, & Walker, 1985). Inadequate communication can lead to patient dissatisfaction and to the increased likelihood of nonadherence.

It is important for HCPs to keep in mind that in most instances patients have basic concerns:

> Will I be all right?
> What caused my illness?
> Am I responsible for getting sick?

One must attend to such questions or patient dissatisfaction and treatment nonadherence will increase. In order to reduce the likelihood of patient nonadherence a thoughtful set of guidelines or questions that HCPs can ask themselves has been offered by

Stoudemire and Thompson (1983). Tables 13 focuses on questions HCPs should consider in fostering adherence, whereas Table 14 challenges HCPs to ask themselves about possible reasons for nonadherence when it does occur. To the extent that these probes become second nature for HCPs, treatment adherence will most likely be enhanced.

Patient Expectations about Treatment

Any attempt to assess a patient's current expectations about treatment should be put in some historical context whereby HCPs obtain an *adherence-oriented history*. HCPs have a much better likelihood of predicting treatment nonadherence with regard to the present treatment regimen if they first assess the

---

Table 13   Questions to Ask Oneself in Order to Foster Adherence[a]

Patient factors

Have the basic nature of the illness, rationale for treatment, benefits of compliance, and hazards of noncompliance been explained to and understood by the patient?

Does the patient appear appropriately concerned about the illness and motivated for treatment? (If not, why?)

Have major psychiatric syndromes been ruled out?

Can the patient recite the name of the medication and when and how to take it?

The medical regimen

Is the regimen as simple as possible in terms of number of pills and number of daily doses?

Are doses arranged around daily self-care rituals (at meals, at bedtime)?

Have frequent side effects been anticipated and explained in terms that will not frighten the patient?

The spouse and family

Does the spouse or other support figure understand the illness and the need for medication, and will he or she support compliance?

The doctor–patient relationship

Has continuity of care been established?

Has good rapport been established with the patient? (If not, why?)

---

[a]Reproduced with permission from Stoudemire & Thompson, 1983.

Table 14   Questions to Ask Oneself in Determining Possible Reasons for Nonadherence[a]

The patient

Has a major psychiatric syndrome emerged or been overlooked?
Has the patient become apathetic or frustrated regarding the treatment and
    hopes of symptom relief? (If so, why? Would further educational efforts
    help?)

The regimen

Have unpleasant side effects emerged (e.g., sexual dysfunction, depression,
    oversedation, anticholinergic effects)?
Can the regimen be simplified further?

The spouse and family

Can the spouse or other supportive figure be more actively involved in
    supporting compliance?

The doctor–patient relationship

Has the patient become dissatisfied with some aspect of his or her
    treatment?
Is there a personality conflict between doctor and patient?
Has the physician become frustrated or given up on the patient because of
    suspected noncompliance?

---

[a]Reproduced with permission from Stoudemire & Thompson, 1983.

patient's adherence to previous treatment regimens. The patient's failure to adhere to previous treatment regimens is one of the best predictors of the likelihood of future nonadherence (Seltzer, Roncari, & Garfinkel, 1980). Such questioning about previous attempts at adherence should be conducted in a nonthreatening, nonjugmental fashion, using open-ended questions. Hingson (1977), Matthews and Hingson (1977), and Cummings *et al.* (1981) have provided a comprehensive, clinically sensitive adherence-oriented history that assesses the patient's beliefs about their illness and about the treatment plan (see Table 15).

A much shorter, four-item, self-report scale, included in Table 16, has been developed by Morisky, Green, and Levine (1986). They report both concurrent and predictive validity for their scale in predicting blood pressure control at 2 and 5 years. Seventy-five percent of the patients who scored high on the scale demonstrated adequate blood pressure control five years following treatment in contrast to 47% of patients who scored low on

Table 15 Adherence-Oriented History[a]

What is it that worries you most about having developed X?
What chance do you think there is that you may have X?
How serious do you think it would be if you were to get X?
How likely do you think it is that X will return?
What do you think is causing the problem you described?
Have you known anyone with an X such as yours?
How did things turn out for that person?
What have you been doing for X on your own?
Have you been taking anything for this problem already?
Does anything else worry you about the illness?
Have you had anything similar in the past? If so, what did you do?

After a description of treatment regimen
How effective do you think this treatment (e.g., injections, pills, relaxation) will be for you?
How much do you think the treatment (offer detailed example) will help prevent you from developing X (be specific)?
Can you think of any problems you might have in following the treatment plan?
What can happen if the recommended treatment plan is not followed?
How likely is that to occur?
Did you ever not follow the treatment plan because you felt it was too (demanding, strict, difficult, expensive, etc.)?
For example, is there anything that worries you about coming for monthly visits (or some other feature of treatment plan)?
Are you concerned about any particular side effects of the medication?
What do you think would happen if you forgot to take your medicine one night (or some other feature of treatment plan)?
Do you have any questions about the treatment or how to follow it?

[a]Adapted from Hingson, 1977; Matthews & Hingson, 1977; and Cummings *et al.*, 1981.

Table 16 Self-Report Scale on Taking Medication[a]

Do you ever forget to take your medicine?
Are you careless at times about taking your medicine?
When you feel better, do you sometimes stop taking your medicine?
Sometimes if you feel worse when you take the medicine do you stop taking it?

[a]Reproduced with permission from Morisky *et al.*, 1986.

the scale. The results of this study are particularly significant when other research indicates that more than 80% of physicians overestimate patient's medication consumption (DiMatteo & DiNicola, 1982a). If the Morisky *et al.* results replicate across populations, then this brief instrument will have important applications for the prediction, as well as the assessment, of adherence. Such a scale could be easily integrated into the medical visit in order to diagnose patient adherence behavior. Friedman and Litt (1986) recommend a similar brief early probe of the patient's adherence. They suggest that HCPs, in a nonthreatening and nonjudgmental fashion, ask: "'We all have difficulty at times remembering to take our medication. To what degree is this true for you? (Almost never, approximately half the time, or almost always)" (p. 956). The patients are also asked to estimate their adherence with prescribed medication in the past. When specific problems are evident appropriate adherence-enhancement procedures could be adopted.

As Becker and Maiman (1980) suggest, an adherence-oriented history should be seen as a critical extension of the usual medical history. They encourage HCPs to determine whether the patient

   a. Cares about health (or the degree of priority the patient put on health in his or her life
   b. Agrees with the diagnosis
   c. Perceives the condition as serious
   d. Feels the recommended therapy will work
   e. Fears medication or treatment side effects
   f. Feels the treatment regimen is too hard to follow

HCPs should assess potential barriers for carrying out the treatment recommendations. Thus, instead of waiting for adherence problems to arise, the HCP can develop a collaborative plan with patients to reduce their likelihood. An innovative way to assess barriers to regimen adherence was offered by Glasgow *et al.* (1986) and Schafer, Glasgow, McCaul, and Dreher (1983). Working with insulin-dependent diabetics, they developed a Barriers to Adherence Questionnaire that assesses events that interfere with appropriate adherence to the complex treatment regimen (insulin injections, glucose testing, diet, and exercise). The strategy they used in developing their questionnaire could be used for a variety of populations and was derived in this manner:

1. Diabetic patients (age 11 to 55) were asked to list as many things as possible that make it difficult to adhere to the treatment regimen. ("Generate as many problem situations as possible that occur. Be as specific as possible. Try to think of problem situations that interfere with each of the treatment components.")

2. After eliminating redundancies, refining the wording, and adding items, the authors devised a questionnaire and a rating as to the frequency ("How often does this occur?") and the severity ("How much of a problem is this?") for each item was obtained. Those items rated as occurring less than every other day and as causing less than a moderate degree of difficulty in overcoming the barrier when they did occur were dropped.

3. Patients also recorded as many possible solutions to each problem situation as they could (including both good and bad solutions) and they included ratings of their effectiveness.

Illustrative items include: "It is embarrassing to eat when the people around me are not eating." "Bad weather interferes with my regular exercise routine." "On a weekend, it is difficult to get up at the regular time to take my shot." "I feel out of place testing my urine (or blood) at school or work during the day." In a cross-validation, patients' reports on the Barrier Scale revealed consistent relationships with all areas of regimen adherence. We concur with Glasgow *et al.* (1986) that the behavior-analytic approach that enlists patients (as well as significant others) as collaborators in specifying problems, barriers, and possible solutions has high potential in assessing adherence. Such assessment instruments can also provide specific suggestions for treatment intervention.

Sometimes the nature of the assessment may focus on a general area such as self-control rather than on a specific target behavior such as diabetes. For instance, DiMatteo and DiNicola (1982a) offer the following examples of probing whether patients have ever succeeded in exerting self-control and the outcome of past efforts.

> When have you controlled habitual behaviors like smoking or drinking or eating?
> How did you feel when you stopped smoking? Were you able to breathe better? Was your family proud of you? Did you achieve a sense of personal satisfaction?
> You did control yourself and you reduced your health dangers. You see, when you really put your mind to controlling yourself, you can do it. It seems that you sometimes lose control . . . (give example). But, overall the evidence suggests that you can decide to make a change in your life, and carry out that change with self-control. (p. 192)

In short, one objective of conducting an adherence-oriented history is not to construct a litany of patient failures but instead to search for evidence that patients have indeed exerted self-control. The HCP must demonstrate to the patient that he has a lot going for him. Even though he might have lost control on some occasions there is also evidence that he can make a decision and stick to it.

A similar concern has been expressed by Blackwell (1986) who advised HCPs to

1. Not challenge the patient's conceptualization of their condition
2. Find an acceptable definition of the patient's illness since patients search for disease validation
3. Avoid premature reframing of patient's problems (e.g., that stress causes patient's pain)
4. Discuss how patients' symptoms interfere with their daily functioning
5. Avoid ambiguity (e.g., "okay, but" messages)
6. Offer a "good news, bad news" message to the patient
7. Convey deep conviction in the "wisdom of the body"

The latter two points bear a bit more amplification for they convey nicely how one can engage patients as collaborators. In offering "good news–bad news" statements, HCPs can draw the distinction that although medicine does not fully understand the cause of the patient's specific illness (chronic pain, diabetes, hypertension), a great deal can be done to reduce the discomfort and distress. People can learn to function remarkably well in spite of their illnesses. Blackwell illustrates this point by drawing a distinction between "hurt" and "harm" for pain patients. They can continue to undertake numerous activities and the "wisdom of the body" will tell them when they have gone too far. They may feel some hurt (discomfort) but it does not mean greater harm (injury). The patient is seen as a collaborator in the reha-bilitation process in order to develop symptom control and improve daily functioning. The Blackwell guidelines illustrate the need to support all assessment efforts with an adherence-oriented history and an understanding of patient's expectations about treatment.

The questions and messages conveyed by Hingson, DiMatteo and DiNicola, Cummings, Coleman, and Blackwell are all designed to bolster the patient's sense of self-confidence or self-efficacy (Bandura, 1977). Whether it takes the form of "good news, bad news" messages or direct probes about expec-tations, the HCP's interest and concern about patient treatment adherence is earnestly conveyed. The HCP tries to nurture a sense of hopefulness without building up a false sense of denial or an unrealistically optimistic view. Instead, the focus is on nurturing a warranted optimism that follows from short-term accomplishments that grow out of a day-by-day perspective.

The HCP's interest and concern can be conveyed in an even more direct fashion by explicitly asking patients about their expectations concerning treatment and then repeatedly assessing adherence behavior over the course of the treatment regimen. A number of investigators have suggested questions that could be raised about treatment expectations. For example, Lazare *et al.* (1975) suggest that patients be asked, "How do you hope I (or the clinic) can help?" as compared to a request such as "What do you want?" or "What do you expect?"—both of which are likely to be viewed as confrontational in tone. Some open-ended probes can be followed with more specific questions such as:

> You must have had some idea about what could be done when you decided to come? It is important for me to know what your wishes are, even if I may not be able to fulfill them all.
>
> You said you want me to help you understand things better. What in particular do you want to understand?
>
> "You thought you would feel better if I would fix up your family situation. How do you hope I can fix it up?" (Lazere *et al.*, 1975, p. 554)

The need to assess such patient expectations (or parent expectations if the patient is a child) is illustrated by Korsch *et al.* (1968) and Turk, Litt, Salovey, and Walker (1985), who assessed mothers of pediatric patients who visited an emergency room clinic. The mothers entered the clinic with a variety of expectations (e.g., wanting to be told the diagnosis and cause of the current problem) and a variety of fears or anxieties (e.g., Is my child seriously ill?). If the physician met parental expectations or quelled parental concerns, the parent was more likely to be satisfied with care and more likely to adhere to the prescribed regimen. Another example comes from the work of Burstein (1985), who studied patients' expectations concerning the treatment of depression. Many of the patients felt their depression was influenced by psychosocial factors, and when the treatment was restricted to biochemical means (antidepressive medication) they did not adhere to the treatment regimen. There was a clear need for the HCPs to bring the patients' views of their problems into line with the treatment orientation, or a need for the HCPs to broaden the treatment regimen to match the patients' expectations.

The role of patient expectations is not limited to pharmacological intervention. Sue (1977) reported that minority patients are likely to terminate psychotherapy treatment after the first session. Cultural differences between patient and therapist contribute to misunderstandings, mismatched expectations, and different conceptualizations of the presenting problem and the proposed treatment interventions. Mayerson (1984) has suggested that preparing clients for psychotherapy may be useful as a means of aligning patient's and therapist's expectations and as a means of increasing patient adherence. Klein and Carroll (1986) have highlighted the value of preparation (pretherapy training) for participants in group psychotherapy. They note that examining the nature of the referral process, dealing with patient's fears and unrealistic expectations about group therapy, and articulating a clear contract that identifies mutual goals, role expectations, and responsibilities can reduce the dropout rate.

Patients are active processors and recipients of information; there is therefore a clear need to develop a mutuality of expectations between patients and HCPs. Only when such expectations are congruent will patient satisfaction and accompanying treatment adherence be increased. Such joint consideration of mutual expectations will help to nurture a more equitable relationship between patients and HCPs, a relationship where patients can assume greater responsibility for the outcome of the treatment. The task for the HCP shifts to one of helping patients help themselves, as described by Szasz and Hollender's (1956) mutual participation model.

Finally, several investigators have reported the value of explicitly assessing patient expectations in achieving specific treatment goals. In particular, Bandura (1977, 1986) has proposed the usefulness of drawing a distinction between (a) *outcome expectations*—belief about whether a given behavior will lead to given outcomes or judgments of the likely consequences such behavior will produce—and (b) *efficacy expectations*—belief about how capable one is of performing the behavior that leads to those outcomes or judgments of their capabilities to execute a given level of performance. These can be assessed in a two-step process by asking patients whether they believe a particular behavior could be accomplished and then asking them to rate the strength of their beliefs for each designated task. Operationally, patients are presented with a list of performance activities, usually graded in difficulty, and are then asked to judge those tasks they believe they can accomplish at that time. For each designated task they rate the strength of their belief on a 10-unit interval scale ranging from 0 to 100 from high uncertainty, through intermediate values of certainty, to complete certainty. For example, Kaplan, Atkins, and Reinsch (1984) demonstrated the predictive usefulness of asking patients to rate the strength of their expectations (from 0% to 100%, in 10% units) of being able to achieve and adhere to the various components of an exercise treatment regimen.

Yates and Thain (1985) have developed a self-efficacy questionnaire that asks patients to rate on a scale ranging from completely sure (7) to completely unsure (1) whether they felt they could resist smoking in various high-risk situations (e.g., "when you feel impatient, when someone offers you a cigarette, when you are drinking an alcoholic beverage"). Patients' ratings on this questionnaire were useful in identifying patients who were at high risk for relapse. Such a self-efficacy questionnaire could readily be adapted to a variety of clinical populations (e.g., see Condiotte and Lichtenstein, 1981, an efficacy questionnaire for smokers; Weinberger and Agras, 1984, a weight reduction efficacy questionnaire; and Schneider, O'Leary, and Bandura, 1985, an efficacy scale for bulimics). O'Leary (1985) has also described several examples of cases in which it was helpful to solicit spouse's perceptions of patient's ability to perform various treatment components. Caplan (1979) has used an interview format to assess patients' expectations about the treatment regimen. Consider the following questions that focus on weight control, although similar questions could be used with a variety of other disorders:

> *Assess patients' expectancies that they can perform behavioral act.*
> "To what extent do you think you will be able to limit yourself to just three eating periods a day for the next week?"
> *Assess patients' expectancies that the performance of the act will lead to various outcomes.*
> "To what extent do you think that this change in your eating will lead to a) a loss of five pounds in the next two weeks, b) feelings of being hungry all the time, c) difficulties in preparing meals for the rest of the family?"
> *Assess patients' attractiveness or incentive value attached to each outcome.*

"How important is it to you to lose five pounds in the next two weeks?"

"How important is it to avoid feelings of being hungry all of the time?" (p. 80)

Such probes could be directed at any aspect of treatment adherence. The data indicate that patients' answers to such questions are predictive of their adherence (Caplan, 1979; Hoelscher *et al.*, 1986; O'Leary, 1985). As Bandura (1986) notes, "If people are not fully convinced of their personal efficacy, they rapidly abandon the skills they have been taught when they fail to get quick results or experience some reverses." Not only do questions about self-efficacy provide useful prognostic information, but they also provide a much needed diagnostic tool that can be used in selecting adherence enhancement procedures, as discussed in Chapters 5, 6, and 7. Moreover, the assessment of expectations (whether by questionnaire or interview) conveys a phenomenologically based interest in the patients' appraisals of their disorder and their views about alternative treatment interventions.

HCPs can assess patient self-efficacy ratings for performing specific behaviors in specific situations. The magnitude (order of task difficulty), strength (likelihood of performing specific tasks or confidence that they can attain expected level), and the generality (extent to which the expectation applies to other situations) can each be determined. Moreover, it is important to assess patient expectations over the course of treatment in order to chart patient progress and to identify high-risk situations wherein lapses are likely to occur. Expectational ratings can signal where specific tasks should be broken down into simpler, more readily achievable components.

Strecher, DeVellis, Becker, and Rosenstock (1986) and O'Leary (1985), in thoughtful reviews, document the potential usefulness of patient self-efficacy ratings in predicting health behavior change in such areas as cigarette smoking, weight control, contraception, alcohol abuse, pain management, recovery from myocardial infarction, and adherence to preventive health measures such as exercise programs. In each instance, the patient's perception of his or her capabilities was predictive of adherence behavior. A patient's sense of self-efficacy affects not only the amount of effort devoted to a task and the length of persistence when difficulties are encountered but also the individual's physiological reactions such as heart rate, blood pressure, and serum levels of catecholamines in threatening situations (O'Leary, 1985). Although much controversy still exists concerning the conceptualization and assessment of patient expectations (e.g., see Kirsch, 1982, 1985), the finding that people's perceptions of their capabilities affect how they behave has major implications for facilitating treatment adherence.

The HCP's interest in patient adherence has to be evident not only in the initial session when one queries patients about their explanatory model, worries and concerns, adherence-oriented history, and expectations, but also in subsequent sessions. Since patients' beliefs and concerns can change over the course of treatment there is a need to assess repeatedly for treatment adherence. In fact, if the HCP fails to conduct such an inquiry patients tend to conclude that the practitioner does not attach much importance to adherence to the treatment regimen or they tend to doubt the efficacy of the treatment (Svarstad, 1976).

Podell (1975) notes that querying patients about adherence entails more than merely asking them if they took their medicine. Instead, HCPs must seek information about any possible side effects, dose scheduling difficulties, administrative problems, problems with forgetfulness, and the like. It is essential to ask about adherence explicitly:

> Are you taking your medicine every day?
> How many times a day?
> Do you take it before or after meals?
> Is the dose at lunch hard to take?
> How many pills are left? (Podell, 1975, p. 69)

> People often have difficulty taking their pills for one reason or another. Have you ever had any difficulty in taking your pills? (Sackett, 1979b, p. 33)

Sometimes the nature of the probe about adherence can be a bit more indirect as when the HCP uses the proverbial "imaginary other" patient as a means of raising concerns about possible obstacles to adherence:

> Patients often find it hard to remember about taking their medicine. What happened when you forgot? (Francis, Korsch & Morris, 1969)

Another line of inquiry may arise out of the HCP's observation concerning the patient's limited progress.

> Are you having any difficulty fitting the treatment into your daily life? The reason I ask is . . . ?
> You are not doing quite as well as we had hoped? Is there something about the treatment I failed to explain or that you find troubling?

The continual concern about assessing adherence must emanate not only from the physician but also from all members of the treatment team (nurse, receptionist, technical staff, and other paramedical staff). This is particularly important when there is no continuity of care and when patients are seen on a rotational system as in some large clinics (that is, when patients see different HCPs each visit). In this regard, Hogue (1979) has noted that nurses usually take more time to educate patients than do physicians and are more prone to pay more attention to patients' social problems that could impinge on medical care and treatment adherence. The nurses are also more likely to provide greater continuity of care than physicians in medical clinics.

These observations raise several possibilities as to how nurses, dieticians, and pharmacists can be used more productively as adherence counselors, implementing many of the suggestions offered in this book (e.g., taking adherence-oriented history, assessing patients' explanatory models and expectations). In support of this suggestion is the finding reported by DiMatteo and DiNicola (1982b) that nurses were as effective as physicians in implementing patient self-care programs. More-over, given the tendency toward specialization of medicine in Western industrialized nations, the employment of nurses and paramedical staff for adherence counseling is becoming increasingly attractive. As Francis, Korsch, and Morris (1969) noted:

> Medical care is increasingly fragmented and complex, and the warmth of a long-term association with a single physician has become a luxury for a few rather than the customary setting for the delivery of health care. (p. 535)

Each of the communication skills that we have discussed in this chapter, if it is to be effective, must occur within a trusting relationship. Patients must feel secure enough to express doubts and provide negative feedback about features of the treatment regimen. The HCP must encourage patient self-disclosure, expression of misgivings, and reservations. If such a trusting relationship is not established, then one increases the likelihood, as Hippocrates noted, of patients' falsifying their reports. In the present-day context we can view such falsifying as the patient's way of forestalling anticipated interpersonal stress, disapproval, or censure from an often impatient, not very understanding HCP (Kovacs & Feinberg, 1982). Only by establishing a trusting relationship wherein patients feel free to express misgivings, set-backs, and failures can one reduce the likelihood of falsification.

As noted, a number of communication skills contribute to this relationship. These include empathy, respect, sincerity, warmth, sensitivity, emotional expressiveness (e.g., smiles, eye contact), self-disclosure, compassion, cheerfulness, gentleness, and a sense of humor. Whether it is the ability to release the building tension by means of humor or the ability to empathize with patients, the human factor must be underscored. As Ben-Sira (1976, 1980) has reported, practitioners who establish good rapport and who are informative are viewed as highly competent. They tend to answer questions, insure that their patients have an informed understanding of their problems, and employ a positive, caring manner. The value of such relationship skills is underscored by Fawcett and Epstein (1983) who noted:

If the patient has trust in the physician, believes in his/her knowledge and competence, and maintains a conviction that the medication will be helpful, the patient will persist in the course of
therapy even in the absence of initial improvement. (p. 35)

Although we will focus on specific adherence enhancement
techniques in the next section, there is no substitute for the
HCP's leaning over to a distressed patient and saying:

I think I understand how you feel. You really are doing well taking
your medication. Your condition is nearly under control. (DiMatteo
& DiNicola, 1982a, p. 95)

I think I can appreciate how you feel. You have put out so
much effort and yet your condition (e.g., blood glucose
level) continues to fluctuate. But the disappointment, the
blame, the guilt you express are misdirected. It is not that
you haven't tried; rather, it is that in a small percentage of
cases we don't know what causes such fluctuations. If you
continue to put yourself down or get angry with bad results,
this will only make things worse. Let's work together to
find an agreed-upon goal.

I can understand that at times when you have difficulty
sticking to your treatment program (e.g., diet) you would
feel self-critical and as if you could not change, that it was
no use. If you didn't have such feelings of frustration, disappointment, and at times despair, I would feel there was
no hope. Having such reactions are normal and constructive. It tells us both there is more to do. So it didn't work.
That's what we talked about. Let's find out what was the
"it." Let's explore the "doesn't work"!

These examples illustrate the need to combine empathy and
understanding with a need to marshal hope.

Finally, it is worth noting that a number of HCPs have had
the courage to assess systematically their patients' satisfaction
with their treatment efforts. Such openness to feedback (whether
anonymous or not) conveys to patients a willingness to solicit

arid eventually to benefit from such feedback. Attempts at assessing patient satisfaction have become more sophisticated as investigators have replaced global, nondescript questions—Did the health care professional care enough?   Did the health care professional provide enough information?—with more specific probes:

> Did you feel that the instructions about medication taking were clear?
> Did the health care professional allow you to ask about everything you wanted to know about the cause of your illness? (Leventhal *et al.*, 1984, p. 417)

Additional forms of probes are offered in Table 17. The value of assessing patient satisfaction was also reported by Fontana *et al.* (1986), who found that the degree to which cardiac patients liked the rehabilitation staff was predictive of adherence to a postmyocardial infarction exercise program. Illustrative phrases to assess patient satisfaction included "Staff have been friendly and easy to talk to," "Staff have cared about me as a

Table 17 *Questionnaire Used in Assessment of Patient Satisfaction and Understanding*[a]

Understanding
What did the doctor say was the problem?
What did the doctor say caused the problem?
What did the doctor tell you to do about it?
What did the doctor say about what to expect?
What instructions did the doctor give you?
What suggestions did the doctor have for you?

Satisfaction
What did you think of your experience here today?
How satisfied were you with the visit?
Did the doctor explain in such a way that you could understand?
Did the doctor seem concerned about you as a person?
Did the doctor spend as much time with you as you would have liked?
Did you feel that the doctor listened to you?

[a]Adapted from Korsch *et al.*, 1968.

whole person," "Staff have viewed me as just another heart condition" (scored in the reverse direction). Such patient satisfaction
measures hold much promise for the assessment of adherence.

In summary, the discussion of relationship variables indicates the challenge to health care providers. Their attitude and
communication style are critical in preventing and remediating
nonadherence. They must not only assess patients' adherence
behavior but also allow and encourage open discussion of adherence issues. All of the techniques that we will describe in subsequent chapters are destined for failure if the relationship factors
and rapport-building measures described in this chapter are not
established. In the next chapter we will assume that a satisfactory
patient–HCP relationship has been established and consider how
best to provide information about disease, treatment, and self-
care regimens in order to maximize adherence.

Patient Education: Organizing and Structuring Treatment Programs

Satisfaction of the patient is more likely when the doctor discovers and deals with the patient's concerns and expectations; when the doctor's manner communicates warmth, interest and concern about the patient; when the doctor volunteers a lot of information and explains things to the patient in terms that are understood.

D. PENDELTON (1983)

There is an increasing trend toward patient education in hospitals, group clinics, and other health care institutions. These programs are designed to meet some of the patients' most common complaints that their physicians do not tell them enough about their illness (Skillern, 1977) and that they do not pay enough attention to their ideas about treating their medical problems (Brody, 1980b).

In evaluating patient education programs, however, it is important to appreciate the fact that education involves more than the mere exchange of information about illness and treatment. For example, Mazzuca (1982) performed a metaanalysis of 63 patient education programs and concluded that patients need to know less about the pathophysiology of their disease

and more about integrating new demands into their daily schedules and routines. Similarly, Kasl (1975) has noted that the pos-
session of correct information about the disease and medical
regimen is by itself, at best, weakly related to clinical outcome,
especially in long-term care with chronic disease populations. A
similar point was offered by Dunbar and Agras (1980), who
observed that the lack of knowledge about one's medication
regimen or treatment program, not about one's disease, was a
major factor in accounting for treatment nonadherence.

Increasing the patients' knowledge of medication or disease
does not increase adherence unless they are taught how to implement it in their treatment regimen (Boczkowski *et al.*, 1985;
Graber, Christman, Alagna, & Davidson, 1977). Although general medical knowledge does not appear to be associated with
better adherence, a different kind of knowledge does appear to
be related, namely, the extent to which the patient knows what
behaviors the regimen requires, how and when to perform them,
and what to do if problems arise. Such knowledge is a necessary
but often not a sufficient condition for following the regimen.

The crucial element is not the exchange of information and
facts, but an examination of the nature of the expectations the
patient and HCP have about their respective roles and responsibilities (Kasl, 1975). Therefore any effort to provide patients
with technical information should be supplemented with efforts
that focus on the patients' attitudes and beliefs about both treatment and factors that may affect adherence such as concerns
about side effects, drug dependency, and so forth. There is a
clear need to educate patients about the benefits and consequences of adherence.

Before we consider what should go into patient education
programs and the clinical guidelines to follow in their administration, let us examine briefly some of the reasons why patient
education programs have tended not to be more successful. As
Dunbar and Agras (1980) note, "More often patients do feel
willing to adhere, but other factors interfere with their *ability*
to do so" (p. 116). Stone (1979) has identified several factors or

barriers that contribute to the patient's not utilizing the information conveyed. These include:

1. Impediments of language, vocabulary, and conceptual understanding of the messages given
2. Differences in expectations regarding desirable or possible outcome of treatment
3. Differences in role expectations regarding rights, duties, and responsibilities
4. Failure in patients' reception of information for emotional reasons (e.g., anxiety may interfere with information processing and recall)

Table 18 provides examples of illustrated findings that contribute to the inefficacy of patient education programs. These facts illustrate the need to (1) customize the information to the patient's level of ability and circumstance, (2) anticipate and subsume possible difficulties such as forgetfulness and comprehension difficulties, and (3) have HCPs monitor and control their own behavior (e.g., their use of technical jargon). Cassata (1978) has summarized a number of the findings related to information provided to patients by HCPs:

1. Patients forget much of what the doctors tell them.
2. Instructions and advice are more likely to be forgotten than other information.
3. The more a patient is told, the greater the proportion he or she will forget.
4. Patients will remember (a) what they are told first and (b) what they consider most important.
5. Intelligent patients do not remember more than less intelligent patients.
6. Older patients remember just as much as younger ones.
7. Moderately anxious patients recall more of what they are told than highly anxious patients or patients who are not anxious.
8. The more medical knowledge a patient has, the more he or she will recall.
9. If the patient writes down what the doctor says, he or she will remember it just as well as if he or she merely hears it.
10. Jargon should be kept to a minimum. (p. 498)

Table 18   Illustrative Findings That Help to Explain Why Patient Education Programs Are Not More Effective

- In North America over 12 million adults cannot read beyond the fourth-grade level (Eaton, 1974).
- More than half of the medical instructions given by the physicians could not be recalled accurately by patients immediately after they left the consulting room (Ley & Spelman, 1967). Two-thirds of patients forgot their diagnosis and treatment explanations, and one-half forgot instructional statements immediately after an office visit (Dunbar & Agras, 1980).
- From 35% to 92% of patients will not understand general information given to them, and on the average 40% of this information will be forgotten (Ley, 1982).
- Sixty percent of patients misunderstood what their physicians said about taking medication (Boyd, Covington, Stanaszek, & Coussons, 1974). For instance, the instruction "to take medication with meals" resulted in patients' varying their adherence from one hour before to over one hour after mealtime (DiMatteo & DiNicola, 1982a).
- Sixty percent of patients fail to comprehend or else misinterpret directions on prescription labels (Joubert & Lasagna, 1975; McKenney, 1979).
- 21% to 51% of patients do not read the written materials with which they are provided (Glasgow, Schafer, & O'Neill, 1981).
- Physicians learn approximately 13,000 new technical words during the course of medical education that they often use in talking with patients (Blackwell, 1979).
- One-third of patients are dissatisfied with communication from physicians (Ley, 1982).
- Physicians consistently overestimate the amount of time spent in giving information to patients and frequently underestimate the patient's desire for information (Hanson, 1986). Of a 20-minute patient–physician encounter, less than 2 minutes was spent in the transmission of information (Waitzken & Stoeckle, 1976).
- Patients who felt that their physicians spent an inadequate amount of time with them were less likely to adhere. Interestingly, the patient's perception of the amount of time spent with the physician is more important than the actual amount of time spent (Geersten, Gray, & Ward, 1973).
- An examination of 124 self-help manuals had a mean readability at 10th-12th grade level suggesting that 35% of people might have difficulty with them (O'Farrell & Keuthen, 1983).

The latter point raised by Cassata about the interfering effects of *jargon* was illustrated in a study of gaps in doctor–patient communication by Korsch *et al.* (1968). They noted that although some patients were impressed with the doctors' use of technical, or what one mother called "medical talk," the use of medical jargon often blocked effective communication of ideas and led to lower patient satisfaction and greater nonadherence. Some of the terms used by physicians were obviously technical (e.g., sphincter, labia, edema, biopsy, peristalsis, lumbar puncture, Coombs titre), but the patients' confusion often extended to such terms as *work up*, *follow-up*, and *history*. For instance, one patient did not understand that a work up meant the hospitalization of her child. Similarly, Leventhal *et al.* (1984) reported that the technical term for high blood pressure, *hypertension* is regularly misunderstood to mean "high levels of nervous tension." The important point is not that such misunderstanding can and will occur but the fact that *patients rarely tell HCPs that they do not understand*. They are reluctant to ask questions for fear of appearing stupid and because they may not even be sure of what to ask. Patients may not know what they do not know.

The patient's lack of understanding occurs even when medication or a specific treatment program is prescribed. In many instances, however, the treatment regimen is not explicitly prescribed. For example, Svarstad's (1974) observational study of patient–physician interactions revealed that 17% of the time practitioners failed to state the treatment regimen. To complicate matters even further, 20% of the time when medication prescriptions were written, there was a discrepancy between what the pharmacist wrote on the label and what the physician had prescribed! Although later studies, as reviewed by Leventhal *et al.* (1984), suggest that such prescription errors occur less frequently, the Svarstad findings underscore the need for HCPs to monitor more carefully the way in which treatment regimens are offered. This is especially important when we consider the findings by Mattar, Markello, and Yaffe (1975), who showed that pharmacists dispensed less than the prescribed amount of antibiotic for 15% of their patients. This was attributed to the pharmacists' not stocking the prescribed bottle size.

All too often HCPs think they know patients' needs and wants without asking them. This is particularly evident in how they interact with patients of different socioeconomic classes. Brody (1980a) observed that physicians tended to provide patients of a higher social class with more information than lower-class patients. Patients of lower socioeconomic status tend to ask fewer questions, to be less assertive, and to be more often intimidated by the physician's status. What is unfortunate about these patterns is that patients from all social classes can benefit from both active participation in medical decisions and the provision of information.

Providing Patients with Information

A major feature of patient education is sharing information, but also carefully insuring that what has been offered has indeed been understood and, moreover, will be applied by the patient. The art of treatment is to customize any instruction individually to the level and needs of the patient. The wording, pacing, and manner with which HCPs convey information are critical. In order to illustrate how information may be conveyed when prescribing medication two examples are offered. The first example is for the treatment of an acute disorder, namely, prescribing amoxicillin for the treatment of a childhood ear infection, otitis media. Amoxicillin trihydrate is one of the most common prescriptions written by pediatricians and given to children's parents to administer. The second example concerns the prescription of lithium carbonate for the treatment of a bipolar or manic-depressive disorder. In both cases we will consider what information must be conveyed in order to increase the likelihood of adherence.

Treating an Acute Disorder by Means of Medication

All too often physicians tend to be perfunctory in how they prescribe medication. We authors are fathers to six children ranging in age from 4 to 18, and over the years we have noted what physicians say when prescribing medication. A not unusual message is the following:

> I am prescribing amoxicillin for your son's ear infection. You should give it to him four times a day. It should make him feel better pretty quickly. If he's not better in a few days, give me a call.

Consider an alternative, more comprehensive communication that anticipates and subsumes potential problems contributing to nonadherence. (Although the exact wording may vary depending upon the particulars of the situation, it illustrates how the HCP can address adherence issues.)

> Mrs. Smith, your son Larry has a common ear infection called otitis media. We can treat this disease quite easily and very successfully with an antibiotic called amoxicillin. This medication is given as a liquid and should be given to him *four times a day for 10 full days* not only to make him feel better but to cure the disease. Often, the child's pain and suffering are greatly reduced within a day or so; however, it is very important for him to take the medicine for the full 10 days because the infection can return. Some parents stop too soon. I will give you a prescription for a full 10 days. Therefore, you must make sure that Larry takes all of the medicine in the bottle *until it is empty.*
>
> It is important that you give Larry one teaspoon of the medicine four times a day. Usually it is best to give it first thing in the morning, with lunch, with dinner, and at bedtime. It is important that the medication be kept cool, best if it can be kept in a refrigerator. Make sure you shake the bottle before pouring. Can you see any problem with this type of schedule? What will you do if you forget to give Larry one of his regular doses?
>
> The medicine is a pink liquid that most children find has a pleasant taste. Some children even say it smells a little bit like bubble gum. Have you had any problem in the past with Larry's willingness to take liquid medication? How did you handle that?

Sometimes children spill the medicine or some of it dribbles onto their clothing. If Larry spills a little this is not a big problem, but if he spills a whole teaspoon then you must give him another one. If this happens *more than three times* then let me know, for I will have to give you a prescription for some extra medicine.

You mentioned that you are working part time and a babysitter takes care of Larry from breakfast until dinner three days a week. I am wondering what you will tell the babysitter about Larry's ear infection and what she should do about giving him the medication?

If anything unusual comes up or if Larry doesn't start to feel better in the next two days, be sure to give me a call. Remember, make sure Larry takes his medicine four times a day until you *use up the entire* bottle because we don't want the infection to come back in just a few days. Do you have any questions or concerns?

This example illustrates several important guidelines. The physician

1. Named the child's disorder (otitis media) and named the medication (amoxicillin)
2. Provided reassurance that the child's disorder (ear infection) is readily treatable and curable
3. Carefully reviewed the schedule of medication (dosage, timing, course)
4. Probed about previous adherence problems
5. Anticipated potential problems that might contribute to nonadherence (forgetfulness, spillage, babysitter) and addressed how to handle them
6. Checked patient comprehension
7. Probed for patient's questions and concerns
8. Used repetition of critical points
9. Emphasized the importance of adherence to the full therapeutic regimen

These guidelines are also relevant in the treatment of chronic disorders with more complex therapeutic regimens (e.g., diabetes, end-stage renal disease, schizophrenia). The following example illustrates how a physician can apply these guidelines to the treatment of a chronic psychiatric disorder. In addition to the above nine guidelines, two other features are carefully considered, namely, the role of potential side effects and how these can be handled and the role of significant others in fostering adherence to the treatment regimen.

Treating a Chronic Disorder by Means of Medication

The treatment of patients with chronic disorders provides HCPs with an opportunity to limit the amount of information that is conveyed at any one session. Clearly, one must not overwhelm the patient, and one must pace the discussion to the emotional state and needs of the patient. As we noted in Chapter 2, one of the factors influencing adherence is the stage of the disorder and the state of the patient in coming to terms with his or her condition and its implications. The following example[7] is taken from what might transpire in an initial prescription session with a manic-depressive patient. (Once again, let us reiterate that there is no one correct script. Instead, this example is offered as a means of illustrating how HCPs must address issues of nonadherence. The example is not intended to provide an exhaustive coverage of every medication issue.)

> **Information about Disorder.** Mrs. Smith, I would like to review with you the results of your evaluation. As you know, we spent a good deal of time with you and your husband and also obtained information from your grown children. We appreciate your honesty in giving us this information and the cooperation of you and your family.
>
> The condition that you have is called bipolar illness or manic-depressive illness. This condition is not a rare one and does affect 1% of the population. As you know from your own history, it can be quite debilitating, with periods

[7]The authors are indebted to Dr. John Rush, Betty Jo Hay Professor of Psychiatry at the University of Texas Health Science Center, for his help in formulating this example. Cochran (1986) and Shou (1980) have provided additional suggestions for patients taking Lithium Carbonate.

of severe depression, interspersed with some normal times, and then periods of hyperactivity that we call mania. It often goes unrecognized for some years before a correct diagnosis is made, as in your case.

Provision of Reassurance and Naming and Describing of the Medication. We have a specific treatment for this, which consists of a medication called lithium carbonate. Sometimes we add an additional medication, either an antidepressant or antimanic medication to lithium, but in most cases (about 70%), lithium alone is sufficient. As we shall discuss in a moment, the medication lithium is usually quite effective and it has only modest side effects that we can control. It will be important, however, to take the lithium exactly as prescribed.

At this point the physician explains how lithium is designed to affect the patient's mood swings. *The physician also comments on the need for the patient to expect gradual improvement*, rather than expecting an all or none response. The physician highlights that it will be important to take *lithium on both good and bad days*. (The latter point will be reiterated several times).

Let me describe what we expect as a result of the medication, so that you will know the specific symptoms that we are attempting to treat and can monitor them closely to help us set up the best medication treatment and schedule for you. First, lithium should gradually reduce the depressive symptoms and in fact should help prevent the manic episodes that you have reported. I expect that your sleep will be a normal 7–8 hours per night; I also expect your energy to be normal, your appetite to be normal, and your mood to be normal and appropriate to events that are occurring around you. If something tragic or sad happens, you will feel sad and lithium will not prevent this. On the other hand, if minor events occur which trigger a great amount of sadness, such as when you are depressed, lithium will help prevent this intense emotional reaction. Thus, I expect the lithium to stop both the manic and depressive episodes. Lithium is not addicting nor habit forming. It does not produce either "highs or lows" in people. It just helps *to control marked shifts in mood*.

Dosage Schedule. In thinking about setting a schedule for you to take the medication, we must consider your daily routine. At first, it is best to take your lithium at bedtime. What time do you usually go to bed? Okay, then beginning today and for the next two days you should take your pill at X P.M. (agreed-upon time). *After the first three days*, you will have to take your Lithium pills *twice a day*. It is usually easiest to remember to take the pills at regular times, like bedtime or when getting up in the morning. What time do you usually get up in the morning? Okay, then you should take your medication upon waking in the morning, about X A.M. How does taking one pill in the morning when you wake up and one pill in the evening before going to bed sound? Is this something you think you can do regularly?

After the first week of taking your lithium, I would like to see you again so we can review the effects of your medication. I expect the optimal level to be a total of somewhere between 3 and 5 tablets per day. Lithium must be taken even on days when you are feeling good and your mood seems fine. Taking the medication regularly will reduce the likelihood of a recurrence of your extreme mood swings.

Anticipating Forgetfulness. Sometimes we all forget things we are supposed to do, like taking medication. That is only human. Let us consider what you can do to make sure you don't forget to take your medicine. This is important because if the lithium is to have an effect you must take all of it *as prescribed*, even if you are feeling okay.

At this point the physician considers ways to avoid patient forgetfulness and what the patient should do if she forgets. In a collaborative fashion the physician must customize the reminder procedures (e.g., where to put the medication, what to do when traveling). The physician will then explore any other possible barriers that might interfere with adherence.

Since on your job you travel quite a bit, you might forget to take your lithium with you. If that occurs you should call my office and I will contact a pharmacy near you to insure that you have the lithium. I usually suggest that when the patient is traveling some lithium be kept in the purse and a second source be kept in your suitcase so that if one becomes misplaced you still have access to the other. It is essential, however, that this medication be kept out of the reach of children and in a child-proof container. Do you know how these containers work? Let me show you. Sometimes I think the drug companies make these adult-proof as well as child-proof.

Insuring and Checking Patient Comprehension. Can you think of any other problems, besides possibly forgetting, that you might encounter? If not, then let us review the schedule once again. When will you take the lithium today? What about the next two days? Then what will your regular schedule be? Good!

I have written all this information down for you as well, so you won't get confused. If you wish, you can show it to your family so they can help you remember to take your lithium pills. I have written out the name of the medicine, exactly how many and when you are to take them, and the reasons for taking lithium. Let us go over this informational sheet to make sure you understand what I am prescribing and why. . . . Do you have any questions or concerns so far?

At this point the physician should encourage the patient to express any concerns about taking lithium and elicit any experiences or information she has from other sources. Patients often have read something in the lay literature about lithium and taking medication often has some particular personal or symbolic meaning. Most commonly, patients will incorrectly view taking medication as evidence that they cannot do anything at all to help themselves but rather have to depend entirely on medication. Whether or not these concerns are elicited, they are addressed in subsequent dialogue. In the context of exploring the patient's concerns the physician can obtain the patient's prior history with medication—conduct adherence-oriented history. (As we shall note later in this chapter, it is also important to discuss possible side effects with the patient.)

Discussion of Side Effects. There are some side effects with lithium, as with all medications, and I want first to review the initial side effects and then to discuss any possible long-term side effects. I want also to discuss what we can do to prevent and reduce the likelihood and impact of such side effects. Initially, when people begin taking lithium they often notice an increased amount and frequency of urination. This occurs particularly in the first 7–14 days and is caused by the fact that lithium is a salt and so is managed by the kidneys. This should not cause great concern on your part, but you should be made aware that initially you will have an increased amount of urine that will gradually return to normal over about 2–3 weeks. In addition, during the first few days lithium may cause you to feel sleepy, and for that reason I recommend that the medication be taken at bedtime. It should, however, not make you feel sleepy, groggy, or "drugged out" during the day. People will not notice that you are in a drugged condition. Furthermore some people notice an initial slight metallic taste in their mouths, but most adjust to this and it disappears.

The physician can then consider any other potential side effects (nausea, abdominal discomfort).

If lithium is carefully monitored long-term side effects are extremely rare. At this point the physician reviews with the patient how he or she will keep track of possible side effects (e.g., monitor blood level on weekly basis at first, then once every 2–3 months, in order to check for toxicity, as well discuss the need to check thyroid and kidney functions). In discussing these potential side effects it is important not to scare the patient nor overhwlem her. Whenever a possible side effect is mentioned the physician should reassure the patient that some alternative medication or treatment is available.

As long as we carefully and regularly monitor your reactions to the lithium you should have little or no problem. I have written a list of the benefits you can expect from taking lithium and a list of possible side effects. Next to each potential side effect I have included what we can do to handle it. Such side effects occur quite infrequently. But because each person is unique and each patient's situation is different, I will need your help in reporting your reactions, especially if anything unusual occurs (e.g.,diarrhea, shakiness in the hands). If these symptoms occur you should call me and we will check the lithium level and modify the dose or change the medication. As I mentioned, at the ordinary dosage that we will be using, you should not have any of these side effects. Let me now review this informational sheet with you. . . . Do you have any questions about possible side effects and what we can do about them? *Let me reassure you that the long-term benefits from taking the lithium will outweight any short-term inconvenience.* Do you see it that way as well?

As a team, and with the help of medication and your family, I think you can come to control the extreme mood swings you are experiencing. Once you get into the habit of taking the lithium every day you should begin gradually to see improvement until you are functioning in your normal manner. Now that we have discussed the treatment plan, do you feel that it will help you with your mood swings? Do you feel that you will be able to take the medication as prescribed?

Involving Significant Others. Since you commented on your husband's and children's concern about your medicine, I would like us both to discuss the treatment recommendation of your taking lithium with your family, so that they can better understand why you are taking it, its expected effects, and possible side effects. Is this all right with you? I would like to call them in so that we can discuss your treatment together. I will start us off, but I would like you to contribute as much as possible, describing when you will take the medication, what it is intended to do, and so forth. Is that okay with you? Good!

At this point the physician would bring in family members and encourage the patient to explain in her own words the nature of her illness and the information about lithium (dosage schedule, potential benefits, and possible side effects). Having the patient actively participate provides an opportunity to assess her comprehension, to elicit a public commitment, and to strengthen her adherence-related attitudes.

With the family members the physician would highlight the nature of the patient's condition and the rationale underlying the treatment plan. The physician would solicit their concerns and query them about what, if any, difficulties they foresee in the patient following the treatment regimen. As a group they are encouraged to explore what solutions might work best. It is important to follow the patient's lead and wishes since the family's involvement may not always be viewed as supportive.

Finally, there is one last thing I wish to mention to all of you, namely, that certain medications should not be taken with lithium unless done so under medical advice. So when a doctor prescribes another medication for you, you should always mention that you are currently taking lithium in order to be sure that the additional medication is acceptable.

I would like for all of you to read about lithium. I have given some informational sheets to Mrs. Smith, and I would like you to read this information before our next session so that if you have any questions I can answer them in detail. Do you have any questions or concerns now? Be sure to write down any questions or concerns as they come up and bring them in next time.

Now that we have discussed the treatment plan of your taking lithium, Mrs. Smith, do you feel that it will help you with your mood swings? Do you feel that you will be able to take the medication as prescribed? Feel free, all of you, to call if there are any questions or concerns about the treatment or about Mrs. Smith's condition.

As we shall consider in subsequent chapters, soliciting the patient's prediction or sense of efficacy in carrying out the treatment regimen in the presence of others increases the likelihood of adherence.

From a trained viewpoint, it would be interesting if similar scripts and handout materials (i.e., accompanying information about rationale, dosage schedule, side effects, and *Physicians' Desk Reference* material written in simple non-jargon terms) were available for each major medication offered. Imagine if medical students and pharmacists were exposed to such training materials. What if pharmaceutical companies provided such scripts and accompanying informational packages with each major sample of medication? In fact, we can envisage research efforts to evaluate systematically what is the best instructional script with the long-term result of creating a library of videotape training films on the best way to prescribe medication. What does the physician say to a mother who must give her child a course of antibiotics? What would the script look like if the total amount of time allotted were only two or three minutes rather than the twenty minutes offered above for lithium treatment? What would the script look like for hypertensives, diabetics, schizophrenics? In each case the script would act as a framework or checklist and provide a set of guidelines.

It is feasible that a similar videotape library could be developed for the patient that could be viewed at the doctor's office, or while the patient is in the hospital, or at the pharmacy when he is picking up medication. In this way the busy and harried HCP could say to the patient:

> Since taking medication is important in the treatment of your condition, I want to make sure that all of your concerns and questions are addressed and that you fully understand what you are to do and why. I would like to suggest that you take a few minutes and step next door where my nurse (receptionist) will show you a brief videotape that will describe your condition and specifically review your medication treatment plan. After you watch the videotape, we will have a chance to chat in order to make sure you understood the material. Many of our patients have found these brief films quite helpful. In this way I am sure that the most important information will be reviewed concerning dosage schedule, expected positive effects, possible side effects, and what can be done to prevent and reduce any such side effects. The brief film also examines any possible difficulties that may keep people from taking their medicine such as sometimes forgetting. This information is also summarized in a handout that you will be given to take home. I am concerned that you receive the best treatment and most importantly that you are able to follow through in taking the medication as prescribed. Do you have any questions or concerns about watching this film?

The research on treatment adherence and patient education has contributed to the development of a set of specific guidelines to be followed in prescribing medication and in providing information. Table 19 provides a comprehensive set of guidelines to

Table 19   Guidelines to Follow When Prescribing Treatment Regimens[a]

- Establish a trusting, supportive relationship and demonstrate interest in the patient. Use a warm and empathic manner, conveying competence, confidence, and knowledge concerning treatment regimen, and a sense of hope and optimism. Provide constancy of care and ongoing contact. Integrate concerns about adherence into totality of patient care. Elicit and nurture the patient's confidence in treatment.
- Identify target and accessory symptoms before discussing medication effects. Assess for target symptoms throughout the course of treatment. If there are many symptoms, probe by categories.
- Assess patient's expectations, beliefs about illness (cause, severity, course). Conduct an adherence-oriented history. Obtain a comprehensive history of previous experience with pharmacotherapy (including specific dosages and treatment durations). Assess for barriers to adherence.
- Describe to the patient the condition, how it is to be treated, and the kind of medication or form of treatment required. Give rationale and justification for drug use and treatment strategy and comment on goals of treatment. Include an understandable explanatory model of how and why medication should be effective. Discuss information about treatment options available and specific behaviors required of the patient in order to carry out the treatment regimen.
- Simplify regimen if possible. Minimize different medications, number of doses, and schedule variations. Prescribe the fewest number of medications the least number of times per day. When appropriate, use combination of dosages in single tablets or slow-release preparations. Synchronize the schedule for doses of different medications. When appropriate, be flexible in the dosage, titrating in order to manage side effects.
- Prioritize treatment in a stepwise fashion, introducing components of regimen in a gradual manner. For instance, if treatment requires multiple medication, when adherence appears to be adequate a second medication can be introduced. Keep treatment regimen as simple and nonintrusive as possible.
- Give name of medication or treatment and check to see that patient knows name.
- Describe specific purpose and function (expectec action—in lay language) of prescribed medication or treatment. Tell the patient what the treatment does. When appropriate, indicate that the prescribed dosage may have to be adjusted in order to achieve desired effect. In order to combat patient's false expectations of an "all or none" response to medication, introduce the idea of progressive improvement or gradual response to treatment.
- Review specifics of taking medication or following treatment regimen:
  special directions for preparation
  special directions and any precautions required in administration

(continued)

Table 19 (continued)

Review specifics (*continued*)
    number of pills to be taken, when, dosage, duration
    action to be taken in case of missed dose
    individual tailoring to specific patient and treatment
- Check patients' comprehension. Question directly about medication. Ask the patients to repeat key points. Encourage them actively to reword the instructions. Ask them if they know what they are taking? When they should take it? How much they need to take? What if they miss a dose?
- Counsel about necessity of a complete course of treatment in order to avoid reoccurrence. Anticipate that early in treatment some patients may discontinue medication if they do not observe obvious benefits. Similarly, later in treatment some patients may discontinue if after obtaining a partial or full therapeutic response they do not understand the need to continue therapy (taking medication).
- Consider immediate and delayed beneficial consequences. Make sure the patient understands that some medications take time to exert their effects. Stress that long-term benefits outweigh short-term inconvenience. Communicate expectation of potential benefits of taking medication. When appropriate, indicate the delayed effect of medication or "lag period," when little or no therapeutic response is evident.
- Encourage discussion concerning cost and risks versus benefits of following treatment regimen.
- Assess the patient's attitude toward medication prophylaxis, side effects, fears about being "controlled" by a drug, concerns about addiction and social stigma. Encourage the patient to express his or her concerns, fears, and attitudes regarding medication. Ask if the patient has any questions. Foster an open discussion of doubts and concerns.
- Discuss and reduce fear of possible side effects and problems associated with medication or treatment. Do not engage in premature discussion of side effects prior to a thorough discussion of the therapeutic benefits of the medication, but discuss troubling side effects early in the course of treatment. When appropriate, reassure patient that the severity of side effects usually decreases over time.
- Forewarn patients about potential side effects that may be encountered, including their avoidance and action required if they occur. Encourage patients to report side effects and reassure them that such side effects are not dangerous if reported promptly and managed correctly. Tell them to telephone if any problems arise.
- Monitor the patient's therapeutic response and look for early signs of side effects. Ask about side effects in a nonthreatening, nonjudgmental fashion. Provide patient with positive feedback about his or her behavior (e.g., praise, comment on test results and behavioral signs of improvement). Indicate how following the treatment regimen has led to these results.

Table 19 (continued)

- Discuss ways in which the patient can self-monitor or keep track of drug or other forms of treatment. Help patient devise way to remember medication, utilize your advice, and adjust the treatment regimen to particular circumstances. Adapt treatment to features of the patient's life style. In subsequent sessions ask about self-monitoring and give feedback.
- Caution about drug–drug, drug–food, and other therapeutic contraindications. Caution against taking more than is prescribed and against self-prescribed reduction in dosage.
- Ensure that prescription labels are clear and understood by the patient and that the bottles show the name of the drug.
- Give simple, typed information sheets that outline reasons for taking the drug, the action, dosage schedule, side effects, and what patient should do if side effects occur.
- Write prescription with limited refills in order to keep track of medication the patient takes. Have pharmacy call when refills are needed in order to keep track of dosage. When appropriate, use calendar packaging like that used in birth control pills. Make sure patients understand when you want them to come back and why.
- Insure that easy-to-open packaging is used except where otherwise indicated.
- If appropriate, involve significant others (spouse, family members, community agencies) in supervision of patient's medication schedule. Explain what patient is to do and why it is to be done.
- Encourage patient to write down any questions or concerns as they come up and bring them in the next time.
- Ensure that patients feel they can follow the treatment regimen. In protracted treatments discuss termination and, when appropriate, what are the demands, potential barriers, and skills needed in the maintenance phase. Also consider fears about going off medication.
- Ask about adherence at next session. Ask patient to describe the affects of medication. Note that patients are particularly at high risk to discontinue the medication shortly after initial improvement. Anticipate this in treatment counseling in order to prevent premature discontinuation of medication.
- Never assume that adherence is satisfactory. Make adherence a priority, specifically and routinely inquiring about it. If nonadherence is detected, investigate the cause. Consider any possible obstacles to adherence.
- Treat the whole person, not the disease. When indicated, involve other professionals and social agencies to provide needed training and support.

[a]Suggestions gleaned from Anderson & Kirk, 1982; Chan, 1984; Coleman, 1985; Dunbar & Agras, 1980; Eraker *et al.*, 1977; Fawcett & Epstein, 1983; Hanson, 1986; Matthews & Hingson, 1977; McKenney, 1979; Podell, 1975; Seltzer & Hoffman, 1980; Turk *et al.*, 1983.

be followed when describing a treatment regimen, as in the case of prescribing medication. These guidelines provide a useful framework against which to evaluate how one discusses treatment programs with patients. A major feature is not only how one describes the medication (rationale, dosage schedule, potential side effects), but also the need for follow-up assessment in subsequent sessions.

In recent years many programs have been developed to provide patients with information about both their disorder (e.g., diabetes, hypertension, schizophrenia, hyperactivity) and the treatment regimen. After reviewing the literature on patient education, we were able to identify a set of guidelines HCPs should follow in providing such information to patients and significant others (e.g., their family members). The HCP's adherence to these guidelines (see Table 20) will increase the likelihood of the information being noticed, read, understood, believed, remembered, and capable of producing the desired behavioral changes (Levy, 1986).

In fact, the guidelines offered in Tables 19 and 20 provide a blueprint for the development of a library of videotapes for prescribing medication and treatment programs. The suggestion for developing a videotape series on medication to enhance adherence is merely an extension of an already existing form of patient education, namely, the provision of written instructions and warnings with prescriptions. As Morris and Halperin (1979) conclude, such written medication information may be effective in enhancing adherence for short-term drug therapy, but as a sole intervention with long-term drug treatment it has not led to improved patient adherence.

A compromising factor in the use of such instructions and drug inserts has been their complexity and lack of comprehensibility. Unfortunately, as Pyrczak and Roth (1976) have found, the directions that accompany both prescription and nonprescription drugs are usually too difficult to comprehend for a large segment of the population. For example, they determined that understanding the warning inserts for a variety of over-the-counter drugs (e.g., Ben Gay, Compoz, Di-Gel, Nytol,

Table 20   Guidelines to Follow in Giving Information[a]

- Be selective in information to be given; the fewer the instructions given, the greater the recall. Giving too much as well as too little information can contribute to treatment nonadherence.
- Be specific, clear, detailed, concrete, and simple in communicating and giving instructions. Use short words and short sentences. Limit number of words per sentence and number of syllables per word. Use down-to-earth, non-technical language without medical jargon.
- Be careful about the timing of the information. Give small amounts of information at each visit. Do not overload the patient with details. Information should be dispensed in discrete quantities over time. Individually pace and tailor the program. Different patients need different kinds of information at different intervals. Check for receptivity and understanding.
- Organize material. There is greater recall of information presented in the first third of communication and greater recall of the first instruction offered.
- Include rationale for the treatment regimen, the specific patient behavior required, and the possible consequences of failure to follow the regimen.
- Determine whether the information corresponds with the patient's private theories about the illness and what should be done about it. Evaluate patient's perception of regimen at the time it is instituted and after it has been initiated.
- Provide advance organizers of what you are about to say (e.g., "First, I am going to describe the medication you are to take; then I will describe the changes needed in your diet").
- Whenever possible present information about the course of action to be followed near the beginning of the session. Provide rationale for recommendations and statement of treatment goals.
- Use explicit categorization of topics where possible. Categorize information: for example, diagnosis, diagnostic tests, prescribed treatment. What patient must do. If diagnosis is given before treatment regimen is described, the patient may "tune into" diagnosis that leads to interfering thoughts and feelings and fail to attend and process material on treatment regimen.
- Repeat important information when possible. Reinforce essential points. Emphasized material is recalled better.
- Use concrete illustrations, mnemonic devices, analogies, retrieval cues such as acronyms, anecdotes, self-disclosure. Heighten personal relevance of material and tie into personal experience.
- Use oral and written material together, which is more effective than either alone. Supplement when appropriate with audiovisual material and visual graphic aides (slides, audiotapes, videotapes, films, anatomical models, educational sheets, take-home booklets, newspaper or magazine articles, diagrams, charts) Use memory aides such as summaries and outlines. Be sure that the patient can comprehend written material.

(continued)

Table 20 *(continued)*

- When providing patients with a course of action to be adhered to, stress how important it is.
- Check patient's comprehension. Ask questions and solicit feedback. Also encourage patient to raise questions and take notes or write summaries. Use pre–post tests. Have patient repeat key features of every message.
- Promote active reworking of material (e.g., ask the patient to restate the information given). Patients have to rehearse the information mentally and mechanically so that it is stored correctly and readily retrieved and so that the health care provider can assess whether the patient understands the information and can satisfactorily carry out the instructions.
- Encourage the patient to discuss treatment regimen with health educator and participate in planning their regimen. Quantify patient expectations rather than leaving them vague.
- Help the patient set realistic goals that can be subdivided into easily attained steps.
- Components of the treatment regimen should be taught in a gradual, incremental fashion, rather than prescribed for implementation all at once.
- Insure that the patient has requisite skills required to follow treatment regimen. Where appropriate include strategies to facilitate lifestyle changes.
- Individualize instruction and give feedback and praise for effort. Nurture the patient's self-confidence that he or she can be successful in following treatment regimen.
- Involve the patient and significant other (where appropriate) in therapeutic planning and decisions.
- Do not oversell program.
- Help the patient remove barriers caused by the regimen itself.
- Supplement educational efforts with adherence counseling (e.g., predischarge counseling with a pharmacist, home visits by a nurse).

---

*a*Suggestions gleaned from Becker & Rosenstock, 1984; Blackwell, 1979; Cassata, 1978; DiMatteo & DiNicola, 1982a; Dunbar & Agras, 1980; Eraker *et al.*, 1984; Friedman & Litt, 1986; Holder, 1972; Leventhal *et al.*, 1984; Ley, 1977, 1982; Pendleton & Hasler, 1983; Rosenstock, 1985; Rosensthal & Downs, 1985; Turk *et al.*, 1983; Turk *et al.*, 1986.

Preparation H, and Vick's Cough Syrup) required an 11th-grade reading level. These results are consistent with those reported by Ley (1982), who reported that approximately two-thirds of educational leaflets distributed by HCPs are too difficult for two-thirds of their patients. These findings underscore the necessity for HCPs to assess the readability level of all written material given to patients.

Useful and simple measures of assessing readability level have been offered by Dale and Chall (1948) and Flesch (1948). These formulas take account of the level of difficulty (polysyllabic nature and unfamiliarity) of individual words and of the length of sentence. Although using such readability formulas provides a convenient way to estimate the difficulty of reading material, they should not be the sole means of assessment. As Pichert and Elam (1985) note, most readability formulas were not developed on patients, and other factors besides readability must be considered in writing educational material (e.g., meaningfulness, organization, interest level). The authors also provide useful guidelines for writing easy-to-read texts. In short, there is a clear need carefully to evaluate patient reading materials since the patient's adherence may depend upon the readability of the written information (Ley, Jain, & Stalbeck, 1976; Ley & Spelman, 1967).

Recent studies have indicated that the impact of health-related information can be enhanced by including vivid case history information (Rook, 1986; Taylor & Thompson, 1982). When abstract information (listing of statistical risks of illness, logical arguments referring to patients in general) was compared with vivid, emotionally charged personal case histories, each of which had equivalent information, it was the case histories that had much greater impact. Health information that presents an interesting, compelling, inspiring case history is more persuasive, evokes greater imagery, is comprehended and remembered more easily, is more emotionally arousing, fosters empathy and identification with the case subject and nurtures a more optimistic, hopeful view about the prospects of improving the patient's health status (Rook, 1986). The timely case history, anecdote, metaphor, or analogy can provide an engrossing means to convey information. This is particularly important for people who are complacent about potential health threats, especially if the risk is distant and there are no current actual symptoms.

As one considers these educational guidelines, it is important to remember that the goal of any treatment program is to foster adherence when supervision has been withdrawn. This is a particular problem when the patient's disorder requires life-long medical care (e.g., end-stage renal disease, diabetes, hypertension). As Luscher and his colleagues (1985) note, patient education programs tend to be more effective in short-term therapies than in long-term treatment. HCPs must educate and reeducate patients about the importance of maintenance and ways in which it can be accomplished. This point was further emphasized by Caldwell, Cobb, Dowling, and Jongh (1970), who reported that patients often discontinued treatment when they felt better. Education programs must address the point that *feeling* well does not necessarily mean *being* well. One must help patients understand that treatment should be continuous and should not be stopped prematurely without HCP supervision. In many instances, follow-up interventions to continue education will be required. As Lawrence and Cheely (1980) demonstrated with diabetic patients, over time patients' skills may deteriorate.

It is also important to appreciate the fact that patients' understanding, especially about their condition and the treatment regimen, appears to be a necessary but insufficient condition to ensure treatment adherence. More than education is required. In the next two chapters we will consider just what more is required. However, before we consider these supplemental interventions several specific issues related to patient education are worth considering. These include the need to:

- Simplify and customize the treatment regimen
- Reduce patients' forgetfulness
- Discuss possible side effects of the treatment

Each of these factors has been found to have an impact on treatment adherence, and they bear additional comment.

Simplifying and Customizing the Treatment Regimen

As noted in Chapter 2, one of the more easily replicable findings is that the simpler the treatment regimen, the greater the level of adherence. This observation has led a number of authors (Matthews & Hingson, 1977; McKenney, 1979) to encourage medical practitioners:

1. To reduce the number of daily medications prescribed (e.g., the number of pills to be taken per day)
2. Where applicable, to use long-acting pharmaceuticals
3. To avoid divided doses when once-a-day administration would be equally effective
4. Where applicable, to use a combination of medications
5. To use calendar dispensers when complicated treatment regimens are being used.

The value of such guidelines is underscored by Dunbar and Agras (1980), who report a significant lowering of patient adherence when three or more drugs are prescribed or when medication is combined with other forms of treatment. When patients are asked to take frequent doses scheduling errors often result. However, one must follow this advice to reduce medication demands with a cautionary note: combining medications may of course contribute to possible side effects and obscure specific treatment effects.

The notion of simplifying the treatment regimen applies as well to behavioral life-style programs. Whether it is medication or other forms of treatment, patients may be able to handle only a limited number of demands and changes in their lives at any given time. The importance of gradualism, or introducing incremental treatment demands in a stepwise fashion, will be examined in more detail when we discuss behavior modification interventions in Chapter 5.

The concept of customizing extends from ensuring that the messages offered are appropriate to the patient in terms of age, intellectual or educational level, and cultural background all the way to fitting the prescribed intervention to the specific patient characteristics, circumstances, personal habits, and routines. The treatment should be as convenient, tolerable, and self-determined as possible. The HCP must question the patient about his or her daily routines, and the HCP and the patient must determine together the best times to take medication (within the realities and restrictions of the treatment regimen) or follow the treatment regimen so as to cause the least disruption. Whenever possible, it is helpful to select dosage intervals and packaging and treatment routines (e.g., taking medication after brushing one's teeth) that fit comfortably into the patient's life and meet his or her particular situational characteristics. For example, special drug packaging has been found to enhance adherence in the elderly. Peck and King (1982) noted that "unit-of-use" packaging (i.e., the pill is packaged into separate days or separate doses per day) reduced patient confusion and enhanced adherence. Fox (1977) suggests that with the elderly, medication should be restricted to not more than three prescriptions, each having a distinct color. Such strategies should be worked out collaboratively with the patient. The HCP should not take for granted the regularity of events such as the patient's eating three evenly spaced meals a day when prescribing a treatment regimen (see Schmidt, 1979).

For the accomplishment of such goals it is important that the HCP not merely offer a specific suggestion but instead *collaborate* with the patient in coming up with suggestions. For example, one technique that can be used is what we have come to call the *imaginary other*. As noted previously, this technique involves the HCP's anticipating and solving possible difficulties for a patient by invoking "other patients'" concerns and difficulties. For example, the HCP might say:

> We have discussed the nature of your problem and the reasons why taking the medication will help. . . . I'm not sure this will be an issue for you but I can recall that some patients have had some difficulty just remembering when to take their medication. Although they were well motivated, like you, to get help, somehow their circumstances contributed to their forgetting. I am wondering, do you foresee yourself possibly forgetting to take the medicine? How will you, indeed, go about reminding yourself? Are there any circumstances in which you could see yourself forgetting? Anything you could do about that? That sounds like a good idea, but every once in a while I also tie a string around my finger to remind myself of something, or I write

myself notes. However, I sometimes forget what the string was there for in the first place or I misplace the notes. Has that ever happened to you? And so forth.

The clinical ploy of the imaginary other can be used to treat a variety of factors that might interfere with adherence. HCPs could explore such issues as social pressure, cultural norms and expectations, and conflictual demands. For instance, Olson *et al.* (1985) noted the need to customize the patient's adherence to a diet to his or her family's cultural food choices, or to fit the patient's prescribed exercise program to the family routine. Marlatt and Gordon (1985) have emphasized the need to identify high-risk situations in which lapses and adherence violations may occur and to work with patients to ensure that they have the skills to handle such difficulties (e.g., social pressures). Although we will consider the issue of relapse prevention in some detail in Chapter 6, at this point it is important to emphasize the potential usefulness of the imaginary other in establishing a mutual collaborative effort between the patient and the HCP. Collaboration increases the likelihood that the responsibility for adherence will be shared by patient and HCP.

Finally, another important form of individualizing is the need to pace the nature and form of education to the stage or phase of the patient's illness. During the *initial onset phase*, patients and family members usually deal with the implications of having an illness, especially if it is a life-long chronic disease. Such reactions as depression, anger, guilt, denial, and wishful thinking may be evident. In this frame of mind patients and their family members are less likely to be receptive to complex information about the disorder. Such emotionality can interfere with adherence. As Cox, Gonder-Frederick, Pohl, and Pennebaker (1984) note, the focus of education during this initial phase is usually on basic "survival" information.

During the *management phase* patients and families are capable of dealing with more complex information and routinizing daily regimens. Major preoccupations tend to include consideration of possible complications and a realization of the social consequences of the illness.

The *complication phase* begins when, despite the patient's attempts to adhere, physical and mental complications may occur. Such complications give rise to additional stress that can interfere with adherence.

Reducing Patient Forgetfulness

Patients can forget to take medication, to follow the treatment regimen, to make and/or keep appointments, and everything the HCP has said. Levy and Loftus (1984) have observed that adherence to a treatment program requires three necessary components:

> First, one must remember something is to be done at a particular time. Second, one must remember what the thing is. And third, one must carry out the action. Failure of any of these requirements will result in failure to comply. (p. 94)

The importance of memory to the adherence process is underscored by the following illustrative findings:

1. Patients who had an accurate recollection of instructions imparted by the physician were three times more adherent than were patients with one or more errors in recollection (Svarstad, 1976).
2. 50% of patients cannot correctly report how long they were supposed to continue taking their medication (Svarstad, 1976).
3. There is a greater likelihood of adherence if patients demonstrate specific knowledge of the treatment regimen such as the name of the prescribed medication and how it should be taken (Latiolais & Berry, 1965).
4. When 2 statements are presented to patients both will be remembered, when 4 statements are presented one will be forgotten, and when 8 statements are presented over half will be forgotten (Ley, 1977).
5. Patients, especially elderly patients, often forget to take their medication or take it incorrectly (e.g., wrong dosage, wrong interval, self-medicate). They often misunderstand the treatment regimen (Richardson, 1986).

In order to combat such memory failures a technology of memory prompting has been developed. For instance, Schmidt (1979) has described three types of prompts that can be used to reduce patient forgetfulness:

1. Direct cues: patient leaves medicine by coffee cup; when he takes his morning coffee he is reminded to take the medication.
2. Indirect cues: patient places reminders on frequently used articles (e.g., wrist watch), especially when medication is out of sight (e.g., refrigerated)
3. Built-in cues: the reminders are built into a self-perpetuating system (for instance, patient places medication in a prominent spot by the alarm clock in the morning and on the dinner table at night) and uses reminders (indirect cues) to perpetuate this system.

Given the variety of possible reasons why memory lapses might contribute to treatment nonadherence, there is no simple or single remedy. Table 21 lists the variety of interventions that have been employed to reduce patient forgetfulness with regard to appointment keeping, taking medication and following a treatment regimen. Whichever cuing procedure is employed, the HCP must determine its acceptability to the patient and convey to the patient that such reminders should act as a cue for action.

A number of investigators have demonstrated that a variety of cuing procedures can improve adherence, at least with short-term prescriptions (see Dunbar & Agras, 1980, for a review). Some of the manipulations are quite simple, involving enhanced packaging, whereas others are quite sophisticated and expensive. At the simpler level, Lima, Nazarian, Charney, and Lahti (1976) had a clock printed on the patient's prescription label with appropriate times circled and a 5 × 7-inch, bright red, self-adhering sticker with written instructions affixed to the patient's refrigerator at home. Alfredson and his colleagues (1982) reported that prescribing a medication to be taken either in the morning or evening (as opposed to midday or at no special time of day) increased adherence. In contrast, an example of an expensive, complex reminder was offered by Azrin and Powell (1969), who

Table 21   Interventions Used to Reduce Patients' Forgetfulness

Reminders to keep appointments
  Mail reminders
  Telephone cueing
  Reminder cards with date and time of next appointment
  Verbal and written commitments
  Follow-up file for noting and contacting those who do not keep appointments
  Decreased waiting times
  Limited time interval between screening assessment and initial appoint-
      ment and between telephone reminder and appointment
  Individualized appointments for a specific health care provider at a partic-
      ular time
  Appointments at the most convenient time for the patient
Reminders to take medication
  Wrist watches with alarms or small pocket timers
  Drug reminder charts (e.g., test charts posted on bathroom wall)
  Written memory aides (e.g., stickers on the refrigerator door or a sign
      posted on the medicine chest)
  Tear-off calendars or pill calendars that are kept close to medication
  Special medication dispensers such as homemade dose packs of a separate
      pill bottle for each day's needs or a special pill bottle to be carried in
      lunch box. Such dispensers provide feedback on dosages taken and missed
  Special pill packages that have time alarm reminders or display pills to be
      taken by date
  Strip packages that contain one day's dose of medication
  Prescription stickers on medicine bottles that have the time circled
  Stickers with directions for administration placed in a highly visible place
      in the home
  Highly visible strategic location for placement of medication (e.g., pills
      taped to calendar)
  Daily medication intake coordinated with the patient's specific routine (e.g.,
      medication before brushing teeth or after breakfast)
  Asking the patient to bring in bottle of pills on next visit or to keep a record
      or diary of which pills are taken each day and at what times
  Supervision: call patient, have patient call office once a week, involve family
      members
Reminders to follow treatment regimen
  Posttest performance charts put in a prominent place (e.g., on bathroom
      wall)
  Wristwatch with an alarm on it
  Integration of the treatment adherence behavior into the patient's daily
      routine
  Identification of reminders or cues for action
  Rehearsal of treatment measures so they can be smoothly implemented

developed a portable timer dispenser to strengthen adherence. The apparatus emitted a tone at the time when patients were scheduled to take their medication. In order to turn off the tone, the patient had to turn a knob that would eject the pill. Although this expensive device has not been more fully tested, less expensive reminders in the form of wrist reminders and other pill-dispensing devices have proved just as effective (e.g., see Linkewich, Catalano, & Flack, 1974; Moulding, 1962). As Southam and Dunbar (1986) conclude after reviewing this literature, "The use of complex mechanical equipment does *not* seem to perform very much better than simpler, less costly reminder charts or stickers . . . in reducing missed doses and in reducing errors with medication" (p. 175).

An example of an intervention program to prevent or overcome patient forgetfulness was offered by Boczkowski *et al.* (1985), who attempted to enhance neuroleptic adherence among chronic schizophrenic outpatients. The HCP helped each patient individualize his prescribed regimen so that it suited his or her personal habits and routines. This involved identifying a highly visible location for placement of medications and pairing the daily medication intake with specific routine behaviors. In addition, each patient was given a self-monitoring calendar that featured a dated slip of paper for each dose of the neuroleptic. The patient was instructed to keep the calendar near his medications and tear off a slip each time he took a pill. This program was effective in enhancing treatment adherence.

Another innovative adherence treatment program with schizophrenics was developed by Liberman, Eckman, and Phipps (1986). The feature of this program most relevant to our present discussion is their use of reminder cards to cue patients as to why they should continue taking medication. For example, in order to be reminded of the rationale for continued use of medication, the patient placed in his cigarette pack a card with three reasons for continuing to take his medication: "(1) it makes me calm, (2) it stops my hearing voices, (3) it helps me sleep" (p. 5). The patients are also given the "insurance policy" rationale that taking medication can act as insurance against the high risk of relapse. Similar, reminder programs have been used with older people. For example, Gabriel, Gagnon, and Bryan (1977) successfully used a drug reminder chart, and Wandless and Davie (1977) used tear-off calendars as memory aides with geriatric patients.

Another form of patient forgetfulness that constitutes an expensive and irritating form of nonadherence is broken appointments. It resulted in wasted staff time and poor staff morale. Consider some of the reasons patients offered for missing appointments (as cited by DiMatteo & DiNicola, 1982a):

1. Lost appointment slip
2. Confusion over appointment
3. Difficulty obtaining an appointment
4. Inability to get a babysitter
5. Lack of transportation
6. Weather conditions

Breaking appointments is a serious problem as illustrated by Benjamin-Bauman, Reiss, and Bailey (1984), who estimate that "no shows" among outpatients range from 17% to 52%. They reported that both mail and telephone reminders can bring an improvement of 30% to 70%, although Dunbar, Marshall, and Hovell (1979) reported a more modest improvement in appointment keeping of 13% to 20% as a result of reminders. One variable that may contribute to this difference is the time interval between the screening detection of a patient's problem and the referral appointment or between the reminder call and the appointment date. Benjamin-Bauman *et al.* (1984) found that with increasing delays there was a concomitant decrease in appointment keeping. For example, in a study of patients at a family planning unit of a public health department, the largest drop-off in appointment keeping occurred when the interval between the time the patient made the appointment and the actual appointment was greater than eight days. When the time interval between making an initial call for an appointment and the actual appointment was less than one week the attendance improved significantly. Oppenheim, Bergman, and English (1979) have reported that an interval greater than two weeks between scheduling an appointment and the appointment date significantly reduces adherence.

Telephone and mail reminders have been shown to be of definite value. A number of investigators have reported that telephone calls, taking no more than two or three minutes, and postcards are effective in improving appointment keeping (Brigg & Mudd, 1968; Duer, 1982; Dunbar *et al.*, 1979; Epstein & Ossip, 1979; Schmarak, 1971; Turner & Vernon, 1976), medication compliance (Gabriel *et al.*, 1977; Lima *et al.*, 1976; Shepard & Mosley, 1976), and breast self-examination (Grady, Kegeles, and Lund 1981; Mayer & Frederiksen, 1986). Dunbar and Agras (1980) indicate that such prompting represents a cost-effective means of helping patients keep appointments: "One thousand telephone prompts using a standard message delivered by an appointment clerk cost $162, an amount recovered when just six appointments were kept, when the time wasted by idle staff was taken into account" (p. 122). Several studies have found that phone prompts were more effective in fostering adherence than were mail prompts (Mayer & Frederiksen, 1986; Shepard & Mosely, 1976). But if the repeated telephone calls to remind for adherence are too standardized and predictable, they lose their initial efficacy (Best, Bass & Owen, 1986; Mayer & Frederiksen, 1986). A personalized approach is essential, individually tailored and providing specific patient feedback. Significant others in the patient's life can also be asked to remind the patient of appointments.

Another possibility is to rotate the type of contact (phone call, mail message, personal visit) (Meyers, Thrackwray, Johnson, & Schleser, 1983). Whatever the form of contact it is important that the frequency of contact should be highest at the outset of treatment (Abernathy, 1976).

Once patients show up, however, memory lapses may contribute to their failing to recall the physician's statements. As noted in Table 21, one way to deal with patient forgetfulness is to anticipate such problems and to prepare communications carefully (keeping them simple, clear, well categorized) and to use memory aides (Harris, 1978; Schmidt, 1979). For example, one can personally involve the patient using salient illustrations, analogies, and metaphors that are likely to be retained to convey the relevant information. Consider the following example offered by Rosenthal and Downs (1985):

> To really understand what drinking is doing to you, try and imagine you've become tiny enough to travel in the bloodstream to your brain. I'll describe what's going on, but you try to visualize it. (p. 44)

One can imagine similar approaches for a variety of other disorders. Moreover, one must conduct a *comprehension check* to see if the patient has indeed understood what is being conveyed, namely, the what, how, when, and why of the treatment regimen. Coleman (1985) has noted that patients can be asked for feedback in a way that will not embarrass them. For example, the HCP can say, "I know a lot of people get a bit mixed up with their medicines. Now you tell me what you will be taking in the morning" or "If you feel differently than you usually feel, what are you going to do?" (pp. 69–70). Coleman observes that such probes will not only tap for possible comprehension difficulties but also indicate concern about possible side effects. The use of the imaginary patient can serve a similar purpose.

Another way to assess understanding is to ask the patient to describe to the HCP what has been discussed. One way to manage this tactfully is to use role reversal, whereby the HCP asks patients to view themselves as the expert and to explain in their own words the nature of the treatment regimen (what is to be done, when, why, what difficulties are likely to occur and how can they be prevented or overcome). Questioning the patients about which pills they should take, when, in what sequence and for what purpose will help measure comprehension. The HCP should avoid asking questions that ask for simple yes or no answers such as "You do understand, don't you?" Instead, one should ask questions that encourage the patient to reword the material such as, "Tell me what you heard me say." or "Since we covered quite a bit of material, could you take a moment and put into your own words what it is you are supposed to do and why?" Such queries reduce the likelihood of the HCP's being deceived by a smile and nod implying an understanding that may be only superficial.

Similarly, patients who have been taught about self-care are asked to reverse roles, to pretend that they are the expert and are trying to explain the self-care regimen to a novice patient (a role assumed by the HCP). The role reversal serves three important functions. First, it enables the HCP to learn about patients' understanding of the regimen as well as their misconceptions and confusions. Second, it enables the patient to consolidate the knowledge and the skills surrounding each behavior. Finally, the role reversal allows patients to generate their own arguments and explanations about self-care regimens and thereby convince themselves of their merits. Social psychologists (e.g., Janis & King, 1954) have shown that when asked to play roles subjects will provide just the kinds of arguments that would be required to convince themselves of the merits of some perspective.

A supplemental approach was suggested by McKenney (1979). He found that pharmacists can exert an important influence on patients' medication-taking behavior. If the pharmacist spent as little as two to four minutes in explaining the course of treatment to the patient, treatment adherence improved. Pharmacists can also identify gaps in patients' knowledge and mistakes in their understanding about disease and treatment, can elicit negative feedback about side effects and related matters, can provide educational material such as drug inserts, can recommend changes, and can act as an intermediary with physician. The pharmacist's expressed concern and readiness to help can go a long way in nurturing adherence.

McKenney, Slining, Henderson, and Devins (1973) underscore the need for a coordinated treatment team approach involving office personnel, physicians, nurses, pharmacists, and other HCPs in the task of nurturing treatment nonadherence. Such a multiprong approach is required especially for patients with long-term chronic disorders. The need for such a team approach is highlighted in those patients who suffer from chronic mental disorders where they are referred from one health care setting (e.g., hospital) to another (e.g., outpatient clinic, half-way house). Often due to memory, as well as confusion, fear, and lack of motivation, patients do not follow through on referral appointments. Although the many interventions to enhance memory have improved adherence to short-term treatment regimens for acute illness, the evidence for their efficacy for patients suffering from long-term chronic disorders is less impressive. A number of factors besides forgetfulness may contribute to the gap between the patient's knowing, recalling, and doing. Often the patient's feelings and concerns about the consequences of adherence (pro and con) can not only interfere with the patient's understanding but also heighten fears about possible side effects.

Discussing Possible Side Effects

As we can now surmise, a great deal must go into patient education, much more than providing instructions or giving advice. One important point is what patients expect to happen to their symptoms as a result of treatment and their concerns about possible side effects arising from the treatment. Although such concerns may be germane for patients, it is important to note that many HCPs are reluctant to discuss them with their patients. A survey of physicians by Ascione and Raven (1975) revealed that 75% of physicians did not wish patients to be told about the potential side effects of the medication that was being prescribed. Cyr and McLean (1978) found that 23% of patients were unaware of the purpose of the prescribed medication and possible side effects, even though 92% wanted complete information about the drugs they were taking. Are such attitudes on the part of physicians justified by the data?

A number of authors (Davis, 1966; DiMatteo & DiNicola, 1982a; Haynes, 1979c; McKenney, 1979; Meyers & Calvert, 1976; Roth, 1979) have reported that forewarning patients about possible side effects that may accompany drug treatment and discussing them does not increase their incidence or lead to treatment nonadherence. Moreover, in most instances the side effects accompanying drug treatment do not play a prominent role in contributing to treatment nonadherence. When exceptions do occur, as noted previously in the case of psychiatric patients who have concerns about side effects resulting from neuroleptic medication, these can be addressed in patient education groups.

In addition to having physicians be vigilant for early signs of side effects, Seltzer *et al.* (1980) demonstrated the value of group education in reducing psychiatric patients' fears of side effects and drug dependency. Their nine-session course focused on the nature of the patient's disorder, pharmacological management, and patient's experiences; discussed the relationship between relapse and premature cessation of drugs; reinforced desirable drug-taking behavior; and also explored possible side effects.

The Seltzer *et al.* study as well as other studies reviewed by DiMatteo and DiNicola (1982a) indicate that the discussion with patients and, where appropriate, with significant others of possible side effects can in fact enhance adherence. Providing patients with advanced reassurance that such side effects, if they do indeed occur, may be unpleasant but not serious, can help allay fears. Hearing about such possible side effects from the HCP rather than from others (family members, friends, media, or the readily available *Physicians' Desk Reference*), provides an opportunity to consider patient concerns and possible counterarguments. HCPs must insure that the occurrence of side effects is not a reason for the patient to discontinue treatment. In some instances, HCPs may suggest the best ways to handle side effects should they occur. The issue of side effects is especially relevant in the treatment of the elderly. As Amaral (1986) reports, the elderly often respond differently to medications than do their younger counterparts. Since little research has been conducted on drug effects on the elderly, each assigned prescription becomes "an individual experiment in titration between the physician and his or her patient" (Pfeiffer, 1980).

Clearly, such discussion of possible side effects should be balanced so that the HCP does not overload the patient with negative features or a description of unattained rewards (things the patient will have to give up). Moreover, any inquiry about the patient's potential symptoms must be accompanied by an explanation that such interest derives from concern about possible side effects, or patients may be misled and think these are additional symptoms of their condition. As Blackwell (1973) notes, it is mainly unexpected and alarming side effects of treatment that patients offer as reason for stopping treatment. Most side effects can be anticipated, and forewarning patients of their potential occurrence has not been demonstrated to affect either their incidence or patients' nonadherence.

Fawcett and Epstein (1983) propose that the discussion of side effects should follow a thorough review of the therapeutic benefits of the medication (or other treatment). It should occur early in the treatment regimen and patients should be encouraged to report the presence of any symptoms to the HCP as soon as they occur.

In summary, the research in patient education indicates that providing information to patients, increasing their knowledge about both their illness and the proposed treatment is necessary but often not sufficient to increase the likelihood of adherence. Patient education must take into consideration a variety of related factors if it is to be successful. Patients must be told why it is important for them to carry out recommended action and reassured that the recommended treatment or preventive action will probably be successful and beneficial. Their comprehension of what is expected of them must be carefully evaluated. The literature and our clinical experience indicate that efforts at patient education should include a discussion of possible side effects in the context of a consideration of patient expectations about treatment outcome. If patient education programs are to be improved, the issue of treatment adherence must be addressed throughout. As Dunbar and Agras (1980) conclude, "Even if patients know what to do, however, a number of other factors contribute to their ability to follow through" (p. 111). In the next three chapters we will consider a variety of procedures that can be used to address these additional factors.

Behavior Modification
Approaches

The mammoth literature documenting the extent of the adherence problem is in sharp contrast to the small number of studies of what to do about the problem.

J. M. DUNBAR AND W. S. AGRAS (1980)

Even in light of the discrepancy that Dunbar and Agras deplore we can fruitfully examine the variety of intervention strategies that have been employed to enhance treatment adherence. The most frequently studied approach to the problem is patient education, followed by behavior modification, then increased patient supervision, adherence reminders and cues, and pharmacy interventions (long-acting medication, counseling). Of these several approaches, behavior modification has proved most successful (Epstein & Cluss, 1982; Epstein & Masek, 1978; Wing, Epstein, Nowalk, & Lamparski, 1986; Zifferblatt, 1975). Subsumed under behavior modification are a variety of diverse but often complementary techniques:

- Self-monitoring
- Goal setting
- Corrective feedback
- Behavioral contracting

- Commitment enhancement procedures
- Reinforcement procedures

Before we consider how these various procedures have been used to enhance treatment adherence, let us first examine some underlying concepts. For many the term *behavior modification* conjures up images of cold, insensitive clinicians who manipulate their patients by means of conditioning procedures. Pavlov's dogs, Watson's rats, and Skinner's pigeons may come to mind. The notion of equating behavior modification with brainwashing and mind control has even received some popular notoriety in such works as Anthony Burgess's *A Clockwork Orange.* Nothing could be further from reality. Those who employ behavior modification can do nothing without the individual's knowing participation and active involvement in the learning process. Once we put various myths of manipulation, control, and insensitivity behind us, we can determine what are the basic concepts behind behavior modification and how they can be put to effective use by health care providers.

Some Basic Concepts

A central premise of behavior modification is that an individual's behavior, including health-related behavior, is influenced by its antecedents and consequences. By *antecedents* is meant those external and internal events that trigger or elicit a behavior. In the case of overeating it may be the sight of food, or in the decision not to take one's medication it may be a feeling of fatalism arising from certain health beliefs. In either case, behavior modification encourages HCPs to specify as explicitly as possible the behaviors that are to be changed and to note the situations and occasions when they do and do not occur. As we shall see, patients can be enlisted as collaborators in conducting this careful situational analysis in order to determine the relevant antecedents.

The patient's behavior is influenced not only by antecedent events, but also by consequences and expected consequences.

Quite simply put, behavior modification highlights the fact that one's behavior is influenced by the rewards and punishments that follow. Whether an individual continues to engage in some behavior depends in part on what happens subsequently. These consequences may occur immediately after a behavior occurs, as in the case of social praise, censure, pleasurable experiences, and so forth. Or behavior may be influenced by distal events such as avoidance of losing worker's compensation, concern about giving up one's "sick role." The latter has often been referred to as one of the "secondary gains" that accompany certain illness behaviors.

Not adhering to treatment regimens may be greatly influenced by how patients and significant others appraise and react to the patient's illness-related behavior. Behavior modification programs that attempt to arrange environmental contingencies such that rewards are provided for appropriate behavior and negative consequences for inappropriate behavior are referred to as *contingency management programs*. An example of this program is illustrated by Dapcich-Miura and Howell (1979), who used contingency management procedures with an elderly heart patient in order to increase his adherence with a complex treatment regimen including exercise, medication, and diet. The patient (Mr. A), an 82-year-old retired longshoreman who had suffered a massive myocardial infarction, was living with his granddaughter and was nonadherent to the demands of the complex treatment regimen. The adherence training program entailed Mr. A's earning a token for engaging in walking activities, taking medication, and drinking orange juice. These tokens were later exchanged for specially desired activities (e.g., the privilege of selecting the evening menu or going out to dinner at the restaurant of his own choice). This reinforcement program was effective in increasing adherent behavior, reducing angina pain, and, as a byproduct, contributing to the reduction of family arguments, especially about adherence. Although this case study illustrates the usefulness of contingent rewards, evidence for how one could wean the patient from the reinforcement program for long-term improvement was not reported.

Another interesting case study wherein long-term maintenance was evident was reported by Masek (1982), who used behavior modification to enhance the adherence of a 5-year-old girl hospitalized for leukemia. Because of the seriousness of her condition and the dire consequences of her nonadherence, Masek enlisted the cooperation of the patient's mother, who used her attention and social approval contingently to shape her daughter's adherence behavior. The extension of these efforts to the home setting facilitated the transfer and maintenance of the treatment gains.

Finally, behavior modification underscores the necessity of not only assessing, monitoring, and manipulating the impact of antecedent and consequent events, but also of ensuring that patients have the necessary skills and resources to engage in adherent behavior. Those who use behavior modification techniques emphasize the necessity of integrating behavioral changes into the patient's long-term life patterns. Thus, behavior modification requires a multifaceted intervention to deal with the various features of treatment adherence. Given the promising results of behavior modification in enhancing adherence, especially with patients suffering from chronic disorders, it is worthwhile to examine briefly but critically how the various behavior modification techniques have been used. In describing these procedures we will illustrate their application with a variety of clinical populations.

Self-Monitoring

It is proposed that a central feature in changing one's behavior, whether it is checking one's blood glucose level, taking medication, following a diet, or giving up an addiction, is the need to increase one's self-awareness. The popular conception of "consciousness raising" can apply as much to enhancing treatment adherence as to fostering such social movements as Women's Lib, Black Pride, and Gay Rights. In this context we are certainly not advocating the development of a major social movement, but instead emphasizing the critical role of self-monitoring in changing one's behavior. Just think about changing some behavior of your own, whether something as simple as the number of times you use a verbal expression such as the word *adherence* instead of *compliance*, or something more central, for instance, how you relate to your patients. We would argue that you are unlikely to change unless you *notice* your present behavior and become *aware* of what you are and are not doing. Without such raised consciousness change is unlikely to come about.

Many actions we perform are habitual and occur in an automatic fashion, and only with increased awareness can we deautomatize these acts. For instance, many cigarette smokers light up regularly with a cup of coffee, without even being aware that they do so. A first step in changing such habitual patterns requires making smokers aware of their smoking pattern. To deautomatize the smoking act, Mahoney (1971) placed a weight inside cigarette packs, such that each time a cigarette was removed, the weight fell into the hand of the smoker. This increased their awareness of the rate of smoking and contributed to its reduction. Thus, the assessment of the frequency of smoking behavior was reactive and initiated the change process. Attending to one's behavior is a necessary but, as we shall see, not always a sufficient condition for change. As Southam and Dunbar (1986) concluded, "It appears that the effect of self-monitoring *alone* on compliance is weak at best" (p. 166, emphasis added). The skills of self-monitoring (recording, interpreting, and responding to the results) have to be explicitly taught and often supplemented by other procedures.

Several investigators have reported that behavior modification procedures can be used to improve patients' accuracy in self-monitoring. For example, Wing *et al.* (1986), in work with diabetics, demonstrated that repeated practice in reading urine and blood glucose samples and training in insulin adjustment enhanced treatment adherence. HCPs can help diabetic patients learn to recognize their idiosyncratic symptom–blood sugar relations. Such self-monitoring and feedback training help to establish a collaborative working relationship between the patient and HCP. In some instances, self-monitoring itself proves to be a reactive measure contributing to behavior change and increased adherence (e.g., Gabriel *et al.*, 1977; Southam & Dunbar, 1986).

One useful way to increase treatment adherence is to enlist patients as collaborators by asking, encouraging, and teaching them to self-monitor (e.g., to keep charts recording frequency). As Southam and Dunbar (1986) observe, such self-monitoring can help the patient discover an appropriate focus for intervention, can provide a baseline prior to treatment, can identify antecedents and consequences of behavior problems, can assist the patient in the actual adjustment to the treatment regimen, and can lead to a better understanding of the disease. A sizable literature on self-monitoring has emerged (e.g., see Nelson, 1977) that offers specific suggestions for increasing adherence. These guidelines have been summarized by Dunbar and Agras (1980):

> 1) Asking the patient to observe positively valued behaviors (e.g., recording medication taken rather than medication missed);
> 2) Using readily accessible, easy-to-use records (e.g., calendars);
> 3) Asking the patient to assess readily observable behaviors (e.g., recording the quantity of meat eaten rather than the amount of saturated fat);
> 4) Training the patient in self-monitoring;
> 5) Reinforcing the patient's accuracy rather than any improvements or changes in regimen-related behavior;
> 6) Letting patients be aware that their records will be checked for accuracy;
> 7) Asking patients to record at the time that behavior occurs rather than at the end of the day or the end of the week. (p. 127)

To supplement this list of guidelines Friedman and Litt (1986) suggest also (1) that HCPs should provide immediate feedback and encouragement to the patient about the self-monitoring, (2) that patients should eventually record behavior before rather than after it occurs, and finally (3) that it is better to monitor a behavior (e.g., dietary intake) than a distant goal (e.g., weight loss).

A variety of different forms of self-monitoring can be used to record physiological and behavioral measures, tailored to the characteristics of the people involved. Self-monitoring has ranged from patients' keeping an open-ended diary to their systematically recording or rating specific thoughts, feelings, and actions. Drug intake, blood glucose levels (by means of reflectance meters, reagant strips, and urinanalysis), smoking and eating behavior, stress logs, anger-engendering incidents, depressogenic thoughts, pain intensity and activity ratings, and more explicit health-related treatment adherence activities have been assessed. Often, different self-monitoring procedures are used in combination: for example, an open-ended diary followed by more specific assessment procedures. The focus of our discussion will be on the clinical guidelines for using self-monitoring procedures. All too often clinical descriptions focus on the specific features of a clinical procedure such as self-monitoring without discussing how one prepares, instructs, and uses the procedure. However, before we consider the clinical features, let us first discuss a somewhat different diagnostic use of self-monitoring.

Brownell and Foreyt (1985) reduced the high attrition rate in treatment programs for obese patients by employing a vigorous screening procedure. In order to qualify for the weight loss program, patients had to complete a daily self-monitoring record of food intake as well as lose at least one pound for each of two weeks during the screening phase. A one-week "grace" period was allowed, but if adherence was not achieved within the allotted time the patients were not permitted to enter the treatment program. Brownell and Foreyt indicate that these requirements provide a useful index to assess patient motivation and tend to give the treatment program a welcomed reputation for being "tough but fair." They argue that such screening requirements decrease the likelihood of accepting patients who qualify but do poorly. At the same time it rarely excludes patients who are screened out but who would have done well. The exclusion of unmotivated patients who show little progress is a valuable addition to the adherence enhancement regimen. Such unmotivated patients are likely to have a damaging effect on other patients and on staff. We concur with Brownell and Foreyt's conclusions that "the benefits of screening far outweigh the hazards. In practice the major function of the screening is to produce a motivated group to begin treatment, because most patients satisfy the screening requirements once they begin" (p. 320).

The value of measuring early adherence to minimally imposed demands was also indicated by Pomerleau, Adkins, and Pertschuk (1978) and Lichtenstein (1982), who reported that smokers' ability to adhere to an earlier, less demanding request was a good prognostic indicator of later adherence and treatment outcome. A number of additional clinical techniques could be used to increase the likelihood of patient self-monitoring.

Soliciting Patients' Suggestions and Preferences

It is proposed that efforts at fostering adherence will prove most effective when the HCP can have the patient suggest the specific procedures that are to be undertaken. There is a greater likelihood that patients will, in fact, carry out routines such as self-monitoring if they come up with the suggestion for its use themselves. The HCP is at his or her professional best when the patient is just one step ahead of him or her in suggesting specific procedures; and the patient can view the suggestion for the need to self-monitor as his or her own. In order to accomplish this objective, the HCP must lay the groundwork by means of the questions asked, the reflections offered, and the rationale and examples given. The HCP can lead the patient to suggest self-monitoring by conducting a clinical interview detailing a situational analysis of adherence-related behavior. The HCP can explore with the patient those situations in which he or she has and has not been able to adhere. Together the HCP and the patient can consider what is different about these situations and how the patient can better understand what is going on. Such probing encourages the patient to come up with the suggestion that he or she should collect more information, perhaps "keep track" of different situations. The HCP can reflect, "Keep track, that's kind of interesting. What did you have in mind?" Such an exchange provides the opening for the HCP to introduce the notion of self-monitoring, a suggestion that is consistent with the patient's own initial view that collecting information about the differences between adherent and nonadherent situations may prove helpful.

We have discussed at length (Meichenbaum, 1985; Turk *et al.*, 1983) specific suggestions as to how self-monitoring can be conducted. Some of the more critical points concern the need to involve the patient as a collaborator, acting as his or her own "personal scientist" in understanding the factors and reasons for nonadherence. Keeping the self-monitoring task simple, asking patients to record soon after the occurrence of the target behavior, providing a rationale as to why self-monitoring is important and giving feedback, checking periodically on the accuracy of the self-monitoring, and soliciting patients' thoughts and feelings about completing the task can all contribute to greater adherence. Many examples of such self-monitoring procedures could be offered. For instance, Coleman (1985) successfully used a self-monitoring procedure with hypertensive patients. The patients were asked to carry a wallet-size card on which they recorded changes in blood pressure. Such explicit and immediate feedback acted as a further reinforcer for taking one's medication. Turk *et al.* (1983) described the use of 3 × 5-inch cards with chronic pain patients to record the intensity of their pain, the frequency of medication use, and any accompanying specific thoughts and feelings that might exacerbate the pain. Such self-monitoring helped patients become aware of the patterns of their pain behavior.

When several different methods of self-monitoring are available the HCP should solicit the patient's preference in order that the collaborative relationship can be strengthened. As Kanfer (1986) has documented, providing patients with a choice increases the likelihood of adherence. It is better to tell the patient that there are different ways to self-monitor and then have the patient choose between the methods than to impose a method of self-monitoring that the patient may not follow. Finally, it is worth repeating an observation offered by Southam and Dunbar (1986) that monitoring physiological and behavioral outcomes has not led to exaggerated patient concerns, nor to increased attention and fear of the disease. Instead, it tends to bolster the patients' confidence and hope.

Goal Setting

The discussion thus far underscores the need to involve patients in a collaborative effort if generalized durable changes are to be achieved. This principle is particularly evident when it comes to the task of establishing mutually agreeable treatment goals. As Wing *et al.* (1986) note, the HCP must help patients set appropriate, explicitly defined, achievable goals, provide patients with feedback on their progress, and develop positive reinforcers for self-regulation. Much research has been conducted on goal setting and as a result clinical guidelines have emerged. Following the suggestions of Kirschenbaum (1985), Kirschenbaum and Flanery, (1984), Locke, Shaw, Saari, and Latham, (1981), Miller (1985), Turk, (1985), and Wing *et al.* (1986) a number of specific clinical guidelines can be offered:

1. Negotiated, individualized, and self-determined treatment goals are most likely to be effective.

2. If the necessary skills are not within the patient's repertoire, then easier (more readily attainable) goals should be employed. For example, in the treatment for weight loss it is useful to monitor behavior that leads to weight loss rather than graphing the more difficult weight loss itself. In this way feedback is more rapid and effective.

3. If the required skills are within the patient's repertoire, then establishing more demanding rather than simpler goals is more effective. The treatment goals, however, must be perceived as proximal and attainable. Bandura and Simon (1977) reported that subjects who used short-term or proximal rather than long-term or distal goals were most successful at maintenance. Moreover, the attainment of treatment goals is more likely if performance feedback is included.

4. There is an advantage in specifying what behaviors are needed in order to reach treatment goals and when and how these behaviors should be implemented. Interestingly, moderately specific plans appear to be better than overly specific, rigid plans.

5. Patient involvement must be nurtured and, as noted, patients must be provided with a choice of treatment alternatives. When patients are offered a choice among feasible intervention alternatives and goals the likelihood of treatment adherence is increased. The perception of choice helps to reinforce the patient's sense of personal control. In addition, the HCP should encourage only moderate patient expectations of success. If expectations are too high or too low then any instances of relapse could be perceived as devastating.

6. Whenever feasible, significant others should be involved in the goal-setting task. For example, Lewis and Minich (1977) found that juvenile diabetics who negotiated treatment goals with their parents increased frequency of urine testing.

7. Patients must be taught self-regulatory techniques whereby they can monitor their behavior, to use this information as a basis for making treatment decisions, and to reinforce themselves for their efforts. As Wing *et al.* (1986) comment, patients must be encouraged to view various aspects of the treatment regimen (symptom monitoring, diet, exercise) as tools rather than ends in themselves.

In order to achieve these objectives, Caplan (1979) has provided procedural guidelines to follow in the establishment of treatment goals for both patients and for HCPs. These include:

1. *The goals must be specific.* For example, HCPs should not provide general admonitions to patients to "cut down on smoking" or "do your best" but instead should specify that the patients should "reduce smoking by one cigarette every two days." Similarly, goals for HCPs should be equally specific. The example offered by Caplan is that the nurse will reinforce the patient for keeping appointments by saying something, such as "I am glad you came today. It shows that you care about your

health." The nurse will document this action. The explicit specification of both the goal and documentation is in contrast to a
general prescription "to provide support for the patient." Behavior modification programs emphasize systematic record keeping
of specifiable behaviors and altering them on a trial-and-error
basis.

2. *The goals must be realistic or potentially achievable.*
The inclusion of subgoals that have a high likelihood of success
increases adherence by both patients and HCPs. Patient and
HCP should work out the subgoals and means together. In any
case, the HCP should avoid setting goals *for* the patient. Relatively distal and moderately specific planning can be effective
because it encourages patients to pursue their goals by continually and flexibly choosing their activities, or what Kirschenbaum
(1985) describes as "engaging in protracted choice."

3. *The goals must lead to anticipated meaningful rewards.*
The HCP may use social praise, positive feedback about performance, and other rewards. These should be offered as soon
after the desirable performance occurs. Such consistent application of rewards should come to be expected by both patient
and HCP. Performance feedback facilitates the development of
self-regulation.

Often such goal statements are summarized in the form of
homework assignments. Martin and Worthington (1982b) have
divided the homework assignment task into three stages:
(1) devising the assignment, (2) presenting the assignment, and
(3) monitoring homework performance. They have provided
guidelines for each stage. In agreement with the literature on
goal setting, they note that in devising homework assignments
concrete, specific (operationally devised), manageable tasks that
do not call for personal or environmental resources not readily
available to the patient should be used. One must provide not
only a reason for the homework but also a choice (or the perception of choice) in defining the assignment, rather than auto-
cratically assigning homework. Especially in the latter stages of
treatment the HCP can act more as a consultant in helping and

encouraging the patient to plan and carry out homework assignments.

Greater adherence to homework assignments will ensue if the patient believes that he or she has helped define the assignment and has chosen to carry it out in the absence of external pressure. In presenting the homework assignment the HCP must not only describe the task, present the rationale, and emphasize its relevance to treatment but must also anticipate possible reasons for nonadherence. The HCP might even have patients consider ways in which to avoid the task or have them imagine undertaking the assignment while they are in the HCP's office and then note any potential problems. In exploring these factors realistic expectations must be nurtured. Finally the HCP must explicitly monitor homework performance and the patient's feelings about undertaking the assignment.

The HCP should help patients attribute any improvement to their own effort rather than to some therapeutic technique or to the HCP. It is not enough that patients change their behavior. They must be encouraged to attribute such changes to their own efforts. The HCP can nurture this self-attribution process by asking the patient such questions as: How was he able to carry out the assignment? How did it make him feel? Where else did he evidence such change? How did his present success (e.g., combating social pressure to skip the cigarette, forget the pill) differ from previous efforts at which he had failed? What do such changes mean about him as a person? Such probing questions increase the likelihood that patients will attribute any changes to themselves rather than to some external source. Bandura (1986) has reviewed the literature that indicates greater maintenance of behavior change when patients make such self-attributions.

When the patient fails to do the homework one must explore the variety of reasons for the failure. Is nonadherence due to the absence of explicit instructions? To the patient's perception of the homework as being irrelevant? To lack of patient skills and resources? To interference (sabotaging) by significant others?

Whatever the reason, the patient and HCP must to take appropriate remedial steps.

Table 22 provides an example of what may go into homework assignments. The application of such specific, demanding, but attainable goals, when supplemented with corrective feedback, enhances treatment adherence. Primakoff, Epstein, and Covi (1986) have stressed the need to assess explicitly for homework adherence by means of patient-written logs, reports by significant others, the HCP interview with the patient, and, when feasible, live observations. Several useful homework assessment instruments have been developed. For example, Kazdin and Mascitelli (1982) have developed a homework adherence questionnaire and Martin and Worthington (1982a) have developed a Homework Assignment Report (HAR) that is completed after each session by the HCP. The HAR provides for (1) a description of the assigned homework (e.g., involving doing, bringing, recording), (2) ratings of the degree to which the patient followed the homework and patient's reactions, and (3) the manner in which the HCP determined whether the patient had done the homework (e.g., asking directly, being told spontaneously, inferring). In order to increase the likelihood of patients'

Table 22   *The Format for Homework Includes One or More of the Following Instructions[a]*

- A *do* statement. "Read, practice, observe, say, count, . . . some kind of homework."
- A *quantity* statement. "Talk three times about . . .; spend thirty minutes *three* times . . .; give *four* compliments per day . . .; write a list of at least *ten*. . . ."
- A *record* statement. "Count and *record* the number of compliments; each time he hits, *mark* a ——— on the chart."
- A *bring* statement. "Bring . . . *your* list; the chart; the cards; your spouse . . . to your next appointment."
- A *contingency* statement. "Call for your next appointment after you have done . . .; for each activity you attend, one dollar will be deducted . . .; each minute spent doing _____will earn you _____; one-tenth of your penalty deposit will be forfeited for each assignment not completed."

---

[a]Reproduced by permission from Shelton & Levy, 1981.

complying with homework assignments, Goldfried (1982) has suggested that psychotherapists arrange with patients to call when they have finished the assignment.

Corrective Feedback

Closely related to self-monitoring and goal setting is the use of feedback concerning patients' ability to adhere to the treatment regimen and/or their ability to learn the often demanding and complicated skills required by their treatment regimen.

Several studies have been conducted that provide patients with systematic feedback concerning their adherence by means of mail or direct counseling when they come in for return visits (e.g., digoxin: Gundert-Remy, Remy, & Weber, 1976; anticonvulsant medication: Lund, Jorgensen, and Kuhl, 1964; Sherwin, Robb, & Lechter, 1973). Such feedback is usually accompanied by advice and encouragement from the HCPs.

On some occasions the feedback accompanies behavioral training in specific treatment skills. For example, Epstein, Figueroa, Farkas, and Beck (1981) taught diabetic patients how to determine glucose levels accurately. Following careful training that entailed 10 pretest tubes of different urine solutions, the patients (both children and adults) received explicit instruction in discrimination. Such feedback training reduced inaccuracies and enhanced adherence. Patients can be asked periodically to describe the treatment regimen and to demonstrate the treatment procedure they are using in order to secure feedback.

Some investigators have incorporated corrective feedback training as part of their integrated adherence enhancement program. An exemplary illustration was offered by Sergis-Deavenport and Varni (1982), who used behavioral techniques to teach factor replacement procedures. Hemophilia home care programs place tremendous responsibilities on patients and their families, and it is no wonder that many do not adhere to the demanding factor replacement procedures. Nurses were trained to help hemophilia patients and their families become more proficient in home care therapy. The specific behavioral techniques used were:

1. Observational learning and modeling—the patient's observation of health-related behaviors modeled by the therapist.

2. Behavioral rehearsal—the trainee practices an observed modeled behavior until he/she feels competent in the skill.

3. Social reinforcement and corrective feedback—the instructor intervenes as necessary throughout the procedure, giving positive reinforcement by social praise (head nodding, smiling) for correct behaviors. Appropriate feedback is given for incorrect behaviors, in addition to prompting and aiding the participant when difficulties are encountered. (Sergis-Deavenport & Varni, 1982, p. 417)

Sergis-Deavenport and Varni include detailed procedural guidelines for the nurses to follow indicating when and how to give corrective feedback. The combination of modeling, corrective feedback, and reinforcement proved to be effective in enhancing treatment adherence.

In many instances, however, providing feedback is not sufficient, and more explicit commitment and contingency consequences must be built into adherence enhancement efforts. One such approach is the use of behavioral contracting.

Behavioral Contracting

Each of us has participated in social contracts involving work, marriage, financial loans, as well as informal agreements. Our culture uses such contracts to specify the obligations of each party and the reciprocal consequences. The notion of behavioral contracts has also been used to help patients change a variety of health-related and other behaviors (e.g., adherence to renal disease and antihypertension regimens, diabetes control, weight loss, smoking cessation, physical exercise, alcohol and drug abuse, marital conflict, and academic difficulties).[8] The contingency contract capitalizes on the patient–HCP relationship by actively

[8]The widespread use of behavioral contracting is illustrated by O'Banion and Whaley (1981), who developed a Behavioral Contracting Service. In its first four years they helped to design and monitor over 650 contracts, primarily to improve health and study behavior. Kirschenbaum and Flanery (1984) have reviewed 46 studies involving over 85 different contracts.

involving the patient in the therapeutic decision-making process and by providing additional incentives (rewards) for achievement of treatment objectives. In each of these areas a behavioral contract is drawn up that is a negotiated explicit agreement between the patient and the health care provider that specifies "expectations, plans, responsibilities and contingencies for behavior to be changed" (Kirschenbaum & Flanery, 1983). Such contracts combine formalized goal setting with reinforcements (contingencies) conditional on attaining the goals.

The contracting process involves concrete discussions of specific behaviors that might be beneficial and how they might be carried out in order to fulfill the contract and claim any reward. From this perspective, contingency contracting is a highly precise approach to patient education (Garrity, 1981). For example, Swain and her colleagues (Steckel & Swain, 1977; Swain, 1978) engaged one group of hypertensive patients in a formal negotiation of an adherence contract permitting the patients to choose adherence behaviors that would be faithfully performed during the contract's term and rewarded, if fulfilled. The contracting group, which also received patient education and conventional medical attention, was compared with a group who received only education and medical attention, but no contract, and with a group who received only conventional medical care. The investigators reported that in their 30-month study of 37 contracting patients, there was never a failure to adhere to the contracted behavior. Furthermore, contracting patients never dropped out of care. These results can be contrasted with the conventional care and conventional care plus education groups, from which 28% and 56%, respectively, dropped out of treatment. Moreover, all of the contracting patients demonstrated good blood pressure control at the 15-month and 30-month follow-up, whereas the other groups showed considerable fluctuation over the follow-up period.

Behavioral contracting has been found to be a useful means of enhancing treatment adherence in both adult and child populations, often involving various HCPs and concerned others. With adults, the clinical problems of obesity (Dinoff, Rickard,

& Colwick, 1972; Harris & Bruner, 1971), hypertension (Steckel & Swain, 1977), chronic pain (Sternbach, 1974), and hemodialysis (Keane, Prue, & Collins, 1981; Wenerowicz, 1979) have been successfully addressed. Epstein, Beck, *et al.* (1981) used contracting as a part of a treatment program to increase urine testing in diabetic children, and Claerhout and Lutzker (1981) used contracts to increase dentally prescribed home care. The latter contract was between the patient and a nurse. Lund and Kegeles (1979) reported on the extension of contracts to school personnel to contract children for increased adherence to a preventive dental regimen. Greenan and his colleagues (1985) established a contingency contract that involved hemophiliac children, their parents, and the physical therapists, each whom signed the contract. The contract was periodically renegotiated in order to insure that a written specification of the targeted behaviors and performance contingencies was clear to all.

Although Sheridan and Smith (1975) caution that for some patients a contract has the negative connotation of a cold and formal approach to care (like a business agreement) that impedes the development of a trusting helping relationship and others have suggested that such contracts may lead to falsification in reporting (Wilson & Endress, 1986), the overall evidence indicates that this is not the case (see Kirschenbaum & Flanery, 1983). Instead, contracts provide a useful means by which the patient's mutual participation, responsibility, and accountability can be nurtured. Contracts help to clarify mutually determined treatment goals, minimize confusion, and foster a sharing process or partnership between patient and HCP.

A number of recent reviews[9] have described the short-term benefits in treatment adherence that have been achieved on both an inpatient and outpatient basis by means of behavioral contracting. Dunbar and Agras (1980) observe that contracts have been used successfully to improve blood pressure control, to assist in following diets, and to maintain appointment keeping

---

[9]For example, see DiMatteo and DiNicola (1982a, 1982b); Epstein and Wing (1979); Janz, Becker, and Hartman (1984); Kirschenbaum and Flanery (1983, 1984); O'Banion and Whaley (1981); Shelton and Levy (1981); and Steckel and Swain (1977).

for disulfiram administration among alcoholics. The evidence, however, for the long-term benefits, especially with patients suffering from chronic disorders or from long-term, life-style problems has yet to be fully demonstrated. For example, a number of reviewers (see Cummings *et al.*, 1981; Kazdin & Bootzin, 1972) have noted that changes (e.g., weight loss, smoking cessation) are maintained only for the duration of the contract, and after its termination or when the treatment contract is withdrawn the patient may stop performing health-related behaviors (e.g., pill taking, diet, exercise). Thus, behavioral contracts may be useful but not sufficiently compelling to guarantee long-term maintenance and continued performance of adherence. Even though the long-term effects of behavioral contracting have not, as yet, been fully studied, an examination of what goes into negotiating, implementing, and monitoring such contracts will prove informative. An examination of the many factors that influence the efficacy of behavioral contracts further underscores the difficulties and the options available to achieve treatment adherence.

Although behavioral contracting seems to be a straightforward and relatively simple enterprise, upon further examination one can appreciate that many options are available, each of which may contribute to the clinical outcome. Research has been conducted on whether behavioral contracts should be:

1. Written or verbal
2. Negotiated or not
3. Individualized or standardized
4. Public or private
5. Contingent upon outcome (e.g., lost two pounds) or on process measures (e.g., changing eating and exercise behaviors) that affect outcome

Although many of these issues have not been fully resolved, some useful guidelines have emerged. For example, Kirschenbaum and Flanery (1984) state:

> Negotiated forms of contracts, contracts using process as well as outcome target behaviors, and administration of consequences by the client and/or significant others (as opposed to administration

of consequences only by the therapist) improve therapeutic outcomes. (p. 598)

In a similar vein, Janz, Becker, and Hartman (1984) note
that in a number of studies in which behavioral contracting has
failed to increase treatment adherence:

> the behaviors and reinforcers were seldom negotiated; provider
> responsibilities were often poorly specified; positive reinforcers
> (other than return of clients' own valuables) were infrequently
> used; the client was rarely weaned from the intervention strategy;
> and reinforcement was often provided at fixed intervals (as opposed
> to coming directly after the desired behavior). (p. 177)

These summary evaluations indicate that a technology for
the successful use of behavioral contracts to enhance treatment
adherence is emerging. Any simple selection or "canned" contract that is imposed upon patients is unlikely to produce the
desired effects.

Table 23 provides specific guidelines for developing a
behavioral contract and Table 24 provides a prototypic contract.
An examination of the contract indicates the need to provide a

Table 23 Guidelines to Follow in Formulating a Behavioral Contract[a]

---

1. A clear and detailed description of the required instrumental behavior be
   stated.
2. Some criterion should be set for the time or frequency limitations
   constituting the goal of the contract.
3. The contract should specify positive reinforcements contingent upon
   fulfillment of the criterion.
4. Provisions should be made for some aversive consequences contingent
   upon nonfulfillment of the contract within a specified time or with a
   specified frequency.
5. A bonus clause should indicate the additional positive reinforcements
   obtainable if the person exceeds the minimal demands of the contract.
6. The contract should specify the means by which the contract response is
   observed, measured, and recorded: a procedure is stated for informing
   the client of his or her achievements over the duration of the contract.
7. The timing for delivery of reinforcement contingencies should be
   arranged to follow the response as quickly as possible.

---

[a]Adapted with permission from Kanfer & Gaelick, 1986.

Table 24   An Example of a Behavioral Contract[a]

Health-Care Contract

Contract goal: (specific outcome to be attained)

I, (client's name), agree to (detailed description of required behaviors, time and frequency limitations)

in return for (positive reinforcements contingent upon completion of required behaviors; timing and mode of delivery of reinforcements)

I, (provider's name), agree to (detailed description of required behaviors, time and frequency limitations)

(Optional) I, (significant other's name), agree to (detailed description of required behaviors, time and frequency limitations)

(Optional) Aversive consequences: (Negative reinforcements for failure to meet minimum behavioral requirements)

(Optional) Bonuses: (Additional positive reinforcements for exceeding minimum contract requirements)

We will review the terms of this agreement, and will make any desired modification, on (date). We hereby agree to abide by the terms of the contract described above.

Signed: (Client) _____

Signed: (Significant other, if relevant) _____

Signed: (Provider) _____

Contract effective from (Date) _____

to (Date) _____

[a]Reproduced with permission from Janz *et al.*, 1984.

clearly measurable specification of the behavior to be performed, desired goals, and responsibilities in terms of frequency, topography, setting, and contingencies. Wherever feasible, accuracy checks on patient self-monitoring should be built into the contract. The contract may or may not call for material rewards. When consequences are employed they should be administered immediately after prespecified criteria that may be in the form of rewards, penalties, and bonuses for noteworthy achievements. The reinforcers need not be costly but should be of value to the patient. A variety of reinforcers (e.g., attention from the nurse, reduction in length of treatment sessions, increased television viewing, access to a favorite meal or money) have been used. The patient should help determine the appropriate and most meaningful rewards. The behavioral contract should be signed by at least two parties as well as other interested and relevant parties. With regard to rewards, we concur with Rosenstock (1985), who concludes that the nature of the reward is of less consequence than the sense of pride and self-efficacy that accompanies the achievement.

The research also indicates that there is some advantage in making contracts public and thereby informing significant others of one's intentions, thus increasing the likelihood of fostering patient commitment and the involvement of significant others. Behavioral contracts should also include the specific dates for contract initiation, termination, and renewal. Above all, contracts must be flexible, modifiable, and open to renegotiation. As Southam and Dunbar (1986) observe, at this point it is not clear what features of behavioral contracting contribute to their efficacy, namely, written specification of tasks and goals, goal setting, public commitment to adherence, reinforcement for performance, or the increased supervision that is inherent in contracting. Most likely it is the combination of these multiple processes that contributes to the usefulness of contracting.

Contracts may be between the HCP and two parties or with the patient alone. In some instances, parents have agreed to provide their child with specific privileges contingent upon their youngster's performing a specifiable action. In studies with children a menu of reinforcers (e.g., money, movies, special time with parent, having a friend sleep overnight) has been used to increase treatment adherence. As Gross, Magalnick, and Richardson (1985) note, such explicit negotiation, monitoring, and implementation can replace the often nagging, bickering parent–child conflicts that have been found in families of diabetic and asthmatic children and children who must wear orthodontic appliances. In such programs, as in the case of adults, it is important that the children be actively involved in negotiating, self-monitoring on clearly visible charts, and receiving performance feedback and rewards (e.g., point system, stars, tokens, daily and weekly rewards) so that the contract does not come to be seen as coercive and the consequences do not come to be seen as a form of bribery. These reinforcement procedures should serve as initial motivation and should gradually be withdrawn and replaced by an emphasis on intrinsic motivation. Failure to establish patient self-motivation will probably result in reduced adherence.

Although other features of behavioral contracts have not been found to be significant (e.g., written versus verbal, good faith versus contingency-laden quid pro quo), one feature that appears to be critical is the benefits that accrue from the negotiation process. It is essential to enlist the patient's cooperation in the design of the contract. This negotiation process increases the patient's involvement in the decision-making process and is more likely to lead to the selection of more satisfactory individualized goals. Even the illusion of control can have salutary effects. For example, the insulin-dependent diabetic, can be given some choice about the scheduling of injections depending upon the various speed of activation of insulin. Even though the diabetic patient cannot control his need for insulin, some choice can be shared concerning the form and schedule of medication.

Insofar as the contract permits the patient or a significant other (not the HCP) to self-monitor and deliver the consequences, the likelihood of treatment adherence is increased. As Kirschenbaum and Flanery (1983) note, too much emphasis has been placed on the role of consequences and the important role of cognitive factors (planning, obtaining information, expressing intentions, and commitments) has been overlooked. We would add that affective factors (raising expectations, overcoming helplessness, fostering hope) have also been overlooked. The patient's sense of choice, control, and involvement is critical if the effects of behavioral contracts are to extend beyond the duration of the contract period and the treatment contact time. Moreover,

Kirschenbaum and Flanery (1984) underscore the important role of the relationship between the HCP and the patient in nurturing adherence to behavior contracts:

> A persuasive contract mediator is one who has high prestige and credentials, who is similar to and liked by the client and appears to be motivated by the client's best interest . . . and who is perceived as competent, expert (punctual, attentive, confident, logical and practical in suggesting treatment plans). (p. 600)

Another critical feature is that the HCP must ensure that the patient has the necessary skills and resources to meet the demands of the contract. Often it is necessary to break down complex goals and behavior into smaller achievable components that progressively move the patient toward treatment objectives. In order to achieve treatment objectives HCPs often ask patients to undertake homework assignments. For instance, Martin and Worthington (1982b) suggest that the homework tasks be logically related to the treatment goals and that they be kept brief, concrete, specific, and simple. All homework should be followed up in subsequent sessions. The rate of adherence with previous homework assignments is predictive of future adherence to homework, and problems with adherence at early stages of treatment should serve as a warning to HCPs and underscore the need to examine the difficulty and modify their own behavior or the treatment plan accordingly.

Patients should be involved in choosing the targeted behaviors to be covered in the contract and in devising the self-care regimen. Suggestions should be presented in a way that patients will accept. In fact, as in the case of self-monitoring, if the HCP has laid out the treatment regimen in a collaborative fashion there is a good chance that the patients may come up with the suggested behaviors themselves, in which case there is a greater likelihood of adherence.

In addition to stating specifically goals, expectations, and reinforcements in a summary contract, we have found it helpful to use progress charts of goal attainment. Patients keep charts of their performance of each self-care behavior. This serves as a constant reminder of the behavior to be performed and provides continuous feedback about progress to both the participants and the HCP. In this manner, problems and relapses are readily apparent and can be addressed before they become chronic and intractable problems that undermine adherence.

In negotiating a contract it is worthwhile to keep in mind the social psychological phenomenon that is known as a "foot-in-the-door" technique, whereby adherence to small, reasonable requests increases the likelihood of adherence to greater demands later on (see Craighead & Craighead, 1980; Freedman & Fraser, 1966). Obtaining initial adherence, especially under relatively low-demand conditions, can create the cognitive commitment for active participation and adherence with larger, more demanding treatment requests. Much research has been conducted on how one can solicit such patient commitments. For example, see Cialdini (1984) for a description of social influence techniques.

Commmitment Enhancement Procedures

Since eliciting a public commitment to adherence is such a central feature of establishing a behavioral contract, it is worth examining commitment enhancement procedures in a bit more detail. Each of us has no doubt made such public commitments that, in fact, have had little effect. It is always easier said than done. Consider how many times all of us have failed to adhere to New Year's resolutions. Our own experience is supported by the literature. For example, Marlatt and Kaplan (1972) examined the effects of self-initiated New Year's Eve resolutions on weight loss efforts. They found that half of the individuals who made written resolutions broke them within 15 weeks, and as for those who did initially lose weight, after an additional 15 weeks they were back to their initial weight. Moreover, unfulfilled resolutions resulted in lowered self-concept and a decreased sense of the importance of following such resolutions. Such repeated failures can lower self-esteem and the likelihood of sticking to future commitments. Consider the example of Mark Twain, who said that giving up smoking was quite easy; after all, he had given it up many times. The individual who repeatedly tries and fails may begin to loose faith in himself, view behavior change as an insurmountable task, and have less motivation to persevere, especially if success may take an extended period. This point illustrates the importance of conducting an adherence-oriented history (as described in Chapter 3). Those with a history of repetitive failure are likely to be more pessimistic about their chances of success and this skepticism may undermine efforts to undertake and maintain adherence.

Since the objective of adherence enhancement interventions is to help patients become more self-reliant and independent, a number of specific recommendations based on research (e.g., Bandura, 1977; Janis, 1983; Kiesler, 1971) can be offered. These guidelines parallel those described for developing contracts.

1. Public commitment leads to greater adherence than does private commitment. Insofar as patients can be encouraged to inform one or more people (in addition to the HCP) of their intentions to follow the treatment regimen, there is an increased likelihood of adherence.

2. The more specific the commitment or intention statement that the patient makes, in terms of the frequency, duration, and self-initiated consequences for specific behaviors, the higher the likelihood of change. Thus, announcing that one intends to stop smoking, lose weight, or take one's medicine is not so effective as specifying exactly how, where, when, and with what consequence (both positive and negative) such behavior changes may come about. For example, DiMatteo and DiNicola (1982a) recommend eliciting a verbal or written public commitment to adhere as well as specific behavioral instructions rather than general statements (e.g., "eat only at meal time" rather than "lose weight"). As noted, a behavioral contract provides the most explicit public commitment.

HCPs can nurture such commitments by asking the patient directly about his or her intentions to adhere and asking also about past efforts to stick to intentions. By asking the patient questions such as "What it is you are going to do?" and "Do you intend to follow (adhere to) the assignment (request)?" the HCP conveys his or her interest and concern in fostering treatment adherence. Such specific queries can be followed by an exploration of whether the patient has tried to follow such intentions in the past: "What kinds of things in the past have you tried that were unsuccessful? How is what you have agreed to do now different?"

Exploring such material will help to pinpoint potential difficulties and to ensure that the necessary skills and resources to meet the commitment intentions are indeed in the patient's repertoire.

3. Such commitments have been solicited in verbal, written, or in both forms. At this point it is not clear that one mode is better than the other or whether some combination is more effective. Although the point is not settled, it does appear that soliciting a commitment in both an oral and written form increases the likelihood of treatment adherence. As noted in the previous discussion of behavioral contracts, soliciting a written commitment may prove effective only during the course and terms of the contract. Therefore something more is required. That something more requires the patient to adhere not for the sake of pleasing the HCP but in order to avoid self-disapproval and obtain self-reinforcement.

4. As noted, the research indicates that greater adherence is achieved if the patient is given a choice in making a decision. If the HCP provides patients with a limited range of assignments from which to choose, then the likelihood of adherence is increased.

5. Another variable identified as important is whether the HCP provides the patient with mild counterarguments about the reasons to comply with the treatment regimen. As Janis (1983) notes, such arguments should indicate possible obstacles and drawbacks to be expected if the patient adheres (e.g., may have to give up so many treats or privileges, or change lifestyle, or engage in certain short-term discomforts). It is more effective if patients hear these arguments from the HCP rather than hearing them from others or to having to come up with them themselves. In the patient's discussion with the HCP such arguments

can usually be minimized, countered, and overcome, thus fostering the patient's sense of control, commitment, and degree of hope. As Janis (1983) notes:

> Research on commitment indicates that if a person is given the opportunity to consider the alternatives and then announces his or her intention to an esteemed other, such as a physician or a health counselor . . . , the person is anchored to that decision by anticipated social disapproval from the practitioner and also by anticipated self-disapproval. (p. 157)

6. The HCP must not only elicit statements of commitment from patients but must also ensure that there are salient cues to remind patients of their commitment efforts. One way to achieve this goal is to have patients self-monitor their behavior frequently, thus enhancing the cues, reminders, or salience of commitment.

7. Finally, when change does come about as patients behave in accord with their intention and commitment statements, the HCP must ensure that the patients make *self-attributions* about the change. In short, it is not enough to have patients adhere; the HCP must be certain that the observed changes are attributed by patients to themselves and not to some external events or persons (Kopel & Arkowitz, 1975). That is why the least powerful reward or punishment should be used to elicit behavior change. In the next chapter we will consider attribution retraining.

The integrated application of the various features of commitment procedures is illustrated in the work of Dishman (1982), who reported that the amount of patients' expressed commitment predicted their perseverance in adhering to a physical fitness training program. Similarly, Atkins, Kaplan, and Timms (1981) reported that commitment enhancement efforts improved adherence to exercise in chronic obstructive pulmonary disease patients.

Reinforcement Procedures

The suggestion that health-related behaviors are significantly influenced by both immediate and distal consequences has provided a powerful medium of change for HCPs. As Southam and Dunbar (1986) note, an effective system of reinforcement requires:

1) The establishment of clear definitions of requested behaviors;
2) Behavioral criteria for reinforcement;
3) A predesignated system of rewards for prompt reinforcement; and
4) And a well-established record-keeping system for recording target behaviors. (p. 137)

Reinforcement procedures have been used in a variety of ways to increase adherence with a wide variety of patients (diabetics, arthritics, asthmatics, hypertensives, renal patients). An examination of some of these applications will illustrate the several alternatives available to the HCPs.

1. *Reward procedures.* Some of the HCPs we surveyed indicated that they make their own services, availability, and fees contingent upon patients' adherence. For example, consider the following comments:

- I reduce my fees if the patient adheres.
- I use praise routinely.
- I post the names of patients on a list of good adherers (that is, with the patient's consent).

The use of material consequences such as money and lottery tickets has been reported by several investigators. For example, in a study by Haynes and his colleagues (1976), patient adherence to a drug program to control blood pressure resulted in a financial bonus toward the purchase of blood pressure recording equipment. Similarly, Masek (1982) reported the successful use of state lottery tickets for patients keeping appointments and demonstrating adherence. Some might consider the use of such tangible rewards as inappropriate or as a bribe or beyond what should be expected of HCPs. These techniques, however, can be used as an initial source of motivation, and with performance of appropriate self-care behaviors they can be gradually withdrawn.

2. *Negative consequence procedures.* Alternatively, HCPs report using the removal of positive reinforcement and the onset

of aversive consequences as a means of increasing treatment adherence:

- I fine the patients for nonadherence.
- If the patient doesn't adhere after a number of repeated warnings I won't see him or her.
- I have the patient make out a set of nonrefundable money orders to a group they despise (e.g., Ku Klux Klan, American Nazi Party). Each time they violate the adherence contract I have the patient send off one of the donations.

In one application, Haynes (1974) used the threat and contingency management of being sent to jail with alcoholics on an Antabuse treatment program. The alcoholics were required to take Antabuse in the presence of a probation officer twice weekly. If patients violated this requirement twice they would be sent to jail. This program resulted in significant reduction of arrests and increased adherence, with few patients missing more than two appointments.

Another form of contingency management has been the use of a *response cost* system (cost to patient for nonadherence). In many of these programs patients must pay a deposit, sometimes on a sliding scale, which is returned for attendance at meetings or for a specified behavior change. For instance, failure to report to the clinic or to adhere to various features of the program results in the loss of the deposit (e.g., $5 to $10 per visit reduced from an initial deposit of $100). Brownell *et al.* (1986) have reported that such contingency management has been used successfully in the control of drug abuse, alcohol intake, smoking, and weight loss. The major focus is on identifying and using meaningful and costly consequences contingent upon the failure to adhere. Examples of cases wherein a response cost system has been used are offered by Bigelow, Strickler, Liebson, and Griffith, (1976); Epstein and Masek (1978), and Hagen, Foreyt, and Durham (1976).

Perhaps the best illustration of the potential usefulness of a deposit–refund response cost system is that offered by Brownell and Foreyt (1985) with obese patients. Their system requires patients to make a financial deposit in addition to the charge for treatment. The deposit is refunded for attendance, weight loss, completion of records, and any other treatment requirements. The amount of the deposit varies with the patient's financial status and the cost of the program. For example, a deposit of $100 may be required for a treatment program costing $200. If patients attend 80% of the initial sessions, $50 is returned and the remaining $50 is returned for attending 80% of the following sessions. Wilson and Brownell (1980) have reported on the effectiveness of the deposit refund program in significantly reducing attrition rates. The amounts used for penalties must be perceived by patients as meaningful and equitable, and this should be individually determined. In setting up such contingency management programs careful consideration must be given to the nature of the reinforcers and the rules of exchange. Patients should be collaborators in setting up such programs or they may sabotage the treatment plan as an effort to exert countercontrol ("reactance").

Although the use of such explicit contingencies can often result in immediate behavioral change, a major concern is the absence of maintenance and generalizability of these changes across settings and over time. As noted before, the evidence, as reviewed by Kazdin and Bootzin (1972) and Leventhal *et al.* (1984), points to the limited effects of such reinforcement programs once the contract with the primary HCP is removed. Moreover, such explicit change efforts are likely to lead to the patient's attributing their adherence to some external feature such as the explicit contingency program or to the efforts of the HCP. As noted, not only must behavior change occur, but patients must attribute the change to their own efforts if it is to endure. In fostering self-attribution a self-control form of reinforcement procedure has emerged as preferable.

3. *Self-reinforcement procedures.* Another way to use the principles of reinforcement procedures is to enlist patients as collaborators so that they will self-monitor, set attainable adherence goals, receive feedback, and reinforce themselves with publicly agreed-upon contingencies. Consider the following procedures reported in our survey of HCPs:

- I have patients keep a flow chart of limited goals they achieve. They also keep a menu of goodies they can have for earning each goal. Slowly, we enlarge the treatment goals.
- I have patients compare their pretreatment and post-treatment results (e.g., lab tests).
- I encourage patients to take pride in what they have accomplished.
- I highlight the self-rewarding features of adhering and bolster the patient's self-confidence.
- I get patients to compete with themselves to improve.

Each of these suggestions is designed to encourage the patient to develop a sense of confidence in his or her ability to perform the appropriate behaviors. Often, however, patients, especially children, may need the help of significant others (e.g., parents, siblings) in order to achieve and maintain adherence.

4. *Involving others in reward procedures.* Another way to expand the efficacy of reward programs has been to teach reinforcement principles to significant others whose assistance is required in the monitoring of patient behavior and in the dispensing of reinforcement. When appropriate, patients should be asked to nominate one or more persons to participate in the program. In fact, the majority of reinforcement programs to increase adherence have involved parents who have been taught behavior modification procedures[10] to use with their children. Table 25 provides guidelines for how parents can establish a reinforcement training program to increase adherence behavior in their children.

An example of such a reinforcement system has been used with the parents of diabetic children who have been trained to employ a reward (point) system. Children could earn a point by

---

[10]Illustrative behavior modification studies of adherence behavior include Barnes, 1976; Carney, Schechter, and Davis, 1983; Dapcich-Miura and Hovall, 1979; Epstein, Beck, *et al.*, 1981; Epstein, Figueroa, Farkas, and Beck, 1918; Gentry, 1976; Hart, 1979; Haynes *et al.*, 1976; Lowe and Lutzker, 1979; Magrab and Papadopoulou, 1977; Masek, 1982; Renne and Creer, 1976; Schaefer, Glasgow, and McCaul, 1982; Sergis-Deavenport and Varni, 1982, 1983.

Table 25 Guidelines for Establishing a Behavioral Parent Reinforcement Program

- The parent should record explicitly all observable, measurable adherence measures in the child's treatment regimen.
- When age permits, the child should keep a performance chart and do the self-monitoring.
- This baseline data (preintervention) should be posted in a prominent place in the home.
- Parents and child should develop an agreed-upon set of reinforcement contingencies (e.g., the child's adherence may result in a special activity, going to movie, having a friend sleep over, various treats).
- Parents should use praise and encouragement to get the child to use self-praise and take pride in his or her adherence behavior, reinforcing the child for effort, not achievement.
- A gradualist approach is necessary; reinforcements should initially be contingent only upon some aspects of the desirable behavior. Over time the criterion for receiving reinforcement should be gradually increased.
- There should be explicit and consistent use of feedback to reinforce the child's attempts to adhere.
- The use of a point, token, or star system (secondary reinforcers) for adherent behavior is usually very helpful. Points can be traded in for primary reinforcers (e.g., desired activities) at a later date.
- In some instances, parents can participate in the same treatment regimen (e.g., a weight loss program for both parents and their obese children).

following a written memo or verbal instructions (e.g., earn one point for doing blood testing, one point for proper foot care). These points are traded in on a daily basis, as well as for bonuses on a weekly basis.

The written memo specifies self-care tasks to be performed and at what times. In simple, easy-to-understand language the memo provides step-by-step instructions as well as reasons why each step is to be taken. Another important feature is the posting of results (feedback) in a prominent place so the child can monitor his or her progress with the self-care tasks. In turn, the child can assume greater responsibility for monitoring and self-reinforcing his or her behavior. This visual information may help the child to become alert to the association between his or her self-care behavior and both positive and negative consequences.

A number of variations of such behavioral programs have been used. HCPs have attempted to involve patients' spouses or siblings in the adherence program. For example, Brownell and his colleagues (1985) have developed a treatment manual for spouses of obese patients, and Epstein and his colleagues (1985) have involved parents in exercise programs with obese children. (See also Israel, Stolmaker, Sharp, Silverman, & Simon, 1984, and Kirschenbaum, Harris, & Tomarken, 1984, for descriptions of parent involvement programs). Insofar as the patient's efforts at treatment adherence can be incorporated into the normal lifestyle of the family, there is an increased likelihood of treatment adherence. (See Baranowski & Nader, 1985a, 1985b, for reviews).

5. *Teaching the patient reinforcement principles and procedures.* Yet another way to use reinforcement principles is illustrated in the work of Gross, Samson, and Dierkes (1985), who noted that often the patient and significant others in the family have different concerns. For example, think of the potentially competing concerns of an adolescent diabetic patient and his or her parents. The meaning of nonadherence to a treatment regimen may be quite different for each. Moreover, in many instances parents are uninterested or unavailable to learn the behavior modification procedures. An interesting way to meet these difficulties has been to teach patients, including children, reinforcement principles. For instance, Gross *et al.* have taught diabetic children how to praise their parents when they employ behavior modification procedures. Given the reciprocal and interdependent nature of parent–child interactions, Gross found that giving children information about behavior modification procedures strengthened their adherence behavior. They used workbooks developed by Brigham (1982) involving nine written lessons (three to five pages each) to teach the children reinforcement principles. They also taught them a variety of negotiation skills to be used with their parents in order to avoid the nagging and conflicts that often surround arguments about adhering to the treatment regimen. The negotiation skills included:

- Identifying what each party wants
- Identifying the reward each party wants
- Setting priorities
- Putting oneself in the other person's place
- Suggesting counterproposals and compromises

The HCP would model and then the children would rehearse (role-play) the use of such negotiation skills. Given the difficulties reported in the literature in having parents carry out behavior modification procedures, the notion of teaching such skills directly to children is indeed attractive. After much parent–child conflict over adherence issues, the children's use of negotiation can act as a powerful reinforcer.

In considering these various reinforcement programs, it is important to emphasize the often observed finding that such behavior change and improved treatment adherence will endure only if the social environment continues to support the program *and* the patient develops necessary intrinsic motivation. Once the contingencies are removed, the patient's behavior may often revert to pretreatment level. For instance, if a patient leaves a hospital setting in which an operant reinforcement program was employed to insure adherence and returns to a family setting that does not sustain the program, the patient's adherence is likely to deteriorate. Such difficulties in maintaining change with reinforcement programs has led behavior modifiers to build in follow-up (booster) interventions, to develop support groups, and to supplement their treatment programs with skills training regimens whereby patients can develop self-regulatory skills required to insure the maintenance of treatment-adherent behavior. The patients' attitudes regarding their own abilities to perform each self-care behavior and the desirability of the outcome are essential for long-care maintenance. This is especially crucial for patients who must live with chronic diseases.

In this chapter, we have focused upon several behavioral techniques that can be employed by HCPs. These techniques should not be used in a rigid manner but should be customized

to the individual patient. Moreover, simple strategies (e.g., contracts) turn out to be significantly more complex than might
initially be expected and must be applied in a thoughtful, clinically sensitive fashion. In the next chapter we will discuss several additional enhancement techniques that place greater
emphasis on the patient as an agent for the maintenance of
control over his or her behavior.

Teaching Self-Regulatory Skills

The problem of maintaining adherence behavior once it has been attained is a dilemma in health care. Not only does there tend to be a persistent decline over time, but the adherence interventions that have been tested have not shown continuation of effects when the intervention is withdrawn.

J. M. DUNBAR and W. S. AGRAS (1980)

The end point of any adherence training program must be maintenance, but as Dunbar and Agras (1980) have noted this is difficult to achieve. Since the objective of an adherence training program is to foster patients' involvement, self-control, and long-term maintenance in the absence of supervision by health care providers, training programs are increasingly focusing on the development of self-regulatory skills (e.g., see Kanfer, 1977, and Leventhal *et al.*, 1984). These programs are designed to foster the patient's self-image of being an effective self-manager. In order to achieve this objective a variety of procedures are included such as:

   a. Establishing a collaborative working relationship with HCP and patient and, where appropriate, with patient's family members
   b. Self-control training that covers self-regulation of medication, planning and problem-solving skills, training in

intrapersonal and interpersonal skills, relapse prevention, and attribution retraining

The objective of each of these efforts is to provide patients
with a greater sense of responsibility and to put them more in
charge of their own treatment regimen. Before we examine how
these procedures are used to nurture self-regulatory skills, it is
worthwhile to repeat a warning offered by Southam and Dunbar
(1986), who comment that self-management procedures may not
be suitable for all patients. As they observe, some patients may
not have the skills, resources, temperament, or outlook to undertake self-help treatment regimens. This is especially true when
adequate training and supervision are lacking. Any effort at fostering self-help skills will require continued commitment and
evaluation from HCPs. When care is taken, however, teaching
self-management skills can prove quite effective, as is evident
in the work by Fireman and his colleagues (1981) with asthmatic
children and their parents, Peterson, Forhan, and Jones (1980)
with diabetics, and Youngren (1981) with pulmonary disease
patients. Although each patient population requires training in
specific disease-related skills, a number of generic skills cut across
the various programs. We will now consider these.

Establishing a Collaborative Relationship

As noted previously in Chapter 3, both the nature and the
quality of the relationship between the patient and HCP are
critical to the treatment outcome. In order to foster self-control
skills the HCP must monitor carefully his or her style of
interaction—what is said and how. Moreover, it is essential to
build up the patient's sense of personal responsibility. Janis (1983)
has provided several guidelines to follow in order to achieve this
objective. These include the need to make the patient feel that
the HCP really does care. For example, consider the message
conveyed by Coleman (1985):

> I am with you in this. It is not going to be easy. I know from
> experience how hard it is to stay on diets, but let's make a plan
> and work together until your blood pressure is at a goal we agree
> on. (p. 71)

Janis also suggests that criticism or feedback be given in a nonthreatening manner. Consider the way feedback was offered by Rodin to patients who had difficulty adhering to the treatment regimen:

> It is quite understandable that you would feel self-critical at such times and would still feel down on yourself. (Cited in Rodin & Janis, 1982)

The HCP then has the patient note the progress that has been made. Such efforts at providing feedback in a constructive fashion are designed to bolster the patients' confidence that they can go further on their own. In this way the HCP become a dependable agent of self-esteem enhancement.

Finally, Janis (1983) suggests a variety of practical considerations that include:

a. Assessing the patient's previous efforts and experience with self-management
b. Ascertaining the patient's preference and capability for each element of the treatment regimen
c. Insuring that the patient has the resources and skills to implement the requisite procedures
d. Introducing changes over the course of several visits
e. Breaking complex tasks into simpler, more manageable demands that can be implemented sequentially
f. Beginning with a single step whereby the patient can gain a sense of accomplishment
g. Enlisting family support
h. Terminating the contract gradually, not abruptly

These guidelines provide the basis for teaching specific self-control skills. Three classes of skills have been identified, namely, problem solving, intrapersonal and interpersonal skills, and coping with and benefiting from lapses.

Skills Training

Any effort to increase patient adherence must insure that patients have the necessary skills to implement the treatment regimen. Often nonadherence derives from the failure to insure that patients do indeed have the requisite component skills for adherence. Such skills as planning, problem solving, information dissemination, assertiveness, stress management, and coping with lapses are germane. In some instances, behavioral feedback training may be used to teach specific treatment-related behaviors such as monitoring one's own physical condition or making changes in one's own treatment regimen (drug selection and dosage). Not only must patients possess skills, but they must also believe in the effectiveness of these responses and have a sense of confidence that they can implement those skills (Bandura, 1977).

Problem-Solving Skills

We begin with problem-solving and planning skills since we view treatment adherence as a result of a personal decision and since problem solving actively involves the patient in the education and treatment process. As Janis (1984a,b) has noted, the patient's decision to follow a treatment regimen is influenced by a number of factors including salient threats, opportunities, and other anticipated consequences, pro and con. "These can be viewed as positive and negative incentives that enter into the patient's decisional balance sheet" (p. 119).

Janis and his colleagues have increased patient adherence by having them engage in a verbal and written evaluation of the anticipated benefits and costs of following a treatment regimen (e.g., Hoyt & Janis, 1975; Janis & Mann, 1977; Winkel & Thompson, 1977). The HCP has the patient describe several alternative ways in which to ensure adherence to the treatment regimen and then consider the gains and losses (pros and cons) to self and others that will follow from such adherence. Table 26 provides an example of such a decisional balance sheet that can be used with almost any patient in order to foster adherence. Such problem-solving training has been used successfully in fostering adherence in several clinical populations (e.g., chronic pain patients, cancer patients, diabetic patients, alcoholics, obese patients). (See D'Zurilla, 1986, and Turk *et al.*, 1986). To illustrate the utility of problem solving to enhance adherence we can

Table 26   Balance Sheet Grid[a]

Treatment alternative:	Positive anticipations	Negative anticipations
Tangible gains and losses for self		
Tangible gains and losses to others		
Self-approval or self-disapproval		
Social approval or disapproval		

[a]Table based on Janis & Mann, 1977, and Slimmer, 1986.

consider a study by Chaney, O'Leary, and Marlatt (1978). These authors successfully employed a cognitive behavioral training program to foster adherence in alcoholics. The training included modeling, role playing, coaching techniques to work through the problem in solving steps of problem definitions and formulation, generation of alternatives, decision making, and then rehearsing optimal alternatives. A major focus was inoculation against backsliding in adherence situations. The HCP focused on identifying high-risk situations and rehearsing ways to cope with them. Another key feature of such training programs was to reinforce a general problem-solving orientation by having patients acknowledge that unforeseen problems will probably occur but that the patient is competent to deal with these as they arise. Similar problem-solving self-control-oriented relapse prevention programs have been developed with smokers by Davis and Glaros (1986) and by Gilchrist, Schinke, Bobo, and Snow (1986).

Slimmer and Brown (1985) used group decision-making counseling and a balance sheet procedure with parents of hyperactive children in order to enhance adherence to the drug regimen. The parents discussed with the HCP alternative ways to handle their hyperactive child and then rank-ordered their decision alternatives. The sessions often included questions such as:

What are the considerations (consequences) in favor (against) placing your child on Ritalin? Will a special education resource room
be as effective as stimulant medication? Will my child be dependent on this drug for the remainder of his life? If I don't use medication, could the condition worsen? (p. 222)

In order to address these questions systematically the HCP
had parents use a balance grid sheet. The HCP said:

We have constructed a list of some of the considerations that
parents think about when deciding to place their child on Ritalin.
I want you to go through this list and see how these considerations
might apply to you. The considerations are grouped under four
headings like those in your balance sheet. Look at the list for a
few minutes.

Let's start with the tangible gains and losses for self that might
be expected for placing your child on Ritalin. Then we will go
through this same category for not placing him on Ritalin. Look
over all the considerations in the first category. Try to see how
they bear on your choice. Some you've already mentioned and
written on your grid. But there will be others you haven't mentioned. I'd like you to concentrate on these. First tell me what
bearing the consideration would have on your choice. Be as specific as possible and say whether this would be an advantage or
disadvantage. I'll ask some questions to try to make sure that we've
touched on all the considerations that might be relevant to you.
(Slimmer, 1986)

The HCP, using the balance grid sheet (see Table 26), provided parents with a list of alternative considerations that were
reviewed and discussed. The use of such a problem-solving,
decision-making approach proved helpful in increasing parent
adherence. Parents were encouraged to talk about their experiences and to seek clarification if they did not comprehend a
specific point. The counseling on decision making helped parents
become more aware of the value and importance of deliberating
about their decisions. The discussion focused on behavioral actions
as well as psychological mechanisms.

Friedman and Litt (1986) have used a similar decisional
balance sheet format with family planning clients in order to
review the advantages and disadvantages of each birth control
method before any method is prescribed. By exploring each of

the options the HCP attempts to inhibit the client's wishful thinking about not getting pregnant and anxious, impulsive behavior that might contribute to nonadherence. Another mode of planning concerns ways in which patients can involve significant others in helping them adhere to the treatment regimen. By means of negotiation the patient can engage other family members in the various treatment management tasks. For example, Kovacs and Feinberg (1982) have noted that parents of diabetic children may not adhere because of logistical obstacles. They report that mothers, who are generally given the sole or prominent responsibility for adherence, may be so fatigued and emotionally drained that they are unable to adhere to the treatment regimen. This is especially true when the diabetic child is young and recently diagnosed and when both parents work, or if the mother is single or there are other siblings in the house. All the demands of parenting and work are now exceeded by the additional requirements of conducting the child's blood and urine testing, insulin shots, dietary regimen, and so forth.

In cases in which the adherence regimen is extensive and demanding (e.g., cystic fibrosis, end-stage renal disease) it is quite evident that the parent must be successful in delegating responsibilities, perhaps with different siblings taking on different activities. In some instances, when one of the older siblings or one of the parents is also suffering from the same disorder they may be able to synchronize testing and insulin injections. By sharing such activities both child and parent may come to see them as less burdensome.

Intrapersonal and Interpersonal Skills

Patients may need explicit social skills training, behavioral rehearsal, and role playing as to how to solicit such cooperation. Assertive behavior rather than passive avoidance of activities can enhance adherence. For example, if the family has been invited to a special function, the parents of the diabetic patient can contact the hosts beforehand in order to assure that proper food is available. Similarly, parents of diabetic children have reported the need to take an active role in the school system so that their child is not stigmatized or treated as different. Kovacs and Feinberg (1982) report the case of a diabetic child who was separated from his classmates and sent to the nurse's office to consume his snack. A powerful motivation for children and adolescents is not to appear different. Sending a child to the nurse's office in this case resulted in the child's being teased by the other children, to his feeling deviant, and to treatment nonadherence. The HCP had to work with the patient and his parents in exploring, practicing, and implementing ways in which the social environment could be changed. This may involve the parents' disseminating information and informing school personnel about the nature of the diabetes and the particular needs of their child. Such actions are required to increase the likelihood of adherence.

The importance of insuring that patients have the required social skills was underscored by the findings of Ary, Toobert, Wilson, and Glasgow (1986). In their study of nonadherence in adult diabetics they found that the patients required socially appropriate refusal skills when being tempted to violate their treatment regimen and assertive skills when eating in restaurants. In the latter instance, there is a need to initiate requests for alternative menu selections. In a collaborative fashion, patients and HCPs can identify high risk situations and then help patients nurture effective coping strategies and skills to anticipate and overcome barriers to adherence. Once patients have had some experience with the treatment regimen and have had time to identify specific problem areas, additional follow-up sessions can be conducted. Many patients and significant others may require specific training in problem solving along the lines described in Table 27 in order to put such efforts into effect.

Often such discussion and training are conducted on a group basis. Various patient groups and groups of significant others (parents, siblings, friends) have proved helpful in fostering adherence. Although we will consider the use of social supports in more detail in the next chapter, at this point it is worth noting that the shared experience and informational exchange that occur in such groups can prove quite valuable. At such meetings patients

Table 27   Problem-Solving Skills

Review the steps of problem solving:
 Define the problem clearly in behavioral terms (give examples).
 Encourage patient to substitute general statements that they cannot do
 something with a specific analysis of exactly what they cannot do and
 why.

 Generate possible solutions to each problem or task and consider a wide
 range of possible alternative courses of action. To facilitate this, have the
 patient imagine and consider how other might respond if asked to solve
 similar problems.

 Evaluate the pros and cons of each proposed solution and rank them
 from least to most practical and desirable.

 Try out the most acceptable and feasible solution. Encourage flexibility.

 Reconsider the original problem in light of this attempt at problem
 solving. Does the problem look different? Can the patient see anything
 positive about the situation?

Adopting a problem-solving method of this kind may involve:

 Talking to others to obtain information.

 Recalling things you have done before that required similar skills

Imagine how someone else might cope

Dividing stressful events into smaller manageable tasks

Thinking of what lies ahead and making contingency plans

Practicing coping by rehearsing skills

Looking to support systems for advice and support

 Gradually exposing yourself to small amounts of stress before entering
 high-pressure situations

Using coping skills but not "catastrophizing" if things do not work out.
Failure or disappointment should be viewed as necessary feedback to help
the problem-solving process resume.

---

and family members can catch up with current management practices, share information about treatment materials and obstacles, and explore and deal with the stress inherent in a demanding treatment regimen. They can also practice and hone the specific intrapersonal and interpersonal skills needed to develop and implement an adherence plan.

Coping and Benefiting from Lapses

Inherent in every effort to adhere are failures, setbacks, and backsliding. A critical feature of adherence counseling is the need to teach patients how to anticipate and prepare for high-risk situations and to cope, and even benefit, from such lapses.

Relapse prevention (RP) is a self-control program designed to teach individuals who are trying to change their behavior how to anticipate and cope with the problem of relapse (Marlatt & George, 1984). The RP model was initially developed as a behavioral maintenance program for use in the treatment of patients with addictive behaviors (see Marlatt & Gordon, 1985), but, as we shall see, it has broad application to the area of adherence. Since a major obstacle of most treatment regimens is long-term maintenance, especially for patients suffering from chronic disorders, the development in patients of a coping repertoire designed to handle lapses (slips, setbacks, backsliding, and failures) is most relevant.

As developed by Alan Marlatt and his colleagues, the RP model has focused on identifying high-risk situations, namely, any situation that presents a threat to the person's sense of control. Since patients may lapse, the RP model insures that patients have appropriate skills to anticipate, avoid, and reduce the impact of lapses so that these do not escalate into full-blown relapses. Lapses may occur for many different reasons including social pressure, interpersonal conflict, cultural norms, dysphoric emotions, physiological cravings, and logistical and/or financial difficulties. The essential point is to help patients anticipate occasional lapses that may occur. They must learn to appreciate and control the inadvertent decisions, rationalizations, and accompanying feelings that contribute to lapses (e.g., "I owe myself a drink or cigarette." "Only if I have that drink or cigarette will I be able to cope."). In addition, Marlatt and Gordon (1985) suggest that patients be "inoculated" for failure so that when lapses do indeed occur they will not panic or engage in self-degnigration, "catastrophizing" thoughts, and guilty feelings. Each slip should be viewed as an incremental learning experience. In order to convey the view that an instance of nonadherence should not be seen as a complete failure, or as an occasion for withdrawal from the treatment regimen, a number of metaphors are used. Several examples convey the spirit of this approach.

It is like the situation of a scientist who conducts an experiment. Sometimes the experiment works and that is fine. But sometimes the experiment fails. Now, when does the scientist learn most? Often when the experiment fails. That is the occasion to reassess what went wrong. Without such failures there would be little progress. The same applies in your following the treatment program. You may indeed have occasional lapses, slips, but without them I would feel we are not making progress. It is not that you occasionally backslide, but how you view such slips, what you say to yourself about them that is important. If indeed they occur they should be viewed as learning experiences and as opportunities to determine what went wrong and what you can do about it next time.

It is like teaching my young son to ride a two-wheel bicycle. I run along side holding onto the seat of the bike as firmly as possible and at some point he says, "It is okay, let go." Most of the time he continues fine, but occasionally he falls. Now when does he learn most? Often when he falls. Did he fall because he was going too fast, turned too rapidly, the ground was too wet, or will he grow up and ride a three-wheel bike at the age of 23? The same applies in your case when you attempt to follow the treatment regimen. An infrequent lapse is the occasion when we can learn most about your condition and what can be done to help you. Remember, each person is unique and everyone's situation is different. It will be our job to find out what works best for you. There may be ups and downs, but working together we should find the best treatment regimen for you.

As we noted earlier, it is essential to find the right metaphor or analogy for each patient. If the notion of the scientist or the boy riding the bicycle does not work for your patient, create a relevant example. For instance, Marlatt and Gordon (1985) use the example of a fire drill (i.e., practicing to escape a fire even though fires are rare); Brownell (in press) uses the example of a forest ranger whose job it is to prevent and contain fires to convey the notion of preparing for handling lapses. Marlatt and George (1984) illustrate the RP model by reminding patients of the admonition "Forewarned is forearmed" and the proverb "An ounce of prevention is worth a pound of cure." In any case, the objective is to help patients cognitively reframe deviations and adherence lapses as a learning experience (e.g., violating abstinence in the case of those who have problems with addiction), rather than as an occasion for complete relapse.

According to the RP model, the HCP must help patients anticipate and plan for high-risk situations wherein lapses are likely and to insure that patients have the intrapersonal and interpersonal skills to handle such situations. Although high-risk situations vary widely across individuals and settings, Marlatt and Gordon (1985) found that they often include (1) social pressures (e.g., peer-induced temptations), (2) negative emotional states (e.g., boredom, anger, frustration), and (3) interpersonal conflicts (e.g., disagreements with employer, spouse). Patients have to work out possible solutions to challenges and temptations ahead of time and be able to deal with them when they arise. For example, Kaplan, Chadwick, and Schimmel (1985) taught groups of adolescents with Type I diabetes to identify and enact problem-solving situations (e.g., peer pressure) and their solutions.

The HCP may use a variety of skills-training procedures (videotape demonstrations, modeling, behavioral and imagery rehearsal, role playing, corrective feedback, and the like) in order to insure that patients have the requisite repertoire. For instance, what is the patient likely to say if his buddies challenge or tempt him to deviate from the treatment regimen? The HCP must forearm patients against the changes in beliefs and behaviors that may interfere with treatment adherence. A customized relapse prevention plan or an individualized "road map" is required so that the patient can predict specific potentially difficult situations and plan advance strategies for coping, identifying potential traps and pitfalls. Marlatt and Gordon (1985) even suggest that patients carry reminder cards of what to do if a slip occurs. The RP model is designed to foster increasing levels of patient responsibility, especially as the degree of supervision is reduced. Patients with addictions may also learn to change their life style and to develop "positive addictions," such as exercise or relaxation, and to modify the balance between activities that are perceived as external demands ("shoulds") and activities engaged in for pleasure or self-fulfillment ("wants").

After the patient has made a decision to adhere the HCP can present him or her with mild challenges by calling attention to potential unpleasant consequences of the treatment program. In overcoming a challenge of this sort, the patient achieves a personal accomplishment that bolsters the sense of self-efficacy.

Interestingly, Brownell *et al.* (1986) reported that in the treatment of patients with addiction problems success for most individuals came after prior lapses (e.g., a second relapse). In fact, those patients who struggled with adherence did better in the long run than those patients who adhered perfectly from the outset. Those patients who had a record of perfect adherence had trouble recovering from the inevitable slip that early perfection merely postponed. Those who had faltered were learning how to cope with setbacks so that a single slip would not necessarily become a full-blown relapse or permanent failure. This finding is consistent with the observations of Schachter (1982), who found that multiple attempts often occur before many people succeed in adhering, as in the case of smoking reduction and weight control. Cures in many cases followed several relapses. Initial lapses permit patients to acquire information and learn ways to prevent lapses in the future. Thus, in some instances lapses can provide useful learning opportunities and bolster adherence; whereas on other occasions, if the laspes are repetitive and are perceived as catasatrophes, they may lead to feelings of inadequacy and helplessness. Rather than blaming themselves for slips and thus viewing themselves as failures with no willpower, patients are encouraged to analyze the situation and resolve to try again. An attributional style that examines environmental circumstances as being partly responsible for the slip is nurtured. In this way patients can learn how to anticipate, prevent, and cope with future high-risk situations. It is not the failure to adhere *per se*, but what patients say to themselves, the meaning they attribute to occasional setbacks, that determines future patterns of adherence.

The HCP can help patients better understand and cope with the stress and negative emotional states (disappointment, frustration, depression, anxiety) that accompany lapses. Lapses must be viewed as constructive instrumental learning experiences and as a problem to be solved. As Brownell *et al.* (1986) note, the need for such a systematic learning approach is particularly indicated for those patients who begin treatment programs with a burst of enthusiasm but who do not appreciate the long-term effort involved. In particular, some patients enter treatment because of external social demands (e.g., mandated patients) and lapses are the occasion for treatment withdrawal. HCPs must anticipate and overcome such patient reactions.

A critical feature in determining whether lapses will escalate into total relapse is the nature of the patients' cognitive and emotional reactions following a setback or slide. If the patient tends to attribute the lapse to an internal disposition or to stable personal characteristics in the form of self-blame (e.g., "I lack will power." "It goes to show you I am an addict." "There is nothing anyone can do for my disease."), then there is a greater likelihood of total relapse. It is important that patients not view their relapses as constituting moral failures or pesonal weak-nesses. For example, in working with diabetics, the educator must help patients appreciate that a percentage of patients (approximately 10%) have unexplained glucose fluctuations for no obvious reason, even though they are adhering. Trying and failing again and again can result in discouragement and non-adherence that must be counteracted by a supportive patient–HCP relationship. In many instances, relapses are affected by physiological factors over which the patient has little, if any, direct control. HCPs must foster realistic expectations of what can be achieved in terms of preventing lapses.

Unrealistic expectations and overstringent criteria can set the patient up for failure. High levels of self-efficacy are required to maintain change (Strecher *et al.*, 1986). Some adherence pro-grams have employed booster sessions in order to maintain pro-tection and bolster such coping skills, but Brownell *et al.* (1986) indicate that the evidence for their efficacy is still equivocal. In several RP programs the HCPs have included life-style change programs (e.g., exercise) to nurture a replacement for maladap-tive habits that interfere with adherence. No matter what the form of intervention, there is a need for explicit efforts at main-tenance procedures (e.g., therapist-initiated phone calls, mail reminders, patients mailing in self-monitoring data, and general posttreatment contact with the HCP). (See Spevack, 1981, for a review of this literature.)

In summary, the increasing body of research on RP pro-vides a useful model for helping patients develop self-regulatory skills. Whether one is treating patients with addiction problems or chronic medical health disorders, there is a high likelihood that they will at some point falter. The HCP must help patients anticipate, prepare for, cope with, and learn from such experi-ences. Such lapses must be incorporated, if not programmed, into the treatment program. The HCP must explore with patients specific high-risk situations in which lapses may occur and rehearse specific ways to handle them. For example, working on the skills required to deal with such factors as social pressure, interpersonal conflicts, and dysphoric feelings can help patients view lapses as learning occasions and problems to be solved rather than as occasions for guilt, thus minimizing the sense of personal failure and reducing the likelihood of total relapse. RP is designed to help patients avoid viewing a slip as evidence confirming that he or she is weak or a failure at self-control.

Another means of anticipating potential barriers that patients may encounter is to use *cognitive rehearsal* and *role playing*. Prior to carrying out a task assignment, a patient could be guided through the proposed activity step by step in his or her imagination too see what obstacles might prevent its completion. The patient and HCP together could try to come up with ways to overcome each barrier and thus complete the assignment. Then the patient could reimagine the scene including anticipating, preventing, and handling such obstacles. This mental rehearsal could act as a guide for the real-life application and fulfillment of the homework assignment.

A closely aligned training procedure is the use of role playing in which the HCP reverses roles with the patient during the discussion of situations the patient faces. The HCP may even think aloud, "I'll never be able to follow through on my plan. Nothing will help me with my illness. I'm a complete failure." The patient, acting as the HCP, indicates the inappropriateness of such conclusions. Clinical guidelines for conducting RP training have been offered by Davis and Glaros (1986), Marlatt and Gordon (1985), and Meichenbaum (1985).

Attribution Retraining

Another factor that has been found to relate to the development of self-regulatory skills, the maintenance of behavioral change, and long-term success is the degree of patient self-confidence or what Bandura (1977) has called self-efficacy. As noted in Chapter 3, self-efficacy is belief that one can respond effectively to a situation by using available skills. The individual must believe not only that the treatment will be effective to achieve the desired goals (outcome expectancy), but that he or she can actually implement the skills (self-efficacy). The patient must come to believe not only that the benefits of health actions outweigh the costs but that he or she is capable of learning and performing those actions effectively. As we noted in the discussion of goal setting, the HCP must plan and program for success. This involves helping the patient break large tasks into smaller tasks, building on easier less demanding first steps.

Again, the HCP must make sure not only that patients modify aversive habits or follow the treatment regimen but also that they attribute the reasons for the new behavior to themselves rather than to some external source such as the HCP. The HCP may use a variety of clinical strategies to influence the patient's reattributional processes. These include:

1. The HCP asks the patient how he or she has done in following the treatment regimen since the last session. Any success should be greeted with genuine interest and the patient should receive praise and approval. The HCP can then ask the patient how he or she was able to accomplish the treatment goal. This exchange will encourage the patient to make self-attributions.
2. Moreover, the HCP can ask the patient how well he or she was able to adhere this time as compared with previous occasions when the patient faltered. Asking the patient to draw this comparison will also encourage self-attribution.
3. The HCP can ask patients, "What does such adherence mean about you as a person, especially when there are so many distractions and temptations present?" Once again, such probes by the HCP will increase the likelihood of patients' self-attributions and a self-image of their becoming good self-managers.
4. The HCP can ask patients to maintain records that can then be used as data sources in order to contrast present accomplishments with past performance. Many patients initially perform the appropriate behaviors but use failure or leveling off of accomplishment as evidence of their

inability to behave appropriately. They often lose sight of how far they have come or have unrealistic expectations of what changes can be achieved.

The techniques described in this chapter, problem-solving and skills-training procedures, relapse prevention, and attribution retraining, are designed to enhance the long-term maintenance of the treatment regimen. Although several specific components have been investigated, there is no study of a comprehensive application of these various features in enhancing long-term treatment adherence. We hope that the present chapter will speed along such an evaluation.

Additional Interventions

> *Because biological, psychological, social environmental and economic factors are all likely to influence the decision to adhere, a strategy which integrates several approaches is most likely to produce useful techniques for change. Not only should individuals be considered . . . but strategies and campaigns can focus on small groups, on organizations, or on whole communities. If changes are introduced simultaneously at several levels, the chances of general adoption are greatly increased.*
>
> C. Lee and N. Owen (1986)

In the last two chapters we have examined a number of adherence enhancement procedures that derive from a behavior modification and a self-regulatory perspective. The focus of the present chapter is on a variety of additional procedures that have been used to nurture treatment adherence. Although often having links to a behavioral modification perspective, they go beyond that framework in considering the cognitive, affective, and social factors that contribute to treatment nonadherence. We begin the examination with a consideration of emotional inducements (e.g., use of fear messages, guilt inducements) because they represent one of the most widely used means to try to achieve adherence. Can one scare patients into adhering? Just how effective are such efforts? Are there possible side effects? After an examination of the pros and cons of this approach, we consider how emotional role playing has been employed to improve treatment adherence. Efforts at enhancing adherence occur in a social context and so we examine the social support literature for practical clinical guidelines. The chapter concludes with a collection of diverse techniques that have received recent attention including adherence counseling, psychotherapeutic interventions, paradoxical techniques, and finally, societal levels of intervention. As noted in the opening quotation from Lee and Owen, often a multileveled intervention approach is warranted.

Emotional Inducements

Consider the following answers offered by health care providers to our probe as to how they induce treatment adherence:

Scare them!

When patients (diabetics) are out of control (don't adhere), I tell them I have applied for a seeing eye dog or engaged a surgeon who is excellent in performing amputations.

I ask patients to write their obituaries.

I put up a bulletin board in my waiting room of articles and pictures of what happens if people don't adhere.

I give patients articles to read of what happens if they don't adhere.

Paint a grisly, awful, horrible picture of what will happen if patients don't adhere.

Ask patients whether they want to live long enough to see their grandchildren.

I point out what happens to other patients who did not adhere.

I tell them to floss only the teeth they want to keep!

I tell them the truth. If they don't do the exercises then we will have to try surgery. Then I explain that although such surgery is necessary, it is often not successful.

A classic example of the "scare the hell out of a patient" approach was reported by Janis and Rodin (1979). They reported on the approach of a medical specialist who sought to have patients suffering the early stages of cirrhosis of the liver stop imbibing alcohol. He would hospitalize the patient for medical tests and deliberately arrange for them to be placed in rooms where they would see the agony of other patients dying of the same disease. He told the patient that this would happen to them if they did not stop alcohol intake completely.

Although a number of HCPs in our survey described the use of such fear inducement messages, others employed guilt induction:

> You are paying good money and you are wasting my valuable time when you don't follow the treatment plan.
>
> I tell them what they need to do. I then tell them that if they do it or not, it is their business.
>
> I tell them, The disease is yours and I can only serve you. You make the decisions and you live with the consequences.
>
> I want you to see me as an advisor. You may take my advice or reject it and then you must accept the outcome as your choice.
>
> Present patient with the choice to be well or ill. "You have the ball. It's your body. If you don't want to feel better, then ignore me."
>
> I make clear from the outset that failure to follow treatment instructions will result in the end of my seeing them. I will only give two warnings. I convey that they are not only letting me down but also themselves.

A number of studies have been conducted on the relative effectiveness of such emotional inducements, especially scare tactics. Do such procedures work? Are there dangers in using them? The literature indicates that such procedures represent a double-edged sword. On the one hand, they can sometimes motivate patients (especially complacent and unconcerned patients) to implement change. On the other hand, however, such tactics may have just the opposite effect, reducing treatment adherence and increasing the likelihood of dropping out of treatment. In other words, fear- and guilt-arousing measures affect the intention to follow recommendations, but there is less evidence for the actual change of behavior (Hanson, 1986). There is a breakdown between intention and action, especially when the behavior change required is sustained.

Consider how you might feel and what psychological processes might be set in motion if such fear-engendering messages were conveyed to you. The literature (DiMatteo & DiNicola, 1982a; Higbee, 1969; Holder, 1972; Janis, 1984a; Leventhal, 1965; Leventhal *et al.*, 1984; Miller, 1985; Rogers & Mewborn, 1976; Sutton, 1982) indicates that fear-inducing communications can trigger a variety of defensive reactions that interfere with adherence. These patient reactions include:

1. A feeling of being overwhelmed and demoralized
2. A desire to reduce fear by means of behavioral and/or psychological avoidance (avoid the source of the communication by not visiting the HCP)
3. Perception of helplessness and uncontrollability
4. Diminished self-esteem
5. An attempt to deny or rationalize not only the emotional message but also the accompanying treatment advice
6. An increased sense of anxiety that interferes with the reception and processing of treatment-related information
7. A feeling that the treatment recommendations are too weak or ineffectual to prevent such dire consequences
8. The strengthening of old habits rather than encouraging the adoption of adaptive behavior (e.g., it may lead to increased use of alcohol, smoking)

As Holder (1972) noted, for individuals to be influenced by communication, they must not only be exposed to the message, but they must perceive the message correctly, must retain the content, and must decide to comply. "Yet we know that people expose themselves selectively to messages, perceive selectively, retain or forget selectively, and decide selectively" (p. 344). A major concern in using emotional inducements such as fear and guilt is that they often elicit reactions that interfere with the communication process.

Such concerns, however, do not preclude the possibility that fear and guilt inducements may be useful under certain conditions and with certain patients. As DiMatteo and DiNicola (1982a) note, if special conditions are met then fear induction procedures may enhance adherence:

> Research has found that threatening communications will produce belief change only when: (1) the warnings actually convince people that their health is in danger; (2) the recommended responses are perceived as efficacious (i.e., people are convinced that the threat to their health will be reduced if they take the recommended action); and (3) people believe that they themselves are indeed capable of carrying out the recommended responses. (p. 187)

In other words, patients must believe that the suggested steps or the "specific action instructions" for dealing with illness threats are available and efficacious and that they themselves are fully capable of carrying them out (see Leventhal, Singer, & Jones, 1965). If fear arousal communications are not fully relieved by reassurances, then patients will be motivated to minimize, ignore, or deny the importance of the threat (Janis, 1984a; Rogers, 1983). As fear dissipates, the change in attitude will also diminish unless additional features are included. For example, asking patients to relate fear to already existing attitudes and values can enhance the persuasiveness of a message. Conroy (1979) had patients list cherished values and then examine how each identified risk helped or hindered realization of such values. Clearly, any warnings given by HCPs must do more than scare the patient. They must also carry specific concrete behavioral recommendations and must bolster the patient's sense of efficacy in carrying out instructions. For example, while pointing out that negative consequences could occur, the HCP must also indicate that if the patient performs specific behaviors they are less likely.

In addition to focusing on the emotions of fear and guilt, HCPs may also consider focusing on positive emotions as inducements to adherence. These include pleasurable feelings that are likely to follow from treatment adherence (e.g., feelings of personal satisfaction, pride, self-control, parental responsibility, caring, and joy). Table 28 summarizes a variety of compliance-gaining strategies. A perusal of the table indicates the variety of alternatives available to HCPs besides fear inducements.

Whether one focuses on negative or positive emotions, there is a clear necessity for HCPs to empathize with patients concerning the difficulties in adherence. Before judging our patients, we must ask ourselves how many of us could adhere to the difficult and demanding tasks we ask our patients to follow. In order to appreciate this point, consider a study by Warren-Boulton (1982). They asked HCPs to perform a typical diabetic regimen for four days. They were requested to administer daily saline injections, conduct daily urine tests, and comply with a special diet. The adherence rates for the professionals was quite low, especially in adhering to the prescribed diet (as is the case with actual diabetic patients). The experiment proved most revealing to the HCPs, yielding a patient's perspective toward the demands of treatment adherence. As HCPs, we are unlikely to participate in such experiments. This is unfortunate because doing so might provide us with a different perspective on how we communicate and what we ask patients to do.

As we have emphasized many times, the HCP must not be a prescriber of a set of rules, but a collaborator and adviser, individually responding to the needs of a particular patient. The important thing is to negotiate an acceptable and workable treatment plan wherein the quality of life is considered as well as the specific features of the patient's illness (e.g., blood glucose level). The use of emotional inducement procedures must be considered in this larger context. A similar concern is raised when we consider other specific adherence enhancement procedures, expecially those designed to have strong emotional impact, such as emotional role playing.

Emotional Role Playing

Although using fear-engendering messages can often backfire, a variation called emotional role playing has been found to be a useful means of increasing adherence. Janis and Mann (1977)

Table 28   Compliance-Gaining Strategies[a]

Promise	If you comply, I will reward you.
Threat	If you do not comply, I will punish you.
Expertise, positive	If you comply, you will be rewarded because of the nature of things.
Expertise, negative	If you do not comply, you will be punished because of the nature of things.
Liking	Practitioner is friendly and helpful in order to put patient in a good frame of mind so that he will comply with request.
Pregiving	Practitioner rewards patient before requesting compliance.
Aversive stimulation	Practitioner continually punishes patient, making cessation contingent on compliance.
Debt	You owe me compliance because of past favors.
Moral appeal	You are immoral if you do not comply.
Self-feeling, positive	You will feel better about yourself if you comply.
Self-feeling, negative	You will feel worse about yourself if you do not comply.
Altercasting, positive	A person with good qualities would comply.
Altercasting, negative	Only a person with bad qualities would not comply.
Altruism	I need your compliance very badly, so do it for me.
Esteem, positive	People you value will think better of you if you comply.
Esteem, negative	People you value will think worse of you if you do not comply.

[a]Adapted from Baglan, LaLumia, & Bayless, 1986, and Marwell and Schmitt, 1967.

have reported that having patients enact the part of someone who suffers aversive consequences as a result of their behavior can motivate patients to adhere to treatment regimens. Emotional role playing involves creating a scenario in which the patient is confronted with an "as if" experience of being a victim. For example, a patient who is a heavy smoker may be asked to play the role of a lung cancer patient at the moment when he or she receives the bad news from a physician (Janis, 1984a). This scenario is designed to instill the feeling of personal vulnerability and to puncture the patient's feeling that "it can't happen to me." Janis and Rodin (1979) also suggest having patients list various rationalizations or excuses they might use to avoid following the health-engendering measure such as giving up smoking. Labeling such excuses or reasons as "rationalizations" may help to remove some of their impact and strength.

An example of such an approach was offered by Reed and Janis (1974), who directed patients' awareness to the rationalizations they use in order not to adhere to medical advice. They presented patients with a list of excuses and asked them if they were aware of using any of them in order to avoid adherence. They then exposed patients (in this case, smokers) to a taped lecture and discussion that refuted each excuse. This procedure was effective in improving adherence.

In order to challenge and undermine the patient's accompanying feeling that it is impossible to change, a reversal of roles is undertaken whereby the patient plays the role of the physician and the HCP plays the role of the patient. During this role reversal the patient is encouraged to participate actively with aroused emotion in offering counterarguments and specific suggestions about why and how one can change (e.g., give up smoking, take medication, alter one's life style). The patient not only has to provide arguments for adhering, specifying precisely a course of action, but also consider possible obstacles, high-risk situations, and ways in which these can be anticipated, avoided, and, when necessary, overcome. (This is an example of the inoculation or relapse prevention model described in Chapter 6.) The HCP can challenge the patient, subsequently asking such questions as

> Are you telling me that you are going to be able to change, (e.g., to take your medicine, to give up smoking, to test your blood regularly, etc.)? What about the social pressure, the possible side effects, the simple fact that you often feel too busy or at times too overwhelmed to follow the treatment plan?

The HCP can tailor the specific challenges to the patient's situation. The evidence reviewed by Janis and Mann (1977) indicates that greater behavioral change is achieved and maintained if patients are required to instigate and provide self-generated arguments, challenges, and rebuttals to their initial attitudes and behavior, and when this is done in an emotionally involving manner.

Yet another means of nurturing patient involvement is the use of psychodrama. Janis and Mann (1977) provide a detailed outline of how one can use emotional role playing or what they call psychodrama (see Appendix B in their book). For example, what they call "outcome psychodrama" is a kind of role playing in which the patient is asked to play the role of himself or herself at some moment in time after making a decision to adhere (e.g., upon hearing that one has developed complications because of not adhering to the treatment regimen). In addition, the HCP may suggest specific situations, or "best case" and "worst case" scenarios, for the patient to imagine. A typical psychodrama might have the patient going through the events of an average work day or weekend day and imagining specific situations and his reactions. This can be an effective method for generating the kinds of problem situations that might be stressful and demoralizing but that could be anticipated.

In most instances psychodrama is used in combination with the decisional balance sheet whereby patients have been asked to weigh the consequences of several alternative decisions. The psychodrama provides a means for the patients to project themselves into the future when making an important decision (e.g., not to adhere to treatment program). By using an emotionally involving scenario the HCP can have patients reconsider risks and benefits that might materialize. The role playing is often followed by a readministration of the decisional balance sheet and a discussion of the decision, commitment, and skills required to adhere.

In short, the efforts to nurture adherence are not merely an intellectual exchange about the pros and cons of adhering. It is necessary to underscore the emotional features of the role playing exercise. This is furthur illustrated in what has been called a *videotape self-confrontation* procedure that has been used with alcoholics (Miller, 1985). In this procedure the HCP videotapes the patient during a period of peak insobriety and then plays it back later. Such efforts to motivate patients by means of emotional role playing and videotape self-confrontation must be supplemented with other techniques such as relapse prevention training. If not, the improvement in adherence will probably be only limited and transitory (e.g., Mausner & Platt, 1971). Such emotionally charged interventions are often required in order to foster patients' sense of self-dissatisfaction with their present state and thus motivate them for other interventions. It is not sufficient to know the facts and to possess behavioral skills. It is essential to establish what has been called an "emotional hooker," a "motivator," in order to change belief into action. Emotional role playing has been used successfully to accomplish this task.

Social Support

As noted previously, it is important to keep in mind the patient's social environment. Any request made by the HCP is only one input among many the patient receives. An appreciation of the attitudes of significant others and the potential support and rewards they can provide can have a significant impact on the adherence process.

In many instances, patients are dependent on others in their families to be able to carry out adherence behavior (e.g., following a diet, administering medication in the case of a child). In her review of the social support literature, Levy (1983) notes that family members can act as sources of potential rewards as well as transmitters of beliefs and motives and agents of behavioral change. What the HCP may consider deviant or nonadherent may not be viewed as deviant by the patient's reference group. Better understanding of these pressures will help efforts at improving adherence.

Before we consider how one can mobilize the patient's social supports, a few observations are germane:

1. Social support refers to personal contacts available to an individual from other individuals, groups, and the community. Social support is complex, consisting of multiple components—tangible, emotional, and informational support. Significant others in the patient's life may prompt, remind, aid, and support but may also undermine the patient. In addition, social supports can provide the patient with the means of expressing feelings, finding meaning and a sense of belonging, receiving material aid, providing information, developing realistic goals, receiving feedback and encouragement, and providing feelings of success. Generally, the support system can act as a buffer to stress, but it can also inhibit adherence.

At this point we are not able to determine which feature of social support contributes to treatment adherence. Although Levy (1983) has noted that "it is very difficult to draw any conclusions on the specific effects of social support on medical regimen compliance" (p. 1335), a number of investigators (Baekeland & Lundwall, 1975; Baranowski & Nader, 1985a; Becker & Green, 1975; Brownell, Heckerman, Westlake, Hayes, & Monti, 1978; Colletti & Brownell, 1982; DiMatteo & DiNicola, 1982a; Dunbar & Agras, 1980; Janis, 1983) have highlighted the potential usefulness of social supports in fostering treatment adherence in such areas as weight reduction, smoking, physical fitness programs, dental visits, alcoholism treatment, dietary habits in diabetics, taking antihypertension medication, wearing an arthritis splint, and attending psychotherapy sessions.

An illustrative social support intervention was conducted by Morisky (1986) who reported that educating family members of individuals with hypertension about the nature and consequences of elevated blood pressure resulted in improved patient adherence. The social support effort resulted in increased appointment keeping, reduced blood pressure levels, increased preparation of special diets requiring salt reductions, and the family's reminding of medication schedule.

2. The research on social support suggests that it is not the number of social contacts per se, but rather the quality of the relationship that influences the individual's ability to cope with distress and adhere to treatment regimens. Usually, the person or persons with whom the patient has the most frequent contact are considered critical social supports. The potential value of such social support is revealed by Sweeney, Van Bulow, Shear, Freedman, and Plowe (1984) who found greater patient adherence when patients were accompanied by relatives than when they were self-referred. Hogue (1979) also reported lower treatment adherence for those who live in social isolation.

3. Not all families, however, are supportive. Nor is what might be viewed as unsupportive behavior always detrimental to adherence (Funch & Gale, 1986). Like any other factor, social support can be double-edged. Research has indicated that intrusive kin or highly critical, nagging, guilt-inducing spouses or parents can have a "boomerang effect" that results in a deteriorating condition and increased treatment nonadherence (Leff & Vaugh, 1985). Olson *et al.* (1985) also reported that overly anxious, indulgent, rejecting, controlling parents can have a detrimental effect on treatment adherence.

The notion of support should not be confused with involvement. That is, simply bringing in family members or other "supportive people" does not guarantee that these people will be perceived by the patient as supportive. It is particularly important that attention be given to the nature of the support rather than to its mere presence. Family members may have good intentions and may try to be supportive, but they may do so inappropriately. As DiMatteo and Hays (1981) note, family support may have negative consequences for some patients and contribute to nonadherence. (For an extended review of this topic, see Colletti and Brownell, 1982).

The lack of interest and accompanying neglect by significant others represent another obstacle. In a multivariate assessment of long-term adherence in children and adolescents, Babani, Banis, Thompson, and Varni (in press) found that the levels of familial conflict, control (setting of rules), organization (planning of activities and responsibilities), and competitiveness were related to metabolic control and adherence. Heiby and Carlson (1986) report that family instability, lack of resources, interference or concurrent illness of family members also relate to non-adherence. Similarly, Kirschenbaum *et al.* (1984) reported that families who reported chaotic family environments (as assessed by the Moos & Moos Family Environment Scale, 1981) were significantly more likely to drop out of treatment and were less likely to adhere to a weight control program for their obese children. Conversely, Funch and Gale (1986) found that the best predictor of who remained in treatment for temperomandibular pain was the family's attitude toward the patient's pain. They reported that patients who perceived family members as being most irritated or upset with them and as less supportive were more likely to remain in treatment, whereas those patients who indicated that their families were solicitous were more likely to drop out of treatment. Pain in these cases seemed to serve as a source of secondary gain.

An innovative way to assess the impact of family supports on patient adherence was developed by Schafer, McCaul, and Glasgow (1986). Focusing on Type I diabetics, they developed a Diabetes Family Behavior Checklist that assesses family behaviors that may support or interfere with the appropriate conduct or timing of four regimen factors: insulin injection, glucose testing, diet, and exercise. Schafer *et al.* developed a highly sensitive 16-item questionnaire. Illustrative items, each rated on a five-point scale ("never" to "at least once a day") include: "Praise you for following your diet." "Exercise with you." "Nag you about testing your glucose level." The study's results support the promise of assessing family behaviors that are specific to the diabetes self-care regimen. Similar population-specific, behaviorally oriented social support scales could be developed for other disorders. Levy (1986) has highlighted the need to assess specific social supportive behaviors that are directly related to the treatment regimen such as family member's involvement and participation in the treatment program. Bruhn and Phillips (1984) provide a valuable, critical summary of the various social support measures. Assessing social supports may prove a valuable source in formulating adherence intervention programs.

In some instances, however, providing social supports may prove stressful for patients if it threatens their sense of self-sufficiency. Caplan (1979) notes that the need for social support may vary across situations. In some situations patients may view social support as legitimate, whereas in other situations it may be viewed as intrusive. The HCP must discuss this with the patient before the involvement of others is undertaken.

These observations draw attention to the need to assess the patient's social support system and, wherever feasible, to include others in the treatment process only with great care. This clinical observation is consistent with the conclusion drawn by Baranowski and Nader (1985a) that "there may be no aspects of family life that maximize compliance, but many aspects that inhibit and detract from compliance" (p. 69). These factors include lack of family cohesion, interference of the treatment regimen with social role tasks, secondary gains, scapegoating, family expectations, and the like. There is a clear need to define precisely the task demands that are imposed on a family in adhering to a specific treatment regimen. These demands will vary by disease (its form, stage, severity), age and gender of patient, and family ethnicity. With younger children, the character of the mother and the demands she makes on the child may be critical in predicting adherence, whereas with adolescent patients, peer pressure may be a more critical operative factor. The exact manner in which social supports are used to enhance treatment adherence will have to vary depending on the circumstances. Consider the following alternatives:

1. Involve family members in the treatment regimen.
2. Establish a buddy system between patients and/or use the peer group.

3. Introduce the patient to a successful patient who can share knowledge of how he or she handled adherence.
4. Set up group discussions for patients and family members. There can be separate groups for patients (e.g., adolescents) and parents or mixed groups.
5. Use home visits by HCPs.
6. Initiate groups for nonadherent patients.

Most efforts at involving social supports have been at the level of family involvement. Any approach to family members should be done with the patient's approval and involvement. The HCP can ask patients who are the key people in their lives, how can they be involved, and of what help they may be. With the patient's approval the family members or peers should be approached early on so that they may view themselves as collaborators in any attempt to understand the nature of the patient's problems and as possible supporters of the treatment plan.

The significant others can collaborate in identifying and implementing ways in which the patient could be helped in adhering to the treatment regimen (e.g., encourage, remind, assist, supervise, and reinforce patient for engaging in self-care behavior). Significant others can also identify possible obstacles and high-risk situations that might interfere with patient adherence. They might also offer specific recommendations for adherence, especially if they exert some control over the patient's environment. In various programs social support agents have participated in monitoring patient behavior, participating in commitment and behavioral contracts, and engaging in joint activities (e.g., parents exercise with obese children). When such acitivities are shared, the adherence demands may be seen as less burdensome. However, in those instances when the treatment regimen interferes with the parents', especially the mother's, daily routines, adherence is less likely to occur. Moreover, if the parents are dissatisfied with the physician's communication and suggestions they are less likely to adhere with the presented

regimen and more likely to seek other sources of care (Baranowski & Nader, 1985a).

A second form of social support is the use of groups for
either patient, patient's family members, or for both patients
and their parents. A number of such educational and supportive
groups exist for a variety of diverse clinical populations (e.g.,
diabetics, alcoholics, pain, cancer, and ostomy patients). Such
groups provide educational seminars that help patients and family members catch up with current management practices and
share common experiences, information exchange, and social
support.

It is important to realize that extensive self-care regimens
affect not only the patient but also his or her family. All too often
HCPs forget or overlook the demands of the regimen on the
patient's family. For example, we can think of the demands that
an aggressive regimen for cystic fibrosis makes on the family as
an extreme instance. Performing bronchial drainage twice a day,
caring for oxygen tents and related apparatus, and preparing
foods and monitoring medication are extremely time-consuming
and may require up to eight hours a day. There is also a large
literature on the role that an illness or a sick family member
plays in family dynamics, but the discussion of this topic is beyond
the scope of this book. (See Turk & Kerns, 1985). The HCP
must be alert to the impact of the prescribed behaviors on family
functioning, and nonadherence must be viewed in the family
context. In extreme cases, referral to family therapists may be
the most appropriate action on the part of the primary HCP (see
Gervasio, 1986).

In suggesting groups, however, it is important to remember
that such self-help groups are not everyone's "cup of tea." A
number of patients may resist and in fact resent suggestions that
they join such groups. Often HCPs view a patient's rejection of
group participation as negative and put inadvertent pressure on
the patient to join. In some cases, however, patients may view
themselves as self-sufficient and independent and actively avoid
self-help groups (e.g., Turk, Sobel, Follick, & Youkilis, 1980).

It is essential to individualize treatment programs to the patient's needs, attitudes, and circumstances. Different procedures will be useful with different sorts of patients; flexibility is imperative.

In many instances, however, providing patients or their significant others with group outlets can enhance treatment adherence. For example, Gross, Magalnick, and Richardson (1985) report that parents of diabetic children benefited from the opportunity to share their experiences of similar difficulties they had in maintaining health care. The information exchange contributed to changes in their personal performance expectations and to altered self-evaluation of their skills. Such discussion led to a consideration of skills needed to obtain adherence. Other examples are offered by Gonder-Frederick, Cox, Pohl, and Carter (1984), who used peer instructors to enhance adherence to blood glucose monitoring in diabetics, and Jay, Durant, and Shoffitt (1984) who used peer-run groups to improve adherence to contraception by teenagers. These social support groups were mobilized to model and to create a positive peer environment for adherence behavior.

Several studies have demonstrated that home visits to provide support to the family, usually by nurses but sometimes by pharmacists or priests, can increase the likelihood of treatment adherence. Such home visits are particularly valuable when they are part of a more comprehensive program (see Baranowski & Nader, 1985b). In some treatment programs the patient's family members attend educational and supportive meetings either in the home or in the clinic where they are trained in all aspects of regimen adherence. Ways in which family members can promote adherence are discussed. Such involvement is critical, especially in those instances when the demands of the treatment regimen require assistance of family members (e.g., dietary changes). As Baranowski and Nader (1985b) note:

> Pratical ways for families to be supportive without nagging must be identified; methods must be developed for training family members in the performance of these support behaviors and for increasing the frequency of their performance; . . . preexisting

family relationship and interaction patterns must be assessed and
tailored into the intervention program. (p. 102)

Another way in which social supports have been employed
to facilitate adherence is described by Amaral (1986). In a low-
vision rehabilitation center for the elderly, people from the health
provider's patient population were used as on-site peers to wel-
come, socialize, train, and perform follow-up calls in order to
check on the new patients' progress. Although much research
needs to be conducted about the relationship between social
supports and treatment adherence, the present "state of the art"
underscores the importance of social support both in adherence
and nonadherence.

Finally, several recent attempts at the prevention and treatment of health-related behavior have been directed at entire
communities (e.g., Maccoby, Farquhar, Wood, & Alexander,
1977). Multimedia interventions (televisions, pamphlets, group
and community meetings) were employed to foster health promotion and treatment adherence. In coming years, it is likely
that we will witness many more such large-scale community
interventions. The guidelines proved in this volume should prove
helpful in formulating such programs.

Adherence Counseling

Throughout this volume we have commented on the potential usefulness of the primary HCP's calling upon allied health
professionals (public health nurses, pharmacists, lay health workers) and significant others in the patient's life in an effort to
improve patient adherence. For example, McKenney *et al.* (1973)
demonstrated that brief extra counseling (lasting on average six
minutes) by a pharmacist over a five-month period was effective
in facilitating adherence in hypertensive patients. Similarly,
Skoutakis, Acchiardo, Martinez, Lorisch, and Wood (1978)
reported that a combination of education, written reminders to
take medication, and pharmacist consultation over one year
enhanced adherence in hemodialysis patients. Important aspects
of the counseling were the identification and management of

medication side effects and the feedback and attention provided by the pharmacists. However, the improvement in adherence often dissipated once the counseling ended. Perhaps the counseling either must be continuous or should focus on self-management skills with an emphasis on relapse prevention, maintenance, and generalization issues.

In some instances nonadherent patients, as a last resort, may have to be referred to adherence specialists or adherence-oriented treatment groups as described by Nessman, Carnahan, and Nugent (1980). Along these same lines, Sackett (1976) has gone so far as to suggest that a "community compliance service" be established:

> Operated jointly by the regional clinical laboratory program and the local pharmacy and medical associations, the Community Compliance Service will, upon request, measure compliance and achievement of the treatment goal and, after consultation with the referring physician, offer the noncompliant patients who failed to achieve the treatment goal an array of validated compliance—improving strategies and ongoing assistance. (p. 189)

Although to some, such a service might have overtones of "big brother" watching, the notion that a speciality of adherence counselors will emerge is something we can well envisage and support. However, such efforts should not detract from the need for the primary HCP to remain continually responsible for patients' adherence. Surely, seeking assistance from qualified colleagues is a highly regarded, time-honored practice, but in the case of adherence such referral should not be seen as a way of "dumping" recalcitrant and resistant patients. If such a practice occurs, then the community compliance service has the undesirable potential of fostering nonadherence by strengthening further patient reactance.

Psychotherapeutic Interventions

In some instances the HCP may have to seek the assistance of a mental health professional (psychiatrist, psychologist, social worker, psychiatric nurse) in order to deal with the specific psychosocial barriers that contribute to patient nonadherence. The referral may be for a specific difficulty such as fear of needles in the case of a diabetic or for a more general psychiatric or psychological problems. In either case, treatment interventions are available that can prove helpful. For example, in work with some diabetic youngsters and their parents Kovacs and Feinberg (1982) reported a variety of specific reactions that interfered with adherence. The parents reported that they were afraid that they would "hit a vein or bone," or that they would "accidentally break the needle," or "inject the wrong dose of insulin." In a few cases the normal educational training is inadequate to allay these concerns, and psychotherapy, in the form of cognitive-behavior modification, can prove helpful (see Meichenbaum, 1977). The therapist can use a combination of cognitive restructuring, relaxation training, and desensitization procedures to help such patients.

Psychotherapeutic procedures have also proved successful with even more recalcitrant populations such as severely nonadherent diabetics (Boehnert & Popkin, 1986) and with drug addicts (Rogalski, 1984). Boehnert and Popkin stress the challenges of severely nonadherent patients. They indicate that HCPs may be confronted with patients who:

1. Have radically different treatment goals than the HCP (the patient may be seeking or hoping for a "magical cure"
2. Have emotional needs (dependency, rage, fears) that interfere with adherence
3. Feel they can exert control over their illness by not following their treatment regimen
4. Engage in behavior that is designed to split the staff
5. Use excessive denial of illness and falsely believe that "complications could not happen to them"
6. Feel depressed and guilty for not having followed their treatment regimen and feel morally weak for having complied but still experience relapses

In order to deal with these major problems, the intervention often must go beyond the specific adherence-enhancement procedures described in Section II. A variety of psychothera-peutic procedures have been found useful in enhancing treat-ment adherence (e.g., individual psychotherapy, Benson, 1975; group psychotherapy, Powell *et al.*, 1977; Shakir *et al.*, 1979; family psychotherapy, Fitzgerald, 1972; couples group therapy, Davenport *et al.*, 1977). In using a crisis management approach Boehnert and Popkin (1986) suggest that consistent, firm, limit-setting efforts, direct discussion about self-harm attempts, and related psychotherapeutic efforts are helpful. Becker and Green (1975) and Gervasio (1986) describe several examples of how family therapy can be used to deal with behavioral patterns and social conflicts (e.g., family enmeshment, intrusiveness, guilt induction). Under such conflictual conditions patient nonadher-ence may reflect an attempt to assert control over oneself and family members. Cochran (1984) used a cognitive-behavioral intervention to prevent lithium nonadherence in bipolar affec-tive disorder patients. The intervention consisted of six one-hour, weekly individual sessions. The HCP focused on eliciting the patient's maladaptive attitudes toward the mediation and where possible helped patients to develop more functional atti-tudes and adaptive behaviors. Improvement in adherence was evident not only immediately following treatment, but also at a six-month follow-up assessment.

In short, some of our nonadherent patients have problems that require interventions that are beyond the skills or time available to the primary HCP. In these cases the issue of adher-ence has much larger meaning and social ramifications. Two good examples come from the counseling of adolescents and the elderly. In both instances, HCPs must recognize the value of specifically tailoring the intervention to the characteristics of the particular population. In the case of adolescents who are suffering from a chronic disorder such as rheumatoid arthritis, it is necessary to establish a delicate balance between allowing adolescents inde-pendence and responsibility and meeting the concerns of both their parents and the professional staff. There is a need gradually to nurture self-management, putting control into the adoles-cent's hands.

Each age group has particular needs and challenges, and efforts to enhance adherence must take this into consideration. The elderly present a particular challenge to the health care profession. Eighty-six percent of persons 65 or older have one or more chronic disorders, most of which are treated with drugs. Although the elderly constitute only 10% of the population in North America, they consume 25% of all medications (German, Klein, McPhee, and Smith, 1982). As the reader can well imagine, a variety of factors, physical (impaired visual, hearing, reduced manual dexterity), psychological (faulty memory, increased incidence of dysphoric emotions), social (loss of social supports), and economic (diminished financial resources) can each play a role in contributing to nonadherence. Efforts to reduce nonadherence will often require multiresource interventions. Whether it is in the form of easily opened medications, enlarged reminder cues, home visits, or social services that deal with the larger plight of the elderly, the skills and resources of the lone HCP may prove inadequate. Working with the elderly challenges the HCPs to address the question, Just how committed are we to improving treatment adherence in our patients? How often do we prescribe treatment procedures to which we know, deep down, that the patient will not adhere? Just how far are we willing to extend ourselves to improve our patients' adherence? In the case of the elderly, both the degree of the HCP's commitment and his or her skills are surely tested. Richardson (1986), in a thoughtful review, provides guidelines for HCPs who treat the elderly. After examining the psychosocial and biological developmental changes he offers the following suggestions for HCPs:

> Pace presentation, task relevance, and difficulty level to the elderly patient's ability.
>
> Increase time for elderly patient to respond.
>
> Increase time for elderly patient to study visual material.
>
> Slow pace of speech and of medication instruction.
>
> Provide advanced organization to help memory.

Insure that elderly patient can handle packaging.

Insure supports are available especially for the elderly patient living alone.

Nurture patients' hope in medical care and treatment.

Arrange for home visits, involvement of significant others, and support groups where appropriate.

Paradoxical Interventions

An innovative form of psychotherapeutic technique that has been used with resistant patients, especially when secondary gain may be implicated, is paradoxical intervention techniques (PIT). PITs are defined as those interventions in which the HCP or therapist apparently promotes the worsening of the patients' problems or resistance rather than their removal (Dowd & Milne, 1986; Griffin, 1985). In a type of "reverse psychology," the HCP instructs the patient to continue to perform the destructive or nonadherent behavior, often in an exaggerated fashion. Implied in the directive is the notion that engaging in the problem behavior will eventually enable the patient to eliminate it. In this way the HCP uses the patient's uncooperative negativistic behavior in such a way as to eliminate resistance and to produce subsequent therapeutic results. As Haley (1963) notes, accepting patient nonadherence is the hallmark of PITs. "It is difficult to resist someone who is agreeing with you! . . . Joining the resistance has the effect of sabatoging it by rendering it no longer functional" (Dowd & Milne, 1986, p. 241). This approach views patient's resistance and nonadherence as purposive and goal-directed.

By giving the patient permission to resist or not adhere, the HCP places the patient in a double bind. On the one hand, the patient does not wish to comply with the HCP's request, but, on the other hand, the HCP has told the patient to do just that. Thus, caught between the Scylla and Charybis of adherence and nonadherence, the only way to break through is for the patient to go along with the HCP's initial request. Several examples will illustrate this approach.

Ascher and Efran (1978) and Ascher and Turner (1979) treated insomniacs who were having difficulty following the proposed treatment regimen by giving them the paradoxical directive "to stay awake as long as possible when going to bed." Ascher and Turner (1979), in treating patients who could not urinate in public restrooms, told them to visit lavoratories and go through the entire ritual of urinating but to refrain from urinating. With repeated trials and the reduction of performance anxiety, the patients were able to overcome their difficulty. PITs were also used to increase the likelihood of patients' complying with these requests. Many other examples of PITs are described in the writings of Erickson (1965), Haley (1963), Watzlawick, Weakland, and Fisch (1974), and in recent articles by Cade (1984), Dowd and Milne (1986), and L'Abate and Weeks (1978).

PITs include various procedures: symptom prescription, restraint strategy, implying choice, anticipating and forearming, reframing, and humour. A brief discussion of each will illustrate their potential usefulness.

1. *Symptom prescription.* The patient is instructed to perform the problem behavior deliberately or even to exaggerate it. The instruction may even specify the particular time and/or particular place. Usually such scheduling is for periods just before the usual spontaneous occurrence of the targeted behavior. For example, a patient may be told to extend a dysphoric feeling or to sit in a specific chair in his living room and dwell on his particular obsession for a specified period of time. Such symptom prescription or paradoxical directives are used most effectively in facilitating voluntary control over specific, habitual, or reportedly involuntary behaviors (Martin & Worthington, 1982b).

2. *Restraint strategy.* The patient is discouraged from progressing to rapidly or even ordered not to do so. For example, the therapist may say, "I suspect you may very well find the homework too frustrating and difficult to accomplish." Oppositional patients who experience what Brehm (1966) called "psychological reactance" may be determined to prove the therapist wrong and show that they can do the homework (obviously, the therapist's true intent). Another version of this procedure is to

suggest to the patient that he or she may wish to delay the change. A clever use of this approach was offered by Erickson (1965), who indicated that with a reluctant patient who did not wish to self-disclose he explicitly instructed the patient to withhold information until he was ready to provide it and not sooner.

3. *Implying choice.* The object is to switch the issue away from whether the patient will adhere to when and from which behaviors the patient can choose to adhere. Any parent will recognize this social influence procedure, for parents often give children a choice between two alternatives, neither of which the child initially finds attractive. The implied choice may help to stifle any resistance. The HCP may raise the question as to whether the patient wishes to get over the habit this week or next? That may seem too soon. Perhaps you would like a longer period of time, three or four weeks?

4. *Anticipating and forearming.* This technique harkens back to our earlier discussion of the relapse prevention model whereby the HCP helps patient identify high-risk situations and prepare for possible lapses. By doing so the HCP can help patients reframe possible setbacks as learning occasions rather than as personal catastrophes. An example of this approach is offered by Shelton and Levy (1981), as patients are told, "I am very pleased with your rapid progress to date but I have found that most clients have a relapse about this time in treatment." When done effectively, such observation and implied request may prevent a relapse. Such suggestions help patients reframe their behavior.

5. *Reframing.* All PITs are designed to help patients change the ways in which they view their problem behavior. Reframing is designed to shift the meaning the patient has attached to his problems. With a shift in the patient's frame of reference, the patient's nonadherent behavior will begin to be seen as voluntarily produced since the patient must have a choice. In fact, the HCP can ask the patient, "Why did you choose to behave in such a self-destructive fashion?" Instead of battling the patient over adherence the HCP uses any opposition and turns such resistance efforts into productive solutions. Coyne (1984) offers an example of such reframing in a case involving

parents of resistant nonadhering adolescents. The therapist suggested to the parents that if they were going to have any success with their adolescent in applying what they were learning in therapy about being firm and consistent, then they should recognize that their adolescent would test their resolve by performing even more outrageously. The parents are guided and encouraged to view the adolescent's testing of them as a sign of progress. Rather than viewing such confrontations as signs of failure that are discouraging, they are encouraged to view them as learning opportunities.

Moreover, HCPs help patients to break complex tasks into smaller, more manageable ones. The therapist may help a withdrawn, shy person reframe the treatment objective as not overcoming shyness but instead meeting new people, approaching others, making dates. Inherent in every form of psychotherapy is some effort to help patients redefine their presenting problems into more manageable, more hopeful terms.

6. *Use of humor.*   One of the best ways to reframe or to help patients gain some distance is humor. Patients are often so preoccupied with their condition that they do not develop any detachment. As Dowd and Milner (1986) note, many patients are so absorbed in their trouble and its treatment that such preoccupation, with its accompanying anxiety, can contribute to nonadherence.

The behavioral changes that follow from PITs should be taken by the HCP in a matter-of-fact fashion and should not be commented upon (Dowd and Milne, 1986). If the patient has not complied with the request, then the HCP should convey disappointment and the patient should be urged to renew his or her efforts. In most instances PITs should be supplemented with other more conventional counseling techniques.

After comprehensively reviewing the literature, Dowd and Milne conclude that paradoxical intervention techniques should not be used until a very strong counseling relationship has been established. They should be used only after other more conventional techniques have been tried and have failed and when such failure is seen as resulting from patients' resistance. Other cautions include:

1. Not using prescription of symptoms when it might lead to harmful consequences (e.g., smoking, excessive drinking).
2. Not using PITs with patients who are depressed, retarded, paranoid, sociopathic, borderline personality, in the midst of personal crisis or an unstable situation, or possessed of a very negative self-image.
3. Not using PITs with patients who lack skills and resources to carry out prescribed requests.

Although there is much interest in the dramatic and creative nature of such procedures, the data on their efficacy in improving adherence are still quite limited. Much skill is required in giving such directives and on making such requests. PITs should be undertaken with much caution and care.

Another Level of Intervention

The primary focus thus far in facilitating adherence has been at the level of the patient and HCP and significant others (family, adherence counselors). A much broader focus may be required on some occasions. For example, we noted earlier that if HCPs are stressed and harassed and work in settings that provide minimal organizational supports, then this can in turn influence how patients are treated and the resultant level of patient adherence. Similarly, the present reward structure does not usually support efforts at prevention, education, and follow-up interventions. For example, insurance policies do no usually cover diabetes educators who could be instrumental in reducing the costly medical and social consequences of patient nonadherence. Much educational work is needed both within and outside the health care professions to highlight the value of adherence enhancement interventions. All too often much visibility and notoriety accompany the development of new medical techniques. This book points up the need to add a footnote to the headlines accompanying the discovery of each "magic bullet" (i.e., drugs, treatments). The footnote should read: "Approximately 50% of those for whom this is intended won't use it!"

Unfortunately, social policies and societal pressures inadvertently can contribute to treatment nonadherence. For instance, Gerber and Nehemkis (1986) offer the example of low back pain patients who may find themselves adhering to a treatment regimen and becoming functional to the point that they lose eligibility for social security benefits. Unfortunately, these individuals are also unlikely to be hired by many employers because of insurance restrictions. Such a double bind can contribute to nonadherence. Interventions are required that go well beyond the specific patient.

Finally, there are occasions when the health care profession and patients must form an alliance in order to educate legislators and the public about how public policy may affect patient adherence. A recent case in point occurred in Canada when the government decided on a 10% increase in sales tax on all types of medical supplies. For instance, in the case of diabetic patients, it would affect the cost of a wide variety of products required to follow the treatment regimen, imposing a substantial financial burden, especially for those of lower socioeconomic status. Even with minimal coverage of medical supplies by insurance companies, such a move appeared shortsighted and misguided. A reduction in adherence could lead to hospitalization and a much more costly governmental expenditure. Fortunately, the tax was not implemented, largely because of pressure from an alliance between patients and HCPs. There is a clear need for policymakers to be educated as to how their decisions influence adherence behavior on both a preventative and a treatment basis. Adherence must be a more central concern for all.

The recent changes in the United States with the introduction of DRGs (diagnostic related groups) mandates that financial reimbursement for the treatment of specific disorders will be predesignated (i.e., so many days of reimbursement allotted for a specific treatment or disorder). One consequence of DRGs and the emphasis on accountability and efficacy is an increased concern by HCPs with patient adherence. For example, if the DRG for a particular disorder specifies six days of hospitalization, then nonadherence of the patient to the treatment regimen that results in additional days of hospitalization will not be reimbursable. Consequently, the hospital will have to absorb the costs of nonadherence. Thus, an implicit pressure is created to insure adherence. In this case, governmental policy can influence the patient–HCP relationship. The issue of treatment adherence is embedded in a larger social context.

III

Integration of Adherence Procedures and Impediments to Their Use

The Integrated Application of Adherence Enhancement Interventions

> *Research comparing combination approaches is limited. It has been found, however, that single strategies generally have been less effective when compared with combination strategies.*
>
> M. A. SOUTHAM AND J. M. DUNBAR (1986)

Because of the complexity and multidetermined nature of treatment nonadherence and the heterogeneity of the patient population, there is an increasing recognition that integrative interventions are required. No one set of adherence enhancement procedures will be successful across populations. In this chapter we will describe various programs that have combined and integrated the variety of procedures that were discussed in Section II. We will also consider clinical guidelines to follow when applying these procedures.

Epstein and Masek (1976) have catalogued over 30 different techniques designed to increase patient adherence. We have summarized our own list in Table 29. But there is now an increasing awareness that for greatest effectiveness these specific procedures should be combined and employed within a general

Table 29   Summary of General Adherence Enhancement Interventions[a]

Keeping appointments

    Give specific appointment time with name of specific health care
        professional to be seen.

    Use reminders (mail, telephone).

    Use efficient clinic scheduling.

    Use short referral time.

    Insure continuity of care.

    Keep an active follow-up appointment file.

    Elicit and discuss reasons for previously missed appointments.

Following acute medical regimens

    Improve patient–health care professional communication: involve patient
        in planning and implementation of treatment program.

    Customize treatment plan.

    Simplify treatment regimens.

    Use patient education and check for comprehension.

    Anticipate management of side effects.

    Use special reminders and special pill packaging.

    Use adjunctive services (health educator, pharmacist counseling).

    Eliminate and/or reduce pharmacy delays.

    Be aware of medication engineering and packaging (e.g., the color or
        shape of a pill can transmit a message).

Following chronic medical regimens

    Improve patient–health care professional communication, pick up on any
        negative feedback

    Use behavior modification procedures (e.g., self-monitoring, goal setting,
        behavioral contracting, commitment and reinforcement procedures.

    Teach self-management skills (e.g., problem solving, decisional balance
        sheet construction, relapse prevention, attribution training).

    Use graduated regimen implementation.

    Involve significant others.

    Use supervision: home visits, brief hospitalization.

    Use adjunctive services (e.g., adherence counseling, psychotherapeutic
        procedures when indicated).

    Integrate treatment regimen into normal life.

    Use role playing, paradoxical techniques when appropriate.

---

[a]Table organization taken from Haynes, 1979b.

conducive manner designed to foster adherence as described in Chapter 3. Since nonadherence can arise for many different reasons associated with the disease, the self-care regimen, health care provider–patient relationship, organizational-structural variables, and individual variables (e.g., lack of comprehension, forgetfulness, competing expectations and health beliefs, absence of skills and resources), different combinations of strategies will be required. It is essential to diagnose and assess each instance of nonadherence and to be flexible, individually customizing procedures to the specific circumstances and characteristics of the patient.

As we have emphasized repeatedly, the first step before intervening is not only to diagnose the patient's clinical condition but also to "diagnose" or assess the chances and reasons for nonadherence. In Chapter 3, we described specific measures (interviews, questionnaires) that could be used to assess the patient's adherence history, health beliefs, expectations, and possible barriers or obstacles to adherence. Once a diagnosis of the reason(s) for nonadherence has been formulated, the HCP can select from the array of alternative enhancement interventions those that can be customized to the individual case.

Examples of Integrative Adherence Programs

As noted in the quotation that begins this chapter, the number of such integrative adherence programs is limited, but the initial results are encouraging. One of the earliest such attempts was conducted by Haynes and his colleagues (1976), who used a multicomponent treatment package with hypertensive steelworkers. The program included self-measurement of blood pressure and pill intake, tailoring of the treatment regimen to the patient's daily habits, increased supervision, praise, and monetary credits.

Levine and his colleagues (1979) reported on the enhancement of adherence resulting from a comprehensive integrative two-year educational program directed at ambulatory hypertensives. The program consisted of educational counselling, drug clarification, family members involvement in the management of high blood pressure, and group meetings. These efforts resulted in higher levels of appointment keeping, increased weight and blood pressure controls relative to standard medical care. These positive results were maintained at a three year follow-up.

Youngren (1981) developed a multicomponent program with patients suffering from chronic obstructive pulmonary disease. The program included training patients in the individualized preparation, administration, and recording of medication, providing them with feedback about errors, giving them a checklist to coordinate body responses and drug effects, family involvement, and follow-up by a nurse. Of the 32 participants, an impressive 26 followed the treatment regimen with almost perfect accuracy.

Two recent studies (Finnerty, Mattie, & Finnerty, 1985; Williams *et al.*, 1986) have demonstrated the utility of an integration adherence enhancement program for parents of children suffering from acute otitis media. Both adherence enhancement programs included (1) educational handouts that described in simple terms the cause, treatment, possible complications, and the importance of giving the medication for the full period; (2) self-monitoring calendars; (3) reminder stickers; and (4) follow-up telephone calls. In both studies such interventions were effective in fostering treatment adherence.

A sophisticated and effective integrative form of adherence training has been developed by Varni and his colleagues (Sergis-Deavenport & Varni, 1982, 1983; Varni, 1983; Varni & Wallander, 1984). They developed instructional strategies and behavioral techniques to increase parents' long-term adherence to the factor replacement therapy for their hemophiliac children. As described by Varni and Babani (1980),

> the instructional strategies included providing the information in incremental quantities over time, organizing the information into specific categories, and combining verbal and written intructions. The behavioral techniques consisted of the modeling of correct factor replacement procedures by the pediatric nurse practitioner,

with the parent of a hemophiliac child observing these modeled behaviors (observtaional learning). The parent's behavioral rehearsal of the observed techniques was recorded on a reliable and valid behavior checklist of factor replacement procedures. The parent's behavioral response on each task (i.e., reconstitution consisted of 20 behaviors, syringe preparation consisted of 20 behaviors, and infusion consisted of 36 behaviors) was recorded on an occurrence/nonoccurrence basis on the behavior checklist, with proper sequencing required for the correct responding of certain behaviors. (p. 506)

In addition, behavioral feedback, social praise, and group parental support were offered. The effectiveness of this training was reflected in the observation that the accuracy of parents' performance increased from 15% during baseline to 92% by the end of the treatment condition and, most importantly, was maintained at 97% adherence over a long-term follow-up assessment. In contrast, the control group showed an overall adherence rate of only 65%.

Efforts to develop an integrative adherence enhancement program are also under way in other health-related areas. For example, Martin and Dubbert (1986) indicate that although optimal exercise training packages must still be developed, the research suggests that a combination of procedures promotes adherence. These include individual goal setting, low- to moderate-intensity exercise, instruction in cognitive and self-control strategies, contracting, feedback, and social support. In addition, creating a natural environment that is supportive of exercise is helpful (e.g., providing exercise cues and reminders, encouraging others to exercise with the participant). They also note that some of the factors that are important in the aquisition phase of exercise such as immediate personalized feedback, reinforcement, and instruction in low-intensity exercise, may be less important during the maintenance phase, when other factors such as opportunities to socialize, awareness of the relationship between exercise, mood, and energy levels, and planned generalization training to new activities and settings may be more critical. The value of distinguishing between the acquisition and maintenance phases applies to many other target behaviors besides exercise.

The most impressive integrative program to improve treatment adherence in outpatient schizophrenics has been developed by Liberman and his colleagues (Liberman, Eckman, & Phipps, 1986). Their Program combines drug therapy and structured rehabilitation methods. The feature of their comprehensive program that is most relevant to the present topic is their use of skills-training methods to teach patients how to manage their antipsychotic drug regimens. The authors designed an educational and training program to teach medication self-management skills. The program specifically teaches the patient and his or her family about drug action and side effects, regular attendance at the clinic, how to devise reminders to take the drugs, the use of incentives, and cognitive and assertive social skills such as how to negotiate medication issues and problems with the physician. In order to teach such skills a well-organized, multimedia *Medication Management Module* was developed that uses videotaped demonstrations, focused instruction, specialized role plays, social and videotape feedback, and practice in the "real world." A detailed trainer's manual and a patient workbook are included.[11] Each skill is broken into its components. The initial results are quite encouraging (see Liberman *et al.*, 1986), and the *Medication Self-Management Module* is currently being evaluated in a large-scale field test throughout the United States and Canada.

The counselors (e.g., nurses, occupational therapists, psychologists, social workers) receive extensive training. The treatment modules are built around the teaching of problem-solving skills. The module includes an introduction to the topic (the goal, why one needs to achieve the goal, what benefits accrue,

[11]The *Medication Management Module*, including the Trainer's Manual, Patient's Workbook, and Demonstration Videocassette, is available from regional McNeil Pharmaceutical representatives (215/628-5000) and from the UCLA center. Liberman and his colleagues are developing other related models covering such areas as self-care, symptom self-management, leisure and recreation skills, problem solving, and money management.

when the goal is attained, what skills and resources are needed, and what steps are required to obtain the goal). Specific videotape demonstrations of the requisite component skills are modeled followed by role playing and specific behavioral feedback couched in a supportive manner. Problem solving and social skills required to overcome possible obstacles are taught. *In vivo* exercises and homework are also included in each module in order to nurture generalization and maintenance of the desired skills. Table 30 provides an example of one skill included in the training program.

Perhaps the reader could envisage how such a multimedia training program could be used to teach self-management skills to specific patient populations with whom they work. Imagine that some day the HCP may have a library of such training materials for all types of disorders from acute (mothers having to administer antibiotics to their children for 10 days) to chronic (diabetes, hypertension, bipolar disorders). The principles and clinical guidelines for developing such programs are now discernible.

With the development of new effective treatment procedures, as in the case of the management of hemophilia, for instance, comparable breakthroughs are required in adherence training procedures. It would seem to be a wise investment if pharmaceutical companies spent a portion of their research budgets on the development and testing of adherence enhancement procedures, in the same way that they develop and test new drug treatments. We can envisage drug sales representatives visiting HCPs not only with a description of their latest products but also with a description of the tested adherence enhancement procedures to be followed when prescribing the proposed treatment. When pharmaceutical companies come to recognize that the investment in adherence intervention research is not only a reflection of good will and a responsible position but also a means of increasing profits, then we will see major advances in the adherence field. Some promise of this is already evident in the Liberman *et al.* program described above. Their innovative drug self-management program for schizophhrenics

**Table 30   Example of One Skill Taught from Patient Medication
Management Module[a]**

Module: Medication self-management
Skill area: Negotiating medication issues
Requisite behavior
  Greet pleasantly.
  Describe problem specifically.
  Tell length of occurrence.
  Describe extent of discomfort.
  Specifically request action.
  Repeat or clarify advice and/or orders.
  Ask about expected time for effect.
  Thank for assistance.
  Good eye contact.
  Good posture.
  Clear audible speech.
Skills Training
What is your goal in this module?
  "To manage my medication better."
What skills are you going to learn now?
  "How to present medical problems to my doctor."
Watch videotape demonstrating model interactions. What did the patient do
  when presenting information to doctor?
  "He had good eye contact and spoke in a pleasant voice."
  "He described the problem specifically."
  "He specifically requested help with his problem."
If unresponsive to questions:
  Prompt more specifically.
  Replay videotape model.
  Annotate more clearly.
Practice in a role play what you just observed in the videotape (rate
    criterion behaviors) and videotape the reenactment.
Watch replay of videotape and elicit feedback.
What did you do well?
  "I asked to discuss medication with the busy doctor."
  "I told how long the problem had existed."
What must be improved?
  "I should lean forward and not slouch."
Repeat role play to criterion level of performance (100% of requisite
    behavior correct twice in succession).

[a]Reproduced with permission from Liberman *et al.*, 1986.

was supported by the McNeil Pharmaceutical Company, an important and far-reaching step. Similarly, the effort by Boehringer-Mannheim Diagnostics, Inc., to teach diabetes educators ways to improve their patients' adherence is laudable. Much more effort and a partnership between pharmaceutical companies and HCPs are greatly needed.

However, before we become overly enthusiastic about the potential of integrative adherence procedures, a bit of reality testing is warranted. Our efforts still have a long way to go before they are considered fully effective. For example, consider the results of a massive effort undertaken to increase the level of adherence in hypertensive patients (JAMA, 1979). The program provided free drugs, free care, free tests, and, when needed, free transportation. Evening and weekend appointments were available, as was 24-hour care. Patients who missed appointments were contacted and, if necessary, cared for at home. The result of such a massive effort was only a modest level of adherence of 65%.

In short, we might conclude from these results that it did not work. Consistent with the philosophy of this book, this should not be the occasion for us to "catastrophize" or to give up but rather to reexamine the experiment—what did they do, and what can we learn from such an effort? An important omission appears to be the failure to teach self-management skills, to enlist patients more as collaborators in the adherence process. The consideration of the following clinical guidelines ("ten commandments") that summarize the main points of this book may help us develop more effective integrative adherence enhancement procedures in the future. These guidelines are based on a combination of the findings of available research and our clinical experience. In many instances, however, the research data are far from optimal and are often derived from only specific populations. Therefore the generalization of these guidelines is somewhat speculative and awaits further confirmation. We do believe, however, that they are still worthy of enumerating and hope that future empirical evidence will justify our clinical intuitions.

Guideline 1: Anticipate Nonadherence

It is essential to insure that adherence is part of health care. Concerns about adherence must pervade the entire treatment program beginning with the initial meeting with a patient and in some cases beginning with the information provided by a referral source. For example, patients who have been referred to our pain treatment program are often confused and misinformed about why they have been referred and what they can expect. An HCP cannot assume that a referral source has provided patients with appropriate information, and misinformation can impede adherence. The HCP might find it beneficial to begin by asking referred patients why they have been referred, what they have been told, and what they expect.

HCPs should perform an adherence history (see Chapter 3) and educational needs assessment, that is, an assessment of the patient and his or her environment to identify factors that may facilitate or impede rapport, readiness to learn, and willingness and capability for self-management. *The HCP must treat the whole person and not simply the disease!*

The HCP should assess such factors as:

1. The patient's expectations about the clinical encounter
2. Beliefs and misconceptions about the cause, severity, and symptoms of the illness and susceptibility to complications or exacerbations
3. Goals of treatment
4. Perceptions about the costs and risks versus benefits of treatment
5. Existing health-related knowledge, skills, and practices
6. Degree of adaptation to the disease
7. Sense of helplessness, hopelessness versus resourcefulness, and self-efficacy
8. Educational and learning limitations
9. Extent of family involvement
10. Life circumstances that might affect adherence (e.g., financial resources, characteristics of job, and work schedule)

This information should be used in planning an individualized approach with the patient. One must also perform a *task analysis*. What capabilities, skills, and information does the patient need to perform all self-care behavior appropriately? What is the match between the demands of the treatment regimen and the resources (e.g., financial, transportation, intellectual, social support) available to the patient? In short, if the patient does not adhere, it is important to determine whether the patient did not know what to do because of a deficiency in knowledge or skills or did know what to do and how to perform the appropriate behaviors but failed to produce the appropriate behavior when required, that is, a production deficiency? The answers to these questions should guide the choice of the adherence enhancement strategies.

An HCP should not view adherence as a separate topic that can be tacked on at the end of a lengthy self-care program but must remain sensitive to it throughout the period during which the patient is under his or her care. For example, a complex program such as that provided to a newly diagnosed diabetic that includes the provision of information regarding insulin, diet, exercise, and foot care must consider potential problems with adherence from the very beginning. Some programs we have examined go through each of the treatment components in weekly meetings and at the end have a week on adherence. We believe this approach is inadequate and that the problems of adherence must peravde all aspects of the program.

Guideline 2: Consider the Prescribed Self-Care Regimen from the Patient's Perspective

HCPs should not assume that their patients will perceive things in the same way that the HCP does or in the way that the HCP would like. Patients come into the health care relationship with certain attitudes, beliefs, expectations, and available resources. Moreover, they have other commitments, demands, and life circumstances that may be more salient than their health problems and may potentially interfere with the performance of specific health behavior. Health is only one, albeit an important, component of life.

It is all too easy for the HCP to forget that disease occurs in the broader context of an individual's entire life. This was pointed out to us when we discussed the importance of losing weight to an obese diabetic woman. She indicated that losing weight would make her less physically attractive and she worried that she might lose her live-in boyfriend if she lost weight since he preferred his women to be voluptuous. Another overweight diabetic Italian woman explained the difficulty in cutting back on carbohydrates since large meals including pasta were intimately associated with her family and social life.

The HCP must attempt to motivate the patient actively to participate in self-care and cannot assume the patient will be adherent simply because he or she has a health problem or because the HCP advocates it. This can best be accomplished by involving the patient in treatment planning and decisions through the use of mutual goal setting to ensure that patient priorities, life style, and resources are considered. The HCP should encourage discussions concerning the cost, risks, and benefits of acceptable alternatives of treatment. The HCP should attempt to ensure that the patient feels that he or she can be successful with self-management. This can be accomplished by the HCP's assisting the patient to set realistic goals organized in manageable steps with some of the easiest steps first to encourage a sense of success and encourage efforts.

Guideline 3: Foster a Collaborative Relationship Based on Negotiation

From patients' perspectives, the overall goal of any health care behavior is to maximize the quality of life. If they perceive any self-care behavior as counterproductive to this end, if the costs are perceived as outweighing the benefits, patients may well choose not to adhere. Therefore the HCP must consider where the patient can be offered some legitimate choices and where they cannot. That is, giving the patient some decisional control concerning the timing of medication is better than giving no control with the result that the patient does not take the medication. *An acceptable regimen that is carried out appropriately is better than an ideal one that is ignored.* The HCP must be flexible and willing to negotiate, within reason. Autocratic, expert-oriented approaches usually do not prove useful. If the HCP hopes to enhance adherence, he or she must communicate empathy and respect and nurture collaboration.

Guideline 4: Be Patient-Oriented

What are the patients' views, expectancies, and knowledge concerning the disease and the treatment regimen? Does the patient believe that he or she can perform the adherence behavior at the prescribed level (ask for example, "To what extent do you believe that you will be able to limit yourself to eating just three meals a day?")? Does the patient believe that the prescribed performance of the adherence behavior will lead to the desired outcome or undesirable outcome ("Do you believe that eating only three meals a day will lead to the reduction of 5 pounds per week?" "How likely do you think it is that if you give up smoking you will gain too much weight?")? How important does the patient feel it is for him or her to achieve the recommended goal (e.g., lowered blood pressure)? What barriers can the patient forsee that will impede his or her ability to perform the self-care behavior? What does the patient think that he or she and the HCP can do to make adherence easier? What problems can the patient anticipate?

It is important to listen not only to what the patient says but what he or she fails to say. The failure to ask questions or raise problems may indicate that the patient was not listening, does not understand, is embarrassed to admit that he or she does not understand, or does not plan to follow the treatment regimen.

The HCP should use clear and specific verbal and written communications. Information should be presented in different ways. We have found it useful to ask patients to repeat what they are suppose to do, in what manner, and how frequently. The HCP should provide feedback and positively reinforce patients' efforts and goal attainments even if not perfect. In this way HCPs can attempt to shape more appropriate behavior. This approach is likely to have greater impact than threats and negative reinforcements.

Guideline 5: Customize Treatment

There is no such thing as a standard treatment for a standard patient. In considering the set of treatment recommendations, the HCP must consider, adjust, and modify the ideal textbook treatment to meet the needs of each specific patient in an optimal way.

Whenever possible, the HCP should remove barriers caused by the regimen itself by recommending treatment modalities that are clinically effective, simple, convenient, and less costly and that produce the fewest side effects and require the least amount of behavioral change or interference with normal daily activities. Whenever possible, couple adherence behaviors to daily rituals such as meals, bedtime, time of awakening. Use the simplest regimen that is reasonably likely to produce the desired goal. Patients need to be helped to plan how best to integrate new behavioral demands into their daily routines.

The HCP must be certain that the patient has the skills necessary to perform the recommended regimen. It is also useful to provide demonstrations and opportunities for practice and feedback and to reassure patients that the HCP is available for assistance and that the patients themselves can exert appropriate controls.

If the adherence behavior is likely to produce side effects, it is helpful to discuss how the patient should deal with them. Knowledge of the existence of side effects is insufficient: whenever possible, patients should be given a definite plan of action for dealing with them.

It is important to select a combination of adherence enhancement procedures. Such efforts must focus on *patient* (e.g., expectations, beliefs), *treatment* (e.g., simplifying treatment demands), *disease* (e.g., visual impairment), *organizational* (e.g., scheduling of appointments), and *relationship* (e.g., insuring continuity of care) variables.

Guideline 6: Enlist Family Support

Make sure that the family or other significant people in the patient's life understand the disease, the treatment, and the goals of the self-care regimen so that they can be enlisted as allies.

Guideline 7: Provide a System of Continuity and Accessibility

Patients must view the HCP as an ally who is accessible, nonjudgmental, respectful, and sincere in his or her desire to cooperate with them as well as knowledgeable and competent. They have to feel comfortable to ask questions, raise concerns, and be willing to acknowledge that they do not understand.

Provide specific appointments, reduce waiting time, offer quiet, comfortable surroundings, adjust length of appointments to the patient's desire and provide specific reminders, especially when the waiting period is longer than one week. Take an active role in the referral process.

Guideline 8: Make Use of Other Health Care Providers and Personnel as Well as Community Resources

Nurse educators, physicians' assistants, dieticians, pharmacists, secretaries, receptionists, and ward clerks can all be called upon to maximize the likelihhood of adherence. The efforts at increasing patient adherence should be seen as a task for the entire treatment team, not just the primary HCP. All members of the clinic and treatment team must keep in mind the ever present possibility of nonadherence and must understand that their attitudes and communications skills are crucial. The health care team's behavior toward patient, treatment, and adherence can serve to nurture the patient's positive feelings toward the staff and increase the patient's positive identification with the health care facility. Insofar as one is able to mobilize the array of professionals and staff, the challenging task of improving treatment can be successfully met.

There are many community resources for education, support, and assistance in dealing with emotional or social problems. These agencies can provide great assistance to enhance the maintenance of the performance of desirable self-care behavior (e.g., Alcohol Anonymous, Reach for Recovery, American Chronic Pain Association, churches, social agencies).

Varni and Babani (1986) have proposed a health team model of care whereby prevention, diagnosis, treatment, and rehabilitation could be provided in a coordinated, comprehensive manner by specialists representing several disciplines. In this way the biomedical, behavioral, and psychosocial factors that influence the patient's health and treatment adherence can all be addressed. Such an integrated interdisciplinary approach to patient care is surely an ideal we can strive to achieve.

Guideline 9: Repeat Everything

Successful educational and motivational interventions are often relatively short-lived and must be given repetitively, especially for the performance of protective health behavior and the treatment of chronic diseases. Initial adherence does not guarantee that adherence will continue; one should expect some degree of dissipation of adherence over time. Therefore it is important to attend to adherence throughout the continuing process of health care.

Guideline 10: Don't Give Up!

It is all too easy to give up on the nonadherent patients and simply write them off as uncooperative and deserving whatever befalls them. The HCP should reinvite, reeducate, remotivate, and renegotiate with the nonadherent patient as circumstances may require. Do not blame the victim! Review guidelines 2–8. Try to analyze the problem and alleviate barriers using specific techniques described in Section 2. Adherence can be enhanced with a reasonable degree of effort on the part of the HCP. The cost–benefit analyses of this effort indicate that it is worthwhile.

In this chapter we have listed and briefly described ten general principles that should , we believe, on the basis of the available literature and our clinical experience, facilitate adherence. We now turn our attention to a consideration of the reasons why HCPs are unlikely to follow these guidelines or any of the other suggestions offered in this book.

9

Why Health Care Providers Will Not Adhere to the Recommendations Outlined in This Volume (or Perhaps They Will)

> *There is enough evidence of professional noncompliance for it to seem likely that even if clinicians were aware of these techniques, they would not necessarily use them.*
>
> P. Ley (1986)

Throughout this book we have described the number of variables that appear to influence adherence to self-care regimens. We have discussed a number of strategies and techniques for improving patients' adherence to therapeutic suggestions and recommendations. In this chapter we must consider our own behavior. How likely is it that we, health care providers, will adhere to the suggestions and recommendations offered in this book? The available research does not create optimism. In fact, the literature on the behavior of HCPs is strikingly reminiscent of the literature on patient nonadherence. For example, HCPs are no more likely to carry out health-protective behavior than are lay persons, despite their greater knowledge of health, given their occupations (see Salovey, Rudy, & Turk, 1986). Whether it is stopping smoking, flossing teeth, undergoing annual physical examinations, or whatever, those who work in the health care professions are no more likely to engage in these preventive activities than the patients they council. We seldom practice what we preach.

Even at a more serious practical level, the literature indicated that HCPs often do not follow clinical procedures that they know should be implemented. A series of studies on physicians' behavior indicate that clinical performance ranges between 48% to 72% below levels of professional standards (Clute, 1963; Jungfer & Last, 1964; Peterson, Forhan, & Jones 1980). Similarly, in a study conducted by the American Society for Internal Medicine, Hare and Barnoon (1973) found little correlation between the established criteria for delivery of treatment and the physician's performance. Raven and Haley (1982) reported on nurses deviation from infection control rules and Green and Neistat (1983) reported that dentists frequently fail to adequately shield their patients when taking x-rays. Kayne and Cheung (1973) examined the drug preparation and administration to elderly patients in three extended care facilities that provided skilled nursing care after discharge from an acute-care hospital. They reported an error rate of 20%. The errors included missed dosages, wrong drug or dose administered, wrong route of administration, and incorrect dosing interval. The cumulative picture across HCPs is one of widespread nonadherence to advised health care practices.

Attempts to modify HCPs' behavior have, to date, not been rewarding (e.g., McDonald *et al.*, 1984; Wilson, McDonald, & McCabe, 1982). For example, data reported by Williamson (1971) suggested that workshops, conferences, newsletters, and information papers may fail to bring HCP behavior up to optimal standards. Sullivan, Estes, Stopford, and Lester (1980) demonstrated that explicit self-imposed standards and protocols provided to the HCPs at a primary care clinic (including physicians, nurse practitioners, and physicians' assistants) to improve care and facilitate quality assessments of urinary tract infection and upper respiratory illness resulted in adherence rates by the HCPs ranging from 38% to 100%.

In a recent study Cohen, Weinberger, Hui, Tierney, and McDonald (1985) evaluated the efficacy of providing reading materials regarding 13 common preventive care actions to residents in internal medicine. The educational intervention consisted of reading 8–9 pages of text about each of a set of clinical actions, 62–69 pages in total, excerpted from *Action-Oriented Decisions in Ambulatory Medicine* (McDonald, 1981). The written material provided the rationale for specific actions given certain clinical indications and a literature review justifying these recommendations. The authors concluded that the overall effect of the educational intervention was quite modest. Despite the high percentage of residents who indicated that they intended to carry out the recommended procedures, they actually adhered to the recommendations less than 10% of the time. Cohen *et al.* (1985) provide the following commentary on the problem:

> Journal reading is the method preferred by physicians for improving their practices (Guptill & Graham, 1976; Christensen & Wertheimer, 1979; Manning & Denson, 1979; 1980), and in the United States continuing medical education is a multi-billion dollar industry (Haynes, Davis, McKibbon, & Tugwell, 1984). We would like to believe that physicians who update their knowledge about recommended standards of care, and the evidence that supports those recommendations, are more likely to transfer that knowledge into practice. The results of the current study indicate that, while such a relationship exists, it is not straight-forward, and the magnitude is small. (p. 913)

Payne, Lyons, and Dwarshuis (1976) noted that the provision of performance information did not cause a change in physician care delivery patterns. More recently, Tierney, Hui, and McDonald (1986) reported that performance feedback to physicians regarding prescription of recommended preventive diagnostic tests resulted in only 15–30% rates of adherence compared to rates of 10–15% adherence in the absence of feedback. Although the feedback did lead to increases in physician adherence, the incidence remained quite low. As we noted with patients, providing physicians as well as HCPs with information about treatment procedures often does not translate into altered behavior.

Given the large gaps between knowledge, intentions and actions, the reader should pause for a moment and consider:

1. Are the results of reading this book, with its many suggestions for enhancing patient adherence, likely to change the way I relate to and work with patients?
2. Moreover, what would it take for me to change my usual way of dealing with my patients to increase the likelihood of improved rates of adherence?

The literature indicates that the information conveyed in this book will lead to noble intentions which will not readily translate into changed behavior unless accompanying appropriate steps are taken. In fact, in those cases wherein adherence among HCPs has been achieved, many of the same techniques that we reviewed for use with patients have been cited. For example, Brook and Williams (1976) reported that negative reinforcement (i.e., reimbursement sanctions) increased adherence to appropriate use of injections by physicians. A number of papers (e.g., McDonald, 1976; McDonald *et al.*, 1984) have reported on the utility of various reminders such as checklists, "flagged" charts, and computer printouts informing HCPs as to which patients were eligible for a particular clinical action. De Dombal, Leaper, and Horrocks (1974) demonstrated that simple but explicit checklists radically altered physicians' performance associated with diagnosis and treatment of abdominal pain, and Grimm, Shimoni, and Harlan (1975) documented the favorable impact of a protocol checklist on reduction in antibiotics and laboratory use.

Rather than simply bemoaning the existence of the non-adherence problem among HCPs, as has often been the case, we must consider what factors contribute to nonadherence and attempt to modify these, in the same way that we attempt to modify the nonadherent behavior of our patients. Our purpose in this closing chapter is to consider the impediments to HCPs' adherence to the suggestions offered in this volume, with the hope that the examination of these factors may serve as an impetus to behavior change. We are unlikely to increase the rate of patient treatment adherence if we cannot first increase the rate of adherence by HCPs.

Impediments to HCP Adherence

The same factors that contribute to patient nonadherence are likely to influence HCP nonadherence. These include: the beliefs and attitudes of the HCP about their patients and the treatment; the complexity of adherence enhancement procedures; the perceived costs (e.g., effort) versus benefits; perceptions of low outcome efficacy and low self-efficacy; faulty memory; inadequate skills and resources; and previous failures. More explicitly, these factors can be viewed as reasons HCPs offer themselves, and others, as to why following the suggestions offered in this book "won't work":

- The patient *should* take my advice. If they don't want to do what I say then it is their business and they can suffer the consequences. *(Pessimism, not useful)*
- I tried it in the past; it doesn't work with my population. They are . . . too old, too young, too uneducated, too unsophisticated. *(Not applicable)*
- It is too complicated. Who can remember to do all these things? (Stimulus overload, *too many obstacles and barriers*)
- Who has the time to worry about and to do what is suggested? I have to see so many patients per hour or per day and there is no time to do all this adherence stuff. *(Useful but no time)*
- You don't get reimbursed for education and prevention. The system doesn't support adherence counseling. *(No payoffs)*
- I'm not a "shrink." I haven't been trained to do these things. *(Low self-efficacy)*

Whether it is the beliefs held by the HCP, the way the health care profession is structured, or various barriers and obstacles, each can interfere with adherence practice. Let us consider each rationale separately so that they may be better understood, dealt with, and possibly prevented. In some instances, these beliefs are not consistent with the facts, whereas at other times they represent professional challenges that are not easily overcome.

The Beliefs of HCPs

At the level of beliefs, we can consider some of the results of our survey of physicians who worked with diabetes patients. Some comments suggested that the physicians surveyed thought that nonadherence was "the patient's problem" and that the role of the HCPs is to treat and cure disease. Their responsibility ended with the presentation of information and the teaching of relevant skills to their patients. After the HCP's initial effort, it is the patient's responsibility to comply. This position characterizes the classical expert model of medicine. One physician surveyed went so far as to suggest, somewhat facetiously, that he believed in Darwinian theory of the "survival of the fittest! Those who don't adhere deserve the consequences."

Of course, we could reverse this physician's observation and consider survival of the physician in an age of growing consumerism, litigation, and a glut of physicians, as noted by the American Medical Association. For self-preservation, HCPs should be wary of entering an adversarial relationship with their patients. The success of any given practitioner is based upon a network of opinion and reputation. The lay referral system of friends, neighbors, and relatives who help the individual define illness and recommend when to seek care and from *whom* to seek care has great potential to influence the survivability of the HCP. Mechanic (1964) found that 34% of his patient sample choose their physician through the recommendation of a friend or relative as opposed to only 20% who made their decision based on the advice of another HCP. HCPs who hope to survive may find that they must attend more to the attitudes and beliefs of their patients if they wish their patients to enhance their practice through recommendation.

In contrast to what many HCPs may believe, their interactions with their patients may be more important than the extent of their technical expertise. For example, Reader, Pratt, and Mudd (1957) reported that 50% of the outpatients they sampled listed kindness, understanding, sympathy, and encouragement as the most important attributes for a physician, compared to only 20% who rated the physician's ability to treat their disease as most important. As noted in Chapter 3, the likelihood of being sued by a patient for malpractice is often more closely related to the quality of the HCP–patient relationship than to the level of competence of the HCP.

The discussion of relationship raises an interesting related point. If you consider extreme cases is there not a point beyond which an HCP should not have to go in order to nurture patient adherence? The answer is of course, yes. There are surely some patients, as well as some HCPs, with whom nothing we try leads to improved adherence. But before reaching this conclusion the HCP should review his or her own behavior in order to assess what has been tried to enhance patient adherence. What barriers contribute to patient nonadherence? What qualities of the patient, what social or professional resources exist that could be called upon to facilitate adherence? In short, we suggest careful self-examination by the HCP as well as comprehensive case assessment before making a referral to a specialist in adherence or to a mental health professional or giving up altogether.

There is some evidence that even refractory patients can improve their adherence behavior if given attention by an HCP who focuses explicitly on this problem. For example, Nessman and his colleagues (1980) reported that groups of particularly nonadherent, inadequately controlled hypertensive patients were seen by a psychologist and a nurse for eight 90-minute sessions. The adherence enhancement treatment sessions focused on patient responsibility, informed decision making through individually tailored education, discussion, and self-help techniques. At two- and six-month follow-up periods, the patients who participated in the groups had lower diastolic blood pressure, better pill counts, and better attendance at the clinic than control patients who were provided with standard care and who listened to a series of hypertension control tapes.

The length of the adherence enhancement program described by Nessman *et al.* may be prohibitive for an individual HCP; however, the data do suggest that there is some merit in considering adherence enhancement groups conducted by counselors who specifically focus on this problem. Such specialized training groups may be a cost-effective way to enhance patient adherence. The prolonged maintenance of adherence, however, following participation in such groups must still revolve around the primary deliverer of health care. As we noted, adherence must permeate all aspects of care and cannot be merely delegated to a technician with an accompanying expectation that the improvements will be maintained. Instead, we must modify our own behavior to maximize the maintenance of patient adherence.

Low Expectation That Adherence Procedures Will Work

Many of the physicians we surveyed were more altruistic than the Darwinian practitioner cited above, but nevertheless they seemed to feel frustrated and helpless because of their history of limited success. As authors, we may have inadvertently reinforced this belief when we described the range and complexity of variables that appear to be related to adherence. There is a growing body of literature, however, indicating that relatively simple sets of activities and the general attitude and orientation of the HCP can produce marked improvements in adherence, if not a cure for the problem. Whether it is postcard reminders, telephone prompts, behavioral contracts, or just taking the time to discuss medication regimens or potential side effects, the improvement in patient adherence can be clinically significant. Moreover, HCPs can be explicitly taught these adherence enhancement procedures. As noted previously, Inui *et al.* (1976) taught physicians ways to increase patient motivation for adherence with the result of dramatically improving medication adherence and clinical outcome in recalcitrant hypertensive patients.

But in spite of such successes HCPs often point to instances in which the variety of adherence enhancement strategies did not work: "It didn't work, thus why try?" As we discusssed when considering the relapse prevention model in Chapter 6, it is important to determine what did not work and why. It is possible that some adherence enhancement procedures we described have been tried by the HCP, but careful consideration must be given to *how* the techniques were implemented. One goal of the present volume has been to emphasize the important role that the style and manner of presentation plays in implementation. For example, in Chapter 5 we described the clinical skills required for such procedures as behavioral contracting. In fact, the style or manner of presentation may be more important than the specific technique itself.

Another impediment to making use of the material covered in this book is the HCP's feeling of limited self-efficacy: "I'm not a psychologist; I don't have special training in psychological techniques or relationship enhancement procedures." Although some clinical skills are necessary (as described in Chapter 3), the level of skill required is both straightforward and specific and the style of interaction should be both natural and commonsensible. The HCP must put himself or herself in the place of the patient and consider how he or she would like to be treated in such circumstances. No more and no less is being suggested. No great amount of specialized training is required to use these adherence enhancement techniques with the average patient. In a few instances, it may be appropriate to refer a patient with a particular adherence problem to a specialist; however, the general patient-oriented negotiation approach we describe should be of utility with most patients, even the most obstreperous. It is all too easy to "pass the buck," often with a sense of relief. Although experts can be of assistance, they cannot take the place of the primary HCP in fostering adherence.

Memory

Memory is a problem for HCPs, as well as for patients. At first it may be necessary for HCPs to make special efforts to attend to adherence. They may have to monitor their usual manner of interacting with and treating patients and catch themselves up when necessary. Business as usual may be maladaptive. As HCPs begin to change their modus operandi, their new behavior and style will become more automatic and require less attention. In the same way that memory prompts can help patients to adhere, they can also foster adherence in HCPs. We have included in this volume many tables and checklists that can be strategically placed in one's office in order to serve as reminder cues. One can also place such reminders in patient's charts, on the back of prescription forms, and so forth in order to increase the likelihood that the issue of adherence will be addressed throughout the course of treatment. In fact, we can envisage pharmaceutical companies developing an entire supply of office equipment (prescription pads, pens, charts, etc.) with adherence reminders, as well as with their logo. The road to improved services, enhanced public health, and increased profits may be by means of encouraging HCP and patient adherence. Few topics so unify the various health care professions as does treatment adherence.

But providing memory prompts is *not* sufficient. HCPs must monitor themselves in order to determine the frequency with which they employ the different adherence enhancement procedures. Behavioral feedback and performance contingencies must be built into any program to ensure the HCP's adherence. Obviously, we hope that simply placing this book prominently on your shelf and reviewing our tables may serve as a cue to follow those exhortations and enjoinders that are most likely to enhance the adherence of your patients.

Inertia

Finally, there is the potential hazard of inertia. Change in typical modes of behavior is as difficult for HCPs as for their patients. What factors are likely to motivate us to change? For the patient it may be the promise of improved health or quality of life or reduced disease or noxious symptoms. For the HCP it is more complicated, combining both altruistic motives and economic demands. Besides improving one's quality of service, employing adherence enhancement procedures can save time, at least in the long run, and can often result in financial benefits (e.g., reduction in time lost from failure of patients to keep scheduled appointments). It may be difficult to conceive that taking the time to address adherence issues with patients can be more expedient. In earlier chapters we have described how adoption of a problem-solving, collaborative, negotiable relationship with patients can facilitate communication and foster joint responsibility and thus help avoid lengthy, often fruitless HCP-patient exchanges. Such a problem-solving approach allows HCPs to focus on patients' specific requests and desires rather than on more amorphous problems. Taking the few minutes at the outset to get acquainted with the patient's ideas and expectations can save the HCP time later on and make for a more productive relationship (e.g., see Korsch *et al.* 1968).

The research reviewed in Chapter 3 also indicated that when physicians read patients' records while interviewing (out of a desire to be more efficient) this inadvertently lengthens the treatment session. In considering these comments it is important to remember that patient satisfaction and adherence are not tied to the actual length of time of the HCP–patient interaction but rather to the patient's perception of being listened to and cared for. Surely, implementing many of the suggestions offered herein will indeed require more effort and time (at least initially), but we have also documented many examples of cases wherein the responsibility for adherence training can be shared by others besides the primary HCP. Whether it is nurses, pharmacists, physical therapists, psychologists, or specialized "adherence counselors," the time and effort expended will pay handsome rewards. Most importantly, HCPs can share the responsibility for treatment adherence with patients and significant others in their lives. The teaching of self-management skills to patients represents a major challenge for the health care professions.

In considering such a team approach, it is important to keep in mind that medical and institutional systems must support such efforts. As DiMatteo and DiNicola (1982a) note, physicians as well as other HCPs tend to treat patients much as they themselves are treated. They cite research indicating that interns and residents who are alienated, abused, misunderstood, and generally mistreated tend to have little energy or motivation for providing emotional support, understanding, and reassurance for their patients. Any effort significantly to influence the rate of HCP and patient adherence must take into consideration the general medical system and its limited reward structure for counseling adherence. We believe there is a necessity to ensure that the topics covered in this book are part of the educational process of all HCPs. Where in the medical school curriculum, nursing program, or the education of other HCPs do we explicitly teach ways to understand and nurture adherence, in both the practioner and the patient? The data reviewed herein documents that major strides in physical and mental health would accompany an increased level of adherence to procedures that are already available. Although much research is needed to develop and improve adherence enhancement measures, a body of information now exists to provide a promising beginning.

It is our fervent hope, and expectation, that the present volume will help to nurture a growing interest in treatment adherence and, most importantly, help translate such favorable intentions into action. As long as HCPs treat patients and not diseases; as long as they appreciate that they are ineluctably bound in a reciprocal relationship with their patients; as long as they think of collaboration, negotiation, and flexibility in their intercourse with their patients in order to achieve mutually desired outcomes, the level of treatment adherence will improve.

Epilogue

Writing this book has been a learning experience for us. As we tried to synthesize the vast literature on adherence, we became aware of the wide range of factors to be considered in formulating practical adherence enhancement guidelines. The dilemma we faced was that of providing breadth of coverage without overwhelming the reader. We have tried to straddle the fence by being somewhat detailed in our narrative but at the same time employing summary tables for easy access to central points.

Part of the complexity we noted in the available literature derived from the range of health prescriptive activities, acute illness, and chronic disease for which adherence is a central issue. That is, we considered adherence as it applied to the performance of such health-protective behavior as regular performance of breast self-examination, short-term medication regimens (e.g., ten days of amoxicillin for otitis media), self-care regimens necessary in living with chronic illnesses (e.g., diabetes mellitus, hypertension, bipolar affective disorders), termination of disease-promoting behaviors (e.g., cigarette smoking), as well as premature treatment termination and the failure to come to scheduled appointments. Moreover, we considered adherence from the relatively simple regimens (e.g., medication for hypertension) to much more complex self-care regimens (e.g., major life-style changes for people with end-stage renal disease).

Treatment nonadherence may occur for diverse reasons, and we have underscored the value of the HCP's conducting a careful adherence-oriented assessment prior to implementing a treatment regimen. It is essential to consider a *patient perspective* in understanding, preventing, and fostering treatment adherence. Developmental familial, social, and cultural factors have all been implicated and must be taken into account.

Further, we felt it important to emphasize the range of general variables that should be considered in our attempts to facilitate adherence, namely, patient variables, setting variables, HCP variables, and patient–HCP interaction variables. Hence our rationalization for the detail included in this text. Perhaps the most critical point that we hope to have made is that *facilitating adherence is an ongoing process* and not something that can be saisfactorily addressed by a brief discussion or a simple technique. HCPs must be adherence-oriented in all phases of their interactions with patients. A partnership, a collaboration between HCP, the patient, and significant others must be established and maintained if treatment adherence is to be expected.

We hope that the material herein will contribute to the process of adherence enhancement; however, this will occur only if HCPs themselves adhere to the specific behaviors that are prescribed. If there is one thing that we know for certain, it is that attitudinal change and good intentions are necessary but not by any means sufficient to produce the desired outcome. We hope that this book will serve to sensitize health care providers to the issue of adherence in general and to strengthen the adherence enhancement behavior of each reader in particular.

References

Abernathy, J. D. (1976). The problem of non-compliance in long-term anti-hypertensive therapy. *Drugs, 11,* 86–90.

Abram, H. S., Moore, G. L., & Westervelt, F. B. (1971). Suicidal behavior in chronic dialysis patients. *American Journal of Psychiatry, 127,* 1199–1204.

Adelman, H. S., & Taylor, L. (1986). Children's reluctance regarding treatment: Incompetence, resistance, or an appropriate response? *School Psychology Review, 15,* 91–99.

Alderman, M. H., & Schoenbaum, E. E. (1975). Detection and treatment of hypertension at the work site. *New England Journal of Medicine, 293,* 65–68.

Alfredson, L., Bergman, U., Erickson, R., Gronskog, K., Norell, S., Schwartz, E., & Wilholm, B. E. (1982). Theophyllins three times daily—when are the doses actually taken? *European Journal of Respiratory Disease, 63,* 234–238.

Amaral, P. L. (1986). The special case of compliance in the elderly. In K. E. Gerber & A. M. Nehemkis (Eds.), *Compliance: The dilemma of the chronically ill.* New York: Springer.

American Psychiatric Association. (1980). *Diagnostic and statistical manual of mental disorders* (3rd ed.). Washington, DC: Author.

Anderson, R. J., & Kirk, L. M. (1982). Methods of improving patient compliance in chronic disease states. *Archives of Internal Medicine, 142,* 1673–1675.

Ary, D. V., Toobert, D., Wilson, W., & Glasgow, R. E. (1986). Patient perspective on factors contributing to nonadherence to diabetes regimen. *Diabetes Care, 9,* 168–172.

Ascher, L. M., & Efran, J. S. (1978). Use of paradoxical intention in a behavioral program for sleep onset insomnia. *Journal of Consulting Psychology, 46,* 547–550.

Ascher, L. M., & Turner, R. M. (1979). Paradoxical intention and insomnia: An experimental investigator. *Behaviour Research and Therapy, 17,* 408–411.

Ascione, F., & Raven, R. (1975). Physicians' attitudes regarding patients' knowledge of prescribed medication. *Journal of American Pharmacy Association, 15,* 386–391.

Atkins, C. J., Kaplan, R. M., & Timms, R. M. (1981). *Behavioral programs for exercise compliance in chronic obstructive pulmonary disease.* Paper presented at the meeting of the American Psychological Association, Los Angeles.

Azrin, N. H., & Powell, J. (1969). Behavioral engineering: The use of response priming to improve prescribed self-medication. *Journal of Applied Behavior Analysis, 2,* 39–42.

Babani, L., Banis, H.T., Thompson, K. L., & Varni, J.W. (In press). Comprehensive assessment of long-term therapeutic adherence and recurrent pain in children and adolescents. *Educational and Treatment of Children.*

Baekeland, F., & Lundwall, L. (1975). Dropping out of treatment: A critical review. *Psychological Bulletin, 82,* 738–783.

Baglan, T., LaLumia, J., & Bayless, O. L. (1986). Utilization of compliance-gaining strategies: A research note. *Communications Monographs, 53,* 289–293.

Balint, M. (1968). *The doctor, his patient and the illness.* London: Pitman.

Bandura, A. (1977). Self-efficacy: Toward a unifying theory of behavioral change. *Psychological Review, 84,* 191–215.

Bandura, A. (1986). *Social foundations of thoughts and action: A social cognitive theory.* Englewood Cliffs, NJ: Prentice-Hall.

Bandura, A., & Simon, K. M. (1977). The role of proximal intentions in self-regulation of refractory behavior. *Cognitive Therapy and Research, 1,* 177–253.

Baranowski, T., & Nader, P. R. (1985a). Family health behavior. In D. C. Turk & R. D. Kerns (Eds.), *Health, illness, and family.* New York: Wiley-Interscience.

Baranowski, T., & Nader, P. R. (1985b). Family involvement in health behavior change. In D. C. Turk and R. D. Kerns (Ed.), *Health, illness, and family.* New York: Wiley-Interscience.

Barnes, M. R. (1976). Token economy control of fluid overload in a patient receiving hemodialysis. *Journal of Behavior Therapy and Experimental Psychiatry, 7,* 305–306.

Barnlund, D. C. (1976). The mystification of meaning: Doctor–patient encounters. *Journal of Medical Education, 51,* 716–625.

Barofsky, I. (Ed.). (1977). *Medication noncompliance.* Thorofare, NJ: C. B. Slack.

Barofsky, I. (1978). Compliance, adherence and the therapeutic alliance: Steps in the development of self-care. *Social Science and Medicine, 12,* 369–376.

Becker, M. H. (1974). The health belief model and sick role behavior. *Health Education Monograph, 2,* 409–419.

Becker, M. H., & Green, L. (1975). A family approach to compliance with medical treatment: A selective review of the literature. *International Journal of Health Education, 18,* 173–183.

Becker, M. H., & Maiman, L. A. (1975). Sociobehavioral determinants of compliance with health and medical care recommendations. *Medical Care, 13,* 10–25.

Becker, M. H., & Maiman, L. A. (1980). Strategies for enhancing patient compliance. *Journal of Community Health, 6,* 113–135.

Becker, M. H., & Rosenstock, I. M. (1984). Compliance with medical advice. In A. Steptoe & A. Mathews (Eds.), *Health care and human behavior.* New York: Academic Press.

Becker, M. H., Haefner, D. P., Kasl, S. V., Kirscht, M. P., Maiman, L. A., & Rosenstock, I. M. (1977). Selected psychosocial models and correlates of individual-health-related behaviors. *Medical Care, 15,* 27–46.

Ben-Sira, Z. (1976). The function of the professional's affective behavior in client satisfaction: A revised approach to social interaction theory. *Journal of Health and Social Behavior, 17,* 3–11.

Ben-Sira, Z. (1980). Affective and instrumental components in the physician-patient relationship: An additional dimension of interaction theory. *Journal of Health and Social Behavior, 21,* 170–180.

Benjamin-Bauman, J., Reiss, M. L., & Bailey, J. S. (1984). Increasing appointment keeping by reducing the call–appointment interval. *Journal of Applied Behavior Analysis, 17,* 295–301.

Benson, R. (1975). The forgotten treatment modality in bipolar illness: Psychotherapy. *Diseases of the Nervous System, 36,* 634–638.

Best, J. A., Bass, F., & Owen, L. E. (1977). Mode of service delivery in a smoking cessation programme for public health. *Canadian Journal of Public Health, 68,* 469–473.

Bieglow, G., Strickler, D., Liebson, I., & Griffith, R. (1976). Maintaining disulfiram injection among outpatient alcoholics: A security-deposit contingency contracting procedure. *Behaviour Research and Therapy, 14,* 378–38.

Blackburn, S. L. (1977). Dietary compliance of chronic hemodialysis patients. *Journal of American Dietetic Association, 70,* 31–37.

Blackwell, B. (1972). The drug defaulter. *Clinical Pharmacology Therapy, 13,* 841–848.

Blackwell, B. (1973). Drug therapy: Patient compliance. *New England Journal of Medicine, 289,* 245–251.

Blackwell, B. (1979). Treatment adherence: A contemporary viewpoint. *Psychosomatics, 20,* 27–35.

Boczkowski, J. A., Zeichner, A., & DeSanto, N. (1985). Neuroleptic compliance among chronic schizophrenic outpatients: An intervention outcome report. *Journal of Consulting and Clinical Psychology, 53,* 666–671.

Boehnert, C. E., & Popkin, M. K. (1986). Psychological issues in treatment of severely noncompliant diabetics. *Psychosomatics, 27,* 11–20.

Boyd, J. R., Covington, J. R., Stanaszek, W. F., & Coussons, R. T. (1974). Drug defaulting: II. Analysis of noncompliance patterns. *American Journal of Hospital Pharmacy, 31,* 485–491.

Brand, F., & Smith, R. (1974). Medical care and compliance among the elderly after hospitalization. *International Journal of Aging and Human Development, 5,* 331–346.

Brehm, J. W. (1966). *A theory of psychological reactance.* New York: Academic Press.

Brigg, E. H., & Mudd, E. H. (1968). An exploration of methods to reduce broken first appointments. *Family Coordination, 17,* 41–46.

Brigham, T. A. (1982). *Managing everyday problems: A manual of applied psychology for young people.* Unpublished manuscript, Washington State University, Pullman, Washington.

Brody, D. S. (1980a). The patient's role in clinical decision making. *Annals of Internal Medicine, 93,* 718–722.

Brody, D. S. (1980b). Feedback from patients as means of teaching the non-technological aspects of medical care. *Journal of Medical Education, 55,* 34–41.

Brook, R. H., & Williams, K. N. (1976). Effect of medical care review on the use of injections: A study of the New Mexico Experimental Medical Care Review Organization. *Annals of Internal Medicine, 85,* 509.

Brown, R. T., Borden, K. A., & Clingerman, S. R. (1985). Adherence to methylphenidate therapy in a pediatric population: A preliminary investigation. *Psychopharmacology Bulletin, 21.*

Brownell, K. D. (In press). Behavioral, psychological and environmental predictors of obesity and success at weight reduction. *International Journal of Obesity.*

Brownell, K. D., & Foreyt, J. P. (1985). Obesity. In D. Barlow (Ed.), *Clinical handbook of psychological disorders.* New York: Guilford Press.

Brownell, K. D., Heckerman, C. L., Westlake, R. J., Hayes, S. C., & Monti, P. M. (1978). The effect of couples training and partner cooperativeness in behavioral treatment of obesity. *Behaviour Research and Therapy, 16,* 323–333.

Brownell, K. D., Cohen, R. Y., Stunkard, A. J., Felix, M. R., & Cooley, N. B. (1984). Weight loss competitions at the work site: Impact on weight, morale and cost-effectiveness. *American Journal of Public Health, 74,* 1283–1285.

Brownell, K. D., Marlatt, G. A., Lichtenstein, E., & Wilson, G. T. (1986). Understanding and preventing relapse. *American Psychologist, 41,* 765–782.

Bruhn, J. G., & Phillips, B. V. (1984). Measuring social support: A synthesis of current approaches. *Journal of Behavioral Medicine, 7,* 157–169.

Buckalew, L. W., & Coffield, K. E. (1982). An investigation of drug expectancy as a function of capsule color and size and preparation form. *Journal of Clinical Psychopharmacology, 2,* 245–248.

Buckalew, L. W., & Sallis, R. E. (1986). Patient compliance and medication perception. *Journal of Clinical Psychology, 42,* 49–53.

Burstein, A. (1986). Treatment noncompliance in patients with post-traumatic stress disorder.*Psychosomatics, 27,* 37–41.

Burstein, B. (1985). Medication nonadherence due to feeling of loss of control in "biological depression." *American Journal of Psychiatry, 142,* 244–245.

Cade, B. (1984). Paradoxical techniques in therapy. *Journal of Child Psychology and Psychiatry, 25,* 509–516.

Caldwell, J. L., Cobb, S., Dowling, M. D., & Jongh, D. (1970). The dropout problem in antihypertensive treatment. *Journal of Chronic Disease, 22,* 579–592.

Cameron, R. (1978). The clinical implementation of behavior change techniques: A cognitively oriented conceptualization of therapeutic "compliance" and "resistance." In J. P. Foreyt & D. P. Rathjen (Eds.), *Cognitive behavior therapy: Research and application.* New York: Plenum Press.

Caplan, R. D. (1979). Patient, provider and organization: Hypothesized determinants of adherence. In S. J. Cohen (Ed.), *New directions in patient compliance.* Lexington, MA: Lexington Books.

Carney, R. M., Schechter, K., & Davis, T. (1983). Improving adherence to blood glucose testing in insulin-dependent diabetic children. *Behavior Therapy, 14,* 247–254.

Caron, H. S. (1985). Compliance: The case for objective measurement. *Journal of Hypertension, 3,* 11–17.

Cassata, D. M. (1978). Health communication theory and research: An overview of the communication specialist interface. In D. Nimmo (Ed.), *Communication yearbook II.* New York: ICA,

Caton, C. (1984). *Management of chronic schizophrenia.* New York: Oxford University Press.

Cerkoney, A. B., & Hart, K. (1980). The relationship between the health belief model and compliance of persons with diabetes mellitus. *Diabetes Care, 3,* 594–598.

Chan, D. W. (1984). Medication compliance in a Chinese psychiatric outpatient setting. *British Journal of Medical Psychology, 57,* 81–89.

Chaney, E., O'Leary, M., & Marlatt, G. A. (1978). Skill training with alcoholics. *Journal of Consulting and Clinical Psychology, 46,* 1092–1104.

Chapin, C. V. (1915). Truth in publicity. *American Journal of Public Health, 5,* 453–502.

Christensen, D. B., & Wertheimer, A. I. (1979). Sources of information and influence of new drug prescribing among physicians in an H.M.O. *Social Science and Medicine, 134,* 313.

Christensen-Szalanski, J. J. J., & Northcraft, G. B. (1985). Patient compliance behavior: The effects of time on patients' values of treatment regimens. *Social Science Medicine, 21,* 263–273.

Cialdini, R. B. (1984). *Influence: How and why people agree to things.* New York: William Morrow.

Claerhout, S., & Lutzker, J. R. (1981). Increasing children's self-initiated compliance to dental regimens. *Behavior Therapy, 12,* 165–176.

Clute, K. F. (1963). *The general practitioner: A study of medical education and practice in Ontario and Nova Scotia.* Toronto: University of Toronto Press.

Cochran, S. D. (1984). Preventing medical noncompliance in the outpatient treatment of bipolar affective disorders. *Journal of Consulting and Clinical Psychology, 52,* 873–876.

Cochran, S. D. (1986). Compliance with lithium regimens in the outpatient treatment of bipolar affective disorders. *Journal of Compliance in Health Care, 1,* 153–170.

Cohen, S. J. (1979). *New directions in patient compliance.* Lexington, MA: Lexington Books.

Cohen, S. J., Weinberger, M., Hui, L. S., Tierney, W. M., & McDonald, C. J. (1985). The impact of reading on physicians' nonadherence to recommended standards of medical care. *Social Science and Medicine, 21,* 909–914.

Coleman, V. R. (1985). Physician behavior and compliance. *Journal of Hypertension, 3,* 69–71.

Colletti, G., & Brownell, K. D. (1982). The physical and emotional benefits of social support: Applications to obesity, smoking and alcoholism. In M. Hersen, R. M. Eisler, & P. M. Miller (Eds.), *Progress in behavior modification* (Vol. 16). New York: Academic Press.

Condiotte, M. M., & Lichtenstein, E. (1981). Self-efficacy and relapse in smoking cessation programs. *Journal of Consulting and Clinical Psychology, 49,* 648–658.

Conrad, P. (1985). The meaning of medications: Another look at compliance. *Social Science Medicine, 20,* 29–37.

Conroy, W.J. (1979). Human values, smoking behavior, and public health programs. In M. Rokeach (Ed.), *Understanding human values.* New York: Free Press.

Cox, D. J., Gonder-Frederick, L., Pohl, S., & Pennebaker, J. W. (1984). Adult diabetes: Critical issues for applied research and clinical intervention. In K. A. Holroyd & T. L. Creer (Eds.), *Self-management of chronic disease: Handbook of clinical interventions and research.* New York: Academic Press.

Craighead, L. W., & Craighead, W. E. (1980). Implications of persuasive communication research for the modification of self-statements. *Cognitive Therapy and Research, 4*, 117–134.

Croog, S. H., Shapiro, D. S., & Levine, S. (1971). Denial among male heart patients. *Psychosomatic Medicine, 33*, 385–397.

Cummings, K. M., Becker, M. H., Kirscht, J. P., & Levin, N. W. (1981). Intervention strategies to improve compliance with medical regimens by ambulatory hemodialysis patients. *Journal of Behavioral Medicine, 4*, 111–127.

Cyr, J. G., & McLean, W. (1978). Patient knowledge of prescription medication. *Canadian Pharmacological Association, 17*, 361–363.

Czajkowski, D. R., & Koocher, G. P. (1986). Predicting medical compliance among adolescents with cystic fibrosis. *Health Psychology, 5*, 297–305.

Dale, E., & Chall, J. A. (1948). A formula for predicting readability. *Educational Research Bulletin, 27*, 11–20.

Dapcich-Miura, A., & Hovell, M. F. (1979). Contingency management of adherence to a complex medical regimen in an elderly heart patient. *Behavior Therapy, 10*, 193–201.

Davenport, Y. B., Ebert, M. H., Adland, M. L., & Goodwin, F. K. (1977). Couples group therapy as an adjunct to lithium maintenance of the manic patient. *American Journal of Orthopsychiatry, 47*, 495–502.

Davidson, P. O. (1976). Therapeutic compliance. *Canadian Psychological Review, 17*, 247–259.

Davis, J. R., & Glaros, A. G. (1986). Relapse prevention and smoking cessation. *Addictive Behaviors, 11*, 105–114.

Davis, M. S. (1966). Variations in patients' compliance with doctor's advice: Analysis of congruence between survey responses and results of empirical observations. *Journal of Medical Education, 41*, 1037–1048.

Davis, M. S. (1968). Variations in patients' compliance with doctors' advice: An empirical analysis of patterns of communication. *American Journal of Public Health, 58*, 274–288.

Deaton, A. V. (1985). Adaptive noncompliance in pediatric asthma: The parent as expert. *Journal of Pediatric Psychology, 10*, 1–14.

DeDombal, F. T., Leaper, D. J., & Horrocks, J. C. (1974). Human and computer-aided diagnosis of abdominal pain: Further report with emphasis on performance of clinicians. *British Medical Journal, 1*, 376.

DiMatteo, M. R., & DiNicola, D. D. (1982a). *Achieving patient compliance: The psychology of the medical practitioner's role.* New York: Pergamon Press.

DiMatteo, M. R., & DiNicola, D. D. (1982b). Social science and the art of medicine: From Hippocrates to holism. In H. S. Friedman & M. R. DiMatteo (Eds.), *Interpersonal issues in health care.* New York: Academic Press.

DiMatteo, M. R., Hays, R. D., & Prince, L. M. (1986). Relationship of physicians' nonverbal communication skill to patient satisfaction, appointment noncompliance, and physician workload. *Health Psychology, 5,* 581–594.

DiMatteo, M. L., & Hays, R. (1981). Sound support and serious illness. In B. Gottlieb (Ed.), *Social networks and social support.* Beverly Hills, CA: Sage Publications.

Dinoff, M., Rickard, N. C., & Colwick, J. (1972). Weight reduction through successive contracts. *American Journal of Orthopsychiatry, 42,* 110–113.

Dishman, R. K. (1982). Compliance/adherence in health-related exercise. *Health Psychology, 1,* 237–267.

Dowd, E. T., & Milne, C. R. (1986). Paradoxical interventions in counseling psychology. *Counseling Psychologist, 14,* 237–282.

Duer, J. D. (1982). Prompting women to seek cervical cytology. *Behavior Therapy, 13,* 248–253.

Dunbar, J. (1979). Issues in assessment. In S. J. Cohen (Ed.), *New directions in patient compliance.* Lexington, MA: D. C. Heath.

Dunbar, J. M., & Agras, W. S. (1980). Compliance with medical instructions. In J. M. Ferguson & C. B. Taylor (Eds.), *Comprehensive handbook of behavioral medicine* (Vol. 3). New York: Spectrum.

Dunbar, J. M., & Stunkard, A. J. (1979). Adherence to diet and drug regimen. In R. Levy, B. Rifkind, B. Dennis, and N. Ernst (Eds.), *Nutrition, lipids, coronary heart disease.* New York: Raven Press.

Dunbar, J. M., Marshall, G. D., & Hovell, M. F. (1979). Behavioral strategies for improving compliance. In R. B. Haynes, D. W. Taylor, & D. L. Sackett (Eds.), *Compliance in health care.* Baltimore: Johns Hopkins University Press.

D'Zurilla, T. (1986). *Problem-solving therapy: A social competence approach to clinical interventions.* New York: Springer.

Eaton, D. L. (1974). NIE attacks the reading and language skills problem. *American Education,* May.

Edwards, M., & Pathy, N. J. (1984). Drug counseling in the elderly and predicting compliance. *The Practitioner, 228,* 291–300.

Eisenthal, S., Emery, R., Lazare, A., & Udin, H. (1979). Adherence and the negotiated approach to patienthood. *Archives of General Psychiatry, 36,* 393–398.

Epstein, L. H., & Clúss, P. A. (1982). A behavioral medicine perspective on adherence to long-term medical regimens. *Journal of Consulting and Clinical Psychology, 50,* 960–971.

Epstein, L. H.; & Masek, B. J. (1978). Behavioral control of medicine compliance. *Journal of Applied Behavior Analysis, 11,* 1–9.

Epstein, L. H., & Ossip, D. J. (1979). Health care delivery: A behavioral perspective. In J. R. McNamara (Ed.), *Behavioral approaches to medicine.* New York: Plenum Press.

Epstein, L. H., & Wing, R. R. (1979). Behavioral contracting. Health behaviors. *Clinical Behavior Therapy Review, 1*, 2–21.

Epstein, L. H., Beck, S., Figueroa, J., Farkas, G., Kazdin, A. E., Daneman, D., & Becker, D. (1981). The effects of targeting improvements in urine glucose on metabolic control in children with insulin-dependent diabetes. *Journal of Applied Behavior Analysis, 14*, 365–375.

Epstein, L. H., Figueroa, J., Farkas, G. M., & Beck, S. (1981). The short-term effects of feedback on accuracy of urine glucose determinants in insulin-dependent diabetic children. *Behavior Therapy, 12*, 560–564.

Epstein, L. H., Wing, R. R., Woodall, B. C., Penner, B. C., Kress, M. J., & Koeske, R. (1985). Effects of a family-based behavioral treatment on obese 5- to 8-year-old children. *Behavior Therapy, 16*, 205–212.

Eraker, S. A., Kirscht, J. P., & Becker, M. H. (1984). Understanding and improving patient compliance. *Annals of Internal Medicine, 100*, 258–268.

Erickson, M. H. (1965). The use of symptoms as an integral part of psychotherapy. *American Journal of Clinical Hypnosis, 8*, 57–65.

Faberow, N. L. (1986). Noncompliance as indirect self-destructive behavior. In K. E. Gerber & A. M. Nehemkis (Eds.), *Compliance: The dilemma of the chronically ill.* New York: Springer.

Fawcett, J., & Epstein, P. (1983). *Clinical management: Imipramine–placebo administration manual.* Unpublished manuscript, Rush Presbyterian St. Luke's Medical Center, Chicago, Illinois.

Fielding, J. E., & Breslow, L. (1983). Health promotion programs sponsored by California employers. *American Journal of Public Health, 73*, 538–542.

Finn, P. E., & Alcorn, J. D. (1986). Noncompliance to hemodialysis dietary regimens: Literature review and treatment recommendations. *Rehabilitation Psychology, 31*, 67–79.

Fink, D. (1976). Tailoring the consensual regimen. In D. L. Sackett & R. B. Haynes (Eds.), *Compliance with therapeutic regimens.* Baltimore: Johns Hopkins University Press.

Finnerty, J. W., Friman, P. C., Rapoff, M. A., (1985). Improving compliance with antibiotic regimens for otitis media: Randomized clinical trial in a pediatric clinic. *American Journal of Diseases of Childhood, 139*, 89–95.

Fireman, P., Friday, G. A., Gira, C., Vierthaler, W. A., & Michaels, L. (1981). Teaching self-management skills to asthmatic children and their parents in an ambulatory care setting. *Pediatrics, 68*, 341–348.

Firestone, P. (1982). Factors associated with children's adherence to stimulant medication. *American Journal of Orthopsychiatry, 52*, 447–457.

Fitzgerald, R. G. (1972). Mania as a message: Treatment with family therapy and lithium carbonate. *American Journal of Psychotherapy, 26*, 547–554.

Flesch, R. (1948). A new readability yardstick. *Journal of Applied Psychology, 32,* 221–233.

Fontana, A. F., Kerns, R. D., Rosenberg, R. L., Marcus, J. L., & Colonese, K. L. (1986). Exercise training for cardiac patients: Adherence, fitness and benefits. *Journal of Cardiopulmonary Rehabilitation, 6,* 4–15.

Fox, E. M. (1977). Drug compliance in the elderly. *British Medical Journal, 1,* 578.

Francis, V., Korsch, B. M., & Morris, M. J. (1969). Gaps in doctor–patient communication. *New England Journal of Medicine, 280,* 535–540.

Freedman, J. L., & Fraser, S. C. (1966). Compliance without pressure: The foot-in-the-door technique. *Journal of Personality and Social Psychology, 4,* 195–202.

Friedman, H. S. (1979). Nonverbal communication between patients and medical practitioners. *Journal of Social Issues, 35,* 82–99.

Friedman, H. S., & DiMatteo, M. R. (Eds.). (1982). *Interpersonal issues in health care.* New York: Academic Press.

Friedman, I. M., & Litt, I. F. (1986). Promoting adolescents' compliance with therapeutic regimens. *Prevention in Primary Care, 33,* 955–972.

Funch, D. P., & Gale, E. N. (1986). Predicting treatment completion in a behavioral therapy program for chronic temporomandibular pain. *Journal of Psychosomatic Research, 30,* 57–62.

Gabriel, N., Gagnon, J. I., & Bryan, C. K. (1977). Improving patient compliance through use of daily reminder charts. *American Journal of Public Health, 67,* 968–969.

Galazka, S. S., & Eckert, J. K. (1984). Diabetes mellitus from the inside out: Ecological perspectives on a chronic disease. *Current Issues in Family Systems Medicine, 2,* 28–36.

Garfield, S. L. (1980). *Psychotherapy: An eclectic approach.* New York: Wiley.

Garrity, T. F. (1981). Medical compliance and the clinician–patient relationship: A review. *Social Science Medicine, 15,* 215–222.

Garrity, T. F., & Garrity, A. R. (1985). The nature and efficacy of intervention studies in the national high blood pressure education research program. *Journal of Hypertension, 3,* 91–95.

Geersten, H. R., Gray, R. M., & Ward, J. R. (1973). Patient compliance within the context of medical care for arthritis. *Journal of Chronic Diseases, 26,* 689–698.

Gentry, W. D. (1976). Parents as modifiers of somatic disorders. In E. J. Mash, L. C. Handy, & C. A. Hamerlynck (Eds.), *Behavior modification approaches to parenting.* New York: Brunner/Mazel.

Gerber, K. E., & Nehemkis, A. M. (Eds.) (1986). *Compliance: The dilemma of the chronically ill.* New York: Springer.

German, P. S., Klein, L. E., McPhee, S. J., & Smith, C. R. (1982). Knowledge of and compliance with drug regimens in the elderly. *Journal of the American Geriatric Society, 30,* 568–571.

German, E., Powell, C., Varni, J. W. (1985). Adherence to therapeutic exercise by children with haemophilia. Unpublished manuscript, University of Southern California at Los Angeles.

Gervasio, A. H. (1986). Family relationship and compliance. In K. E. Gerber & A. M. Nehemkis (Eds.), *Compliance: The dilemma of the chronically ill.* New York: Springer.

Gilchrist, L. D., Schinke, S. P., Bobo, J. K., & Snow, W. H. (1986). Self-control skills for preventing smoking. *Addictive Behaviors, 11,* 169–174.

Gillum, R. F., & Barsky, A. J. (1974). Diagnosis and management of patient noncompliance. *Journal of American Medical Association, 228,* 1563–1567.

Glasgow, R. E., McCaul, K. D., & Schafer, L. C. (1986). Barriers to regimen adherence among persons with insulin-dependent diabetes. *Journal of Behavioral Medicine, 9,* 65–77.

Glasgow, R. E., Schafer, L., & O'Neill, H. K. (1981). Self-help books and amount of therapist contact in smoking cessation programs. *Journal of Consulting and Clinical Psychology, 49,* 659–667.

Goldfried, M. R. (1982). Resistance and clinical behavior therapy. In P. L. Wachtel (Ed.), *Resistance: Psychodynamic and behavioral approaches.* New York: Plenum Press.

Goldsmith, C. H. (1976). The effect of differing compliance distributions on the planning and statistical analysis of therapeutic trials. In D. L. Sackett & R. B. Haynes (Eds.), *Compliance with therapeutic regimens.* Baltimore: Johns Hopkins University Press.

Gonder-Frederick, L., Cox, D. J., Pohl, S. L., & Carter, W. (1984). Patient blood glucose monitoring: Use, accuracy, adherence and impact. *Behavioral Medicine Update, 6,* 8–11.

Gordis, L. (1976). Methodological issues in the measurement of patient compliance. In D. L. Sackett & R. B. Haynes (Eds.), *Compliance with therapeutic regimens.* Baltimore: Johns Hopkins University Press.

Graber, A. L., Christman, B. G., Alagna, M. T., & Davidson, J. K. (1977). Evaluation of diabetes patient-education programs. *Diabetes, 26,* 61–64.

Grady, K. E., Kegeles, S. S., & Lund, A. K. (1981). Experimental studies to increase BSE: Preliminary findings. In C. Mettlin and G. P. Murphy (Eds.), *Issues in cancer screening and communications.* New York: Alan R. Liss.

Green, L. W. (1979). Educational strategies to improve compliance with therapeutic and preventive regimens: The recent evidence. In R. B. Haynes, D. W Taylor, & D. L. Sackett (Eds.), *Compliance in health care.* Baltimore: Johns Hopkins University Press.

Greenan-Fowler, E., Powell, C., & Varni, J. W. (1986). Adherence to therapeutic exercise in children with hemophilia. Unpublished manuscript, University of Southern California, Los Angeles, California.

Griffin, M. (1985). Paradoxical intervention in psychotherapy. *Australian Psychologist, 20,* 263–282.

Grimm, R. H., Shimoni, K., & Harlan, W. R. (1975). Evaluation of patient care protocol use by various providers, *New England Journal of Medicine, 292,* 507.

Gross, A. M., Magalnick, L. J., & Richardson, P. (1985). Self-management training with families of insulin-dependent diabetic children: A controlled long-term investigation. *Child and Family Behavior Therapy, 7,* 35–50.

Gross, A. M., Samson, G., & Dierkes, M. (1985). Patient cooperation in treatment with removable appliances: A model of patient non-compliance with treatment implications. *American Journal of Orthodontics, 87,* 392–397.

Gundert-Remy, U., Remy, C., & Weber, E. (1976). Serum digoxin levels in patients of a general practice in Germany. *European Journal of Clinical Pharmacy, 10,* 97–100.

Guptill, P. B., & Graham, F. E. (1976). Continuing education activities of physicians in solo and group practices. *Medical Care, 14,* 173–176.

Hagen, R. L., Foreyt, J. P., & Durham, T. W. (1976). The dropout problem: Reducing attrition in obesity research. *Behavior Therapy, 7,* 463–471.

Haley, J. (1963). *Strategies of psychotherapy.* New York: Grune & Stratton.

Hanson, R. W. (1986). Physician–patient communication and compliance. In K. E. Gerber & A. M. Nehemkis (Eds.), *Compliance: The dilemma of the chronically ill,* New York: Springer.

Hare, E. H., & Willcox, D. R. (1967). Do psychiatric inpatients take their pills? *British Journal of Psychiatry, 113,* 1435–1438.

Hare, R. L., & Barnoon, S. (1973). *Medical care appraisal and quality assurance in the office practice of internal medicine.* Paper presented at the meeting of the American Society of Internal Medicine, San Francisco.

Harris, J. E. (1978). External memory aids. In M. M. Gruneberg, P. E. Morris, & R. N. Sykes (Eds.), *Practical aspects of memory.* New York: Academic Press.

Harris, M. B., & Bruner, C. G. (1971). A comparison of self-control and a contract procedure for weight control. *Behaviour Research and Therapy, 9,* 347–354.

Hart, R. R. (1979). Utilization of token economy within a chronic dialysis unit. *Journal of Consulting and Clinical Psychology, 47,* 646–648.

Hays, R., DiMatteo, M. R. (1984). Toward a more therapeutic physician-patient relationship. In S. W. Duc (Ed.), *Personal Relationships* New York: Academic Press.

Hayes-Bautista, D. E. (1976). Modifying the treatment: Patient compliance, patient control and medical care. *Social Science and Medicine, 10,* 233–238.

Haynes, R. B. (1973). Contingency management in a municipally administered Antabuse program for alcoholics. *Journal of Behavior Therapy and Experimental Psychiatry, 4,* 31–32.

Haynes, R. B. (1976). Strategies for improving compliance: A methodological analysis and review. In D. C. Sackett & R. B. Haynes (Eds.), *Compliance with therapeutic regimens.* Baltimore: Johns Hopkins University Press.

Haynes, R. B. (1979a). A critical review of the "determinants" of patient compliance with therapeutic regimens. In R. B. Haynes, D. W. Taylor, & D. L. Sackett (Eds.), *Compliance in health care.* Baltimore: Johns Hopkins University Press.

Haynes, R. B. (1979b). Strategies to improve compliance with referrals, appointments and prescribed medical regimens. In R. B. Haynes, D. W. Taylor, & D. L. Sackett (Eds.), *Compliance in health care.* Balitimore: Johns Hopkins University Press.

Haynes, R. B. (1979c). Determinants of compliance: The disease and the mechanics of treatment. In R. B. Haynes, D. W. Taylor, & D. L. Sackett (Eds.), *Compliance in health care.* Baltimore: Johns Hopkins University Press.

Haynes, R. B., Sackett, D. L., Gibson, E. S., Taylor, D. W., Hackett, B. C., Roberts, R. S., & Johnson, A. L. (1976). Improvement of medication compliance in uncontrolled hypertension. *Lancet, 1,* 1265–1268.

Haynes, R. B., Taylor, D. W., & Sackett, D. L. (1979). (Eds.), *Compliance in health care.* Baltimore: Johns Hopkins University Press.

Haynes, R. B., Davis, D. A., McKibbon, A., & Rugwell, P. A. (1984). A critical appraisal of the efficacy of continuing education. *Journal of the American Medical Association, 251,* 61–64.

Haynes, S. N. (1974). Contingency management in a municipally administered Antabuse program for alcoholics. *Journal of Behavior Therapy and Experimental Psychiatry, 4,* 31–32.

Heath, C. (1984). Participation in the medical consultation: The coordination of verbal and nonverbal behavior between the doctor and patient. *Sociology of Health and Illness, 6,* 311–338.

Heiby, E. M., & Carlson, J. G. (1986). The health compliance model. *Journal of Compliance in Health Care, 1,* 135–152.

Henderson, J. B., Hall, S. M., & Lipton, H. L. (1979). Changing self-destructive behaviors. In G. C. Stone, F. Cohen, & N. E. Adler (Eds.), *Health psychology.* San Francisco: Jossey-Bass.

Hertz, C. G., Bernheim, J. W., & Perloff, T. N. (1976). Patient participation in the problem-oriented system: A health care plan. *Medical Care, 14,* 77–79.

Higbee, K. (1969). Fifteen years of fear arousal: Research on threat appeals. *Psychological Bulletin, 72,* 426–440.

Higbee, M., Dukes, G., & Bosso, J. (1982). Patient recall of physician's prescription instructions. *Hospital Formulary, 17,* 553–556.

Hingson, R. (1977). The physician's problems in identifying potentially noncompliant patients. In I. Barofsky (Ed.), *Medication compliance.* Thorofare, NJ: C. B. Slack.

Hoelscher, T. J., Lichstein, K. L., & Rosenthal, T. L. (1984). Objective vs. subjective assessment of relaxation compliance among anxious individuals. *Behaviour Research and Therapy, 22,* 187–193.

Hoelscher, T. J., Lichstein, K. L., & Rosenthal, T. L. (1986). Home relaxation practice in hypertension treatment: Objective assessment and compliance induction. *Journal of Consulting and Clinical Psychology, 54,* 217–221.

Hoenig, F., & Ragg, N. (1966). The non-attending psychiatric outpatient: An administrative problem. *Medical Care, 4,* 96–100.

Hogue, C. C. (1979). Nursing and compliance. In R. B. Haynes, D. W. Taylor, & D. L. Sackett (Eds.), *Compliance in health care.* Baltimore: Johns Hopkins University Press.

Holder, L. (1972). Effects of source, message, and audience characteristics on health behavior compliance. *Health Services Reports, 87,* 343–350.

Hoyt, M. F., & Janis, I. L. (1975). Increasing adherence to a stressful decision via a motivational balance sheet procedure: A field experiment. *Journal of Personality and Social Psychology, 31,* 833–839.

Hunt, W. A., & Bespalec, D. A. (1974). An evaluation of current methods of modifying smoking behavior. *Journal of Clinical Psychology, 30,* 431–438.

Hussar, D. A. (1975). Patient noncompliance. *Journal of the American Pharmaceutical Association, 15,* 183–190.

Inui, T. S., Yourtee, E. L., & Williamson, J. W. (1976). Improved outcomes in hypertension after physician tutorials: A controlled trial. *Annals of Internal Medicine, 84,* 646–651.

Israel, A. C., Stolmaker, L., Sharp, J. P., Silverman, W. K., & Simon, L. G. (1984). An evaluation of two methods of parental involvement in treating obese children. *Behavior Therapy, 15,* 266–272.

Janis, I. L. (Ed.). (1982). *Counseling on personal decisions: Theory and research on short-term helping relationships.* New Haven, CT: Yale University Press.

Janis, I. L. (1983). The role of social support in adherence to stressful decisions. *American Psychologist, 38,* 143–160.

Janis, I. L. (1984a). Improving adherence to medical recommendations: Prescriptive hypotheses derived from recent research in social psychology. In A. Baum, S. E. Taylor, & J. E. Singer (Eds.), *Handbook of psychology and health. Vol. 4. Social psychology of aspects of health.* Hillsdale, NJ: Erlbaum.

Janis, I. L. (1984b). The patient as decision maker. In W. D. Gentry (Ed.), *Handbook of behavioral medicine.* New York: Guilford Press.

Janis, I. L., & King, B. (1954). The influence of role-playing on opinion change. *Journal of Abnormal and Social Psychology, 49,* 211–218.

Janis, I. L., & Mann, L. (1977). *Decision making: A pschological analysis of conflict, choice and commitment.* New York: Free Press.

Janis, I., & Rodin, J. (1979). Attribution, control and decision making: Social psychology and health care. In G. C. Stone, F. Cohen, & N. E. Adler (Eds.), *Health psychology.* San Francisco: Jossey-Bass.

Janz, N. K., Becker, M. H., & Hartman, P. A. (1984). Contingency contracting to enhance patient compliance: A review. *Patient Education and Counseling, 5,* 165–178.

Jay, S., Litt, I. F., & Durant, R. H. (1984). Compliance with therapeutic regimens. *Journal of Adolescent Health Care, 5,* 124–136.

Jennings, R. M., & Ball, J. D. (1982). Patient compliance with CHAMPUS mental health referrals. *Professional Psychology, 13,* 172–173.

Joubert, P., & Lasagna, L. (1975). Patient package inserts: Nature, notions and needs. *Clinical Pharmacology and Therapeutics, 18,* 507–513.

Journal of the American Medical Association. (1979). Hypertension detection and followup program for HDFP. *242,* 2562–2571.

Jungfer, C. C., & Last, J. M. (1964). Clinical performance in Australian general practice. *Medical Care, 2,* 71.

Kanfer, F. H. (1977). The many faces of self-control, or behavior modification changes its focus. In R. B. Stuart (Ed.), *Behavioral self-management: Strategies, techniques and outcomes.* New York: Brunner/Mazel.

Kanfer, F. H., & Gaelick, L. (1986). Self-management methods. In F. H. Kanfer & A. P. Goldstein (Eds.), *Helping people change* (2nd ed.). New York: Pergamon Press.

Kaplan, R. M., Atkins, C. J., & Reinsch, S. (1984). Specific efficacy expectations mediate exercise compliance in patients with COPD. *Health Psychology, 3,* 223–242.

Kaplan De-Nour, A. (1986). Foreward. In K. E. Gerber & A. M Nehemkis (Eds.), *Compliance: The dilemma of the chronically ill.* New York: Springer.

Kaplan, R. M., Chadwick, M. W., & Schimmel, L. E. (1985). Social learning intervention to promote metabolic control in type 1 diabetes mellitas: Pilot experiment results. *Diabetes, 8,* 152–155.

Kaplan De-Nour, A., & Czaczkes, J. W. (1974). Personality and adjustment to chronic hemodialysis. In N. B. Levy (Ed.), *Living or dying: Adaptation to hemodialysis.* Springfield, IL: Charles C. Thomas.

Kasl, S. V. (1975). Issues in patient adherence to health care regimens. *Journal of Human Stress, 1,* 5–18.

Kayne, R.C., & Cheung, A. (1973). An application of clinical pharmacy in extended care facilities. In R. H. Davis and W. K. Smith (Eds.), *Drugs and the elderly.* Los Angeles: University of Southern California Press.

Kazdin, A. E., & Bootzin, R. R. (1972). The token economy: An evaluative review. *Journal of Applied Behavior Analysis, 5,* 343–372.

Kazdin, A. E., & Mascitelli, S. (1982). Covert and overt rehearsal and homework practice in developing assertiveness. *Journal of Consulting and Clinical Psychology, 50,* 250–258.

Keane, T. M., Prue, D. M., & Collins, F. L. (1981). Behavioral contracting to improve dietary compliance in chronic renal dialysis patients. *Journal of Behavior Therapy and Experimental Psychiatry, 12,* 63–67.

Kendrick, R., & Bayne, J. R. D. (1982). Compliance with prescribed medication by elderly patients. *Canadian Medical Association Journal, 127,* 961–962.

Kiesler, C. A. (Ed.). (1971). *The psychology of commitment.* New York: Academic Press.

Kirsch, I. (1982). Efficacy expectations or response predictions: The meaning of efficacy ratings as a function of task characteristics. *Journal of Personality and Social Psychology, 42,* 132–136.

Kirsch, I. (1985). Self-efficacy and expectancy: Old wine with new labels. *Journal of Personality and Social Psychology, 49,* 824–830.

Kirschenbaum, D. S. (1985). Proximity and specificity of planning: A position paper. *Cognitive Therapy and Research, 9,* 489–506.

Kirschenbaum, D. S., & Flanery, R. C. (1983). Behavioral contracting: Outcomes and elements. In M. Hersen, R. M. Eisler, & P. M. Miller (Eds.), *Progress in behavior modification* (Vol. 15). New York: Academic Press.

Kirschenbaum, D. S., & Flanery, R. C. (1984). Toward a psychology of behavioral contracting. *Clinical Psychology Review, 4,* 597–618.

Kirschenbaum, D. S., Harris, E. S., & Tomarken, A. J. (1984). Effects of parental involvement in behavioral weight loss therapy for preadolescents. *Behavior Therapy, 15,* 485–500.

Kirscht, J. P., & Rosenstock, I. M. (1979). Patients' problems in following recommendations of health experts. In G. C. Stone, F. Cohen, & N. E. Adler (Eds.), *Health psychology.* San Francisco: Jossey-Bass.

Kirscht, J. P., Kirscht, J. L., & Rosenstock, I. M. (1981). A test of interventions to increase adherence to hypertensive medical regimens. *Health Education Quarterly, 8,* 261–272.

Klein, R. H., & Carroll, R. A. (1986). Patient characteristics and attendance patterns in outpatient group psychotherapy. *International Journal of Group Psychotherapy, 36,* 115–132.

Kleinman, A. M. (1980). *Patients and healers in the context of culture.* Los Angeles: University of California Press.

Kopel, S., & Arkowitz, H. (1975). The role of attribution and self-perception in behavior change. *Genetic Psychology Monographs, 92,* 175–212.

Korsch, B. M., Gozzi, E. K., & Francis, V. (1968). Gaps in doctor–patient communication. *Pediatrics, 42,* 855–871.

Korsch, B. M., & Negrete, V. F. (1972). Doctor-patient communication. *Scientific American, 27,* 66–74.

Kovacs, M., & Feinberg, T. (1982). Coping with juvenile onset of diabetes mellitus. In A. Baum & J. Singer (Eds.), *Handbook of psychology and health* (Vol. 2). Hillsdale, NJ: Erlbaum.

Kristeller, J., & Rodin, J. (1984). The function of attention in cognitive models of behavior change and maintenance. In A. Baum, S. E. Taylor, & J. E. Singer (Eds.), *Handbook of psychology and health. Vol. 4: Social psychological aspects of health.* Hillsdale, NJ: Erlbaum.

Krupkat, E. (1983). The doctor–patient relationship: A social psychological analysis. In R. F. Kidd & M. J. Saks (Eds.), *Advances in applied social psychology.* Hillsdale, NJ: Erlbaum.

Krupat, E. (1986). Physicians and patients: A delicate imbalance. *Psychology Today, 20,* 22–26.

L'Abate, L., & Weeks, G. (1978). A bibliography of paradoxical methods in psychotherapy of family systems. *Family Process, 17,* 95–98.

Laolais, C. J., & Berry, C. C. (1969). Misuse of prescription medication by outpatients. *Drug Intelligence and Clinical Pharmacy, 3,* 270–277.

Larkin, E. J. (1974). *The treatment of alcoholism: Theory, practice and evaluation.* Toronto: Addiction Research Foundation Report.

Lawrence, P. A., & Cheely, J. (1980). Deterioration of diabetic patients' knowledge and management skills as determined during outpatient visits. *Diabetes Care, 3,* 214–218.

Lazare, A., Eisenthal, S., & Wasserman, L. (1975). The customer approach to patienthood. *Archives of General Psychiatry, 32,* 553–558.

Lee, C., & Owen, N. (1980). Use of psychological theories in understanding the adoption and maintenance of exercising. *Australian Journal of Science and Medicine in Sport, 18,* 22–25.

Leff, J., & Vaugh, C. (1985). *Expressed emotions in families.* New York: Guilford.

Leventhal, H. (1965). Fear communications in the acceptance of preventative health practices. *Bulletin of New York Academy of Medicine, 41,* 1144–1168.

Leventhal, H., & Nerenz, D. R. (1983). A model of stress research with some implications for the control of stress disorders. In D. Meichenbaum & M. Jaremko (Eds.), *Stress reduction and prevention.* New York: Plenum Press.

Leventhal, H., Singer, R. P., & Jones, S. H. (1965). The effects of fear and specificity of recommendations. *Journal of Personality and Social Psychology, 2,* 20–29.

Leventhal, H., Zimmerman, R., & Gutmann, M. (1984). Compliance: A self-regulation perspective. In W. D. Gentry (Ed.), *Handbook of behavioral medicine.* New York: Guilford Press.

Levine, D. M., Green, L. W., Deeds, S. G., Cualow, J., Finlay, J., & Morisky, D. E. (1979). Health education for hypertensive patients. *Journal of the American Medical Association, 241,* 1700—1703.

Levy, R. L. (1983). Social support and compliance: A selective review and critique of treatment integrity and outcome measurement. *Social Science and Medicine, 17,* 1329–1338.

Levy, R. L., & Carter, R. (1976). Compliance with practitioner instructions. *Social Work, 21,* 188–193.

Levy, R. L. (1985). Social Support and compliance: Update. *Hypertension, 3,* 45–49.

Levy, R. L. (1986). Social support and compliance: Salient methodological problems in compliance research. *Journal of Compliance in Health Care, 1,* 184–198.

Levy, R. L., & Loftus, G. R. (1984). Compliance and memory. In J. E. Harris & P. E. Morris (Eds.), *Everyday memory: Actions and absent-mindedness.* New York: Academic Press.

Lewis, C. E., & Minich, M. (1977). Contracts as a means of improving patient compliance. In I. Barofsky (Eds.), *Medication compliance: A behavioral management approach.* Thorofare, NJ: Charles B. Slack.

Ley, P. (1977). Psychological studies of doctor–patient communication. In S. Richman (Ed.), *Contributions to medical psychology* (Vol. 1). Oxford: Pergamon.

Ley, P. (1979). Memory for medical information. *British Journal of Social and Clinical Psychology, 18,* 245–255.

Ley, P. (1982). Giving information to patients. In J. R. Eiser (Ed.), *Social psychology and behavioral medicine.* New York: Wiley.

Ley, P., & Spelman, M. S. (1965). *Communicating with the patient.* London: Staples Press.

Ley, P., Jain, V. K., & Stalbeck, C. Z. (1976). A method for decreasing patients' medication errors. *Psychological Medicine, 6,* 599–601.

Ley, P. (1986). Cognitive variables and noncompliance. *Journal of Compliance in Health Care, 1,* 171–188.

Liberman, R. P., Eckman, T., & Phipps, C. C. (1986). *Protective interventions in schizophrenia: Combined neuroleptic drug therapy and medication self-management training.* Unpublished manuscript, UCLA Department of Psychiatry, Los Angeles, CA.

Lichtenstein, E. (1982). The smoking problem: A behavioral perspective. *Journal of Consulting and Clinical Psychology, 50,* 804–819.

Liddell, A., Mackay, W., Dawe, G., Galutira, B., Hearn, S., & Walsh-Doran, M. (1986). Compliance as a factor in outcome with agoraphobic clients. *Behaviour Research and Therapy, 24,* 217–220.

Lima, J., Nazarian, L., Charney, E., & Lahti, C. (1976). Compliance with short-term antimicrobial therapy: Some techniques that help. *Pediatrics, 57,* 383–386.

Lindell, S. G., & Rossi, M. A. (1986). Compliance with childbirth education classes in second stage labor. *Birth, 13,* 96–99.

Linkewich, J. A., Catalano, R. B., & Flack, H. L. (1974). The effect of packaging and instructions in outpatient compliance with medication regimens. *Drug Intelligence in Clinical Pharmacy, 8,* 10–15.

Litt, I. F., & Cuskey, W. R. (1980). Compliance with medical regimens during adolescence. *Pediatric Clinics of North America, 27,* 3–15.

Locke, E. A., Shaw, K. N., Saari, L. M., & Latham, G. P. (1981). Goal setting and task performance:1969–1980. *Psychological Bulletin, 90,* 125–152.

Lowe, K., & Lutzker, J. R. (1979). Increasing compliance to a medical regimen with a juvenile diabetic. *Behavior Therapy, 10,* 57–64.

Lund, M., Jorgensen, R. S., & Kuhl, V. (1964). Serum diphylhydantoin (Dilantin) in patients with epilepsy. *Epilepsy, 5,* 51–58.

Lund, A. K., & Kegeles, S. S. (1979). Partial reward schedules and self-management techniques in children's preventive dental programs. In B. Ingersoll & W. McCutcheon (Eds.), *Clinical research in behavioral dentistry.* Morgentown: West Virginia University Press.

Luscher, T. F., Vetter, H., Siegenthaler, W., & Vetter, W. (1985). Compliance in hypertension: Facts and concepts. *Journal of Hypertension (Supplement), 3,* 3–10.

Maccoby, N., Farquhar, J. W., Wood, P. D., & Alexander, J. (1977). Reducing the risk of cardiovascular disease: Effects of a community-based campaign on knowledge and behavior. *Journal of Community Health, 3,* 100–144.

Magrab, P. R., & Papadopoulou, Z. L. (1977). The effect of a token economy on dietary compliance for children on hemodialysis. *Journal of Applied Behavioral Analysis, 10,* 573–578.

Mahoney, M. J. (1971). The self-management of covert behavior: A case study. *Behavior Therapy, 2,* 575–578.

Malahey, B. (1966). The effects of instructions and labeling in the number of medication errors made by patients at home. *American Journal of Hospital Pharmacy, 23,* 283–292.

Manning, P. R., & Denson, T. A. (1979). How cardiologists learn about echocardiography: A reminder for medical educators and legislators. *Annual of Internal Medicine, 91,* 469.

Manning, P. R., & Denson, T. A. (1980). How internists learned about limetidine. *Annual of Internal Medicine, 97,* 80.

Marlatt, G. A., & George, W. H. (1984). Relapse prevention: Introduction and overview of the model. *British Journal of Addiction, 79,* 261–273.

Marlatt, G. A., & Gordon, J. R. (1985). *Relapse prevention: Maintenance strategies in the treatment of addictive behaviors.* New York: Guilford Press.

Marlatt, G. A., & Kaplan, B. E. (1972). Self-initiated attempts to change behavior: A study of New Year's resolutions. *Psychological Reports, 30,* 123–131.

Marston, M. V. (1970). Compliance with medical regimens: A review of the literature. *Nursing Research, 10*, 312–323.

Martin, G. A., & Worthington, E. L., Jr. (1982). *Homework assignment report.* Unpublished assessment instrument, Virginia Commonwealth University, Richmond, VA.

Martin, G. A., & Worthington, E. L., Jr. (1982b). Behavioral homework. In L. Mittersen, R. M. Eisler, & P. M. Miller (Eds.), *Progress in behavior modification* (Vol. 13). New York: Academic Press.

Martin, J. E., Collins, F. L., Hillenberg, J. B., Zabin, M. A., & Katell, A. D. (1981). Assessing compliance to home practice: A simple technology of a critical problem. *Journal of Behavioral Assessment, 3*, 193–198.

Martin, J. E., & Dubbert, P. M. (1986). Exercise and health: The adherence problem. *Behavioral Medicine Update, 4*, 16–24.

Martys, C. R. (1979). Adverse reactions to drugs in general practice. *British Medical Journal, 2*, 1194–1197.

Marwell, G., & Schmitt, D. R. (1967). Dimensions of compliance-gaining behavior: An empirical analysis. *Sociometry, 30*, 350–364.

Masek, B. J. (1982). Compliance and medicine. In D. M. Doleys, R. L. Meredith, & A. R. Ciminero (Eds.), *Behavioral medicine: Assessment and treatment strategies.* New York: Plenum Press.

Mattar, M. E., Markello, J., & Yaffe, S. J. (1975). Inadequacies in the pharmacologic management of ambulatory children. *Journal of Pediatrics, 87*, 137–141.

Matthews, D., & Hingson, R. (1977). Improving patient compliance: A guide for physicians. *Medical Clinics of North America, 61*, 879–889.

Mausner, B., & Platt, E. S. (1971). *Smoking: A behavioral analysis.* New York: Pergamon Press.

Mayer, J. A. (1986). Assessing breast self-examination compliance in the natural environment. *Journal of Behavioral Medicine, 9*, 363–371.

Mayer, J. A., & Frederiksen, L. W. (1986). Encouraging long-term compliance with breast self-examination: The evaluation of prompting strategies. *Journal of Behavioral Medicine, 9*, 179–189.

Mayerson, N. H. (1984). Preparing clients for group therapy: A critical review and theoretical formulation. *Clinical Psychology Review, 4*, 191–213.

Mazzuca, S. A. (1982). Does patient education in chronic disease have therapeutic value? *Journal of Chronic Disease, 35*, 521–529.

McDonald, C. J. (1976). Protocol-based computer reminders, the quality of care and the non-perfectability of man. *New England Journal of Medicine, 295*, 1351–1355.

McDonald, C. J. (1981). *Action-oriented decisions in ambulatory medicine.* New York: Year Book, 1981.

McDonald, C. J., Hui, S., Smith, D. M., Tierney, W. M., Cohen, S. J., Weinberger, M., & McCabe, G. P. (1984). Reminders to physicians from an introspective computer medical record: A two-year randomized trial. *Annals of Internal Medicine, 100*, 130–138.

McKenney, J. M. (1979). The clinical pharmacy and compliance. (1979). In R. B. Haynes, D. W. Taylor, & D. L. Sackett (Eds.), *Compliance in health care*. Baltimore: Johns Hopkins University Press.

McKenney, J. M., Slining, J. M., & Henderson, H. R., Devins, D., & Barr, M. (1973). The effects of clinical pharmacy services on patients with essential hypertension. *Circulation, 48*, 1104–1111.

Mechanic, D. (1964). The influence of mothers on their children's health attitudes and behaviors. *Pediatrics, 33*, 444–453.

Meichenbaum, D. (1977). *Cognitive-behavior modification: An integrative approach*. New York: Plenum Press.

Meichenbaum, D. (1985). *Stress inoculation training*. New York: Pergamon Press.

Meyers, A. W., Thackwray, D. E., Johnson, C. B., & Schlesser, R. (1983). A comparison of prompting strategies for improving appointment compliance in hypertensive individuals. *Behavior Therapy, 14*, 267–274.

Meyers, E. D., & Calvert, E. J. (1976). The effect of forewarning on the occurrence of side-effects and discontinuation of medication. *Journal of Internal Medicine Research, 4*, 237–240.

Miller, W. R. (1985). Motivation for treatment: A review with special emphasis on alcoholism. *Psychological Bulletin, 98*, 84–107.

Mitchell, H. J. (1974). Compliance with medical regimens: An annotated bibliography. *Health Education Monographs, 2*, 75–87.

Morisky, D. E. (1986). Nonadherence to medical recommendations for hypertensive patients. Problems and solutions. *Journal of Compliance in Health Care, 1*, 5–20.

Moos, R. H., & Moos, E. S. (1981). *Family Environment Scale manual*. Palo Alto, CA: Consulting Psychologists Press.

Morisky, D. E., Green, L. W., & Levine, D. M. (1986). Concurrent and predictive validity of a self-reported measure of medication adherence. *Medical Care, 24*, 67–74.

Morris, L. A., & Halperin, J. A. (1979). Effects of written drug information on patient knowledge and compliance: A literature review. *American Journal of Public Health, 69*, 47–52.

Moulding, T. (1962). Proposal for a time recording pill dispenser as a method for studying and supervising the self-administration of drugs. *American Review of Respiratory Diseases, 85*, 754–757.

Nehemkis, A. M., & Gerber, K. E. (1986). Compliance and the quality of survival. In K. E. Gerber & A. M. Nehemkis (Eds.), *Compliance: The dilemma of the chronically ill*. New York: Springer.

Nelson, R. (1977). Assessment and therapeutic functions of self-monitoring. In M. Hersen, R. Eisler, & P. Miller (Eds.), *Progress in behavior modification* (Vol. 5). New York: Academic Press.

Nessman, D. G., Carnahan, J. E., & Nugent, C. A. (1980). Increasing compliance: Patient-oriented hypertension groups. *Archives of Internal Medicine, 140*, 1427–1430.

O'Banion, D. R., & Whaley, D. L. (1981). *Behavior contracting: Arranging contingencies of reinforcement.* New York: Springer.

O'Farrell, T. J., & Keuthen, N. J. (1983). Readability of behavior therapy self-help manuals. *Behavior Therapy, 14,* 449–454.

Oldridge, N. B. (1979). Compliance with exercise programs. In M. C. Pollock & D. H. Schmidt (Eds.), *Heart disease and rehabilitation.* Boston: Houghton-Mifflin.

Oldridge, N. B. (1982). Compliance and exercise in primary or secondary prevention of coronary heart disease: A review. *Preventive Medicine, 11,* 56–70.

O'Leary, A. (1985). Self-efficacy and health. *Behaviour Research and Therapy, 23,* 437–451.

Olson, R. A., Zimmerman, J., & Reyes de la Rocha, S. (1985). Medical adherence in pediatric populations. In A. R. Zeiner, D. Bendell, & C. E. Walker (Eds.), *Health psychology: Treatment and research issues.* New York: Plenum Press.

Oppenheim, G. L., Bergman, J. J., & English, E. C. (1979). Failed appointments: A review. *Journal of Family Practice, 8,* 789–796.

Packard, R. C., & O'Connell, P. (1986). Medication compliance among headache patients. *Headache, 6,* 1416–1419.

Payne, B. C., Lyons, T. F., & Dwarshuis, L. (1976). *The quality of medical care: Evaluation and improvement.* Chicago: Hospital Research and Educational Trust.

Parsons, T. (1951). *The social system.* Glencoe, IL: Free Press.

Peck, C. L., & King, N. J. (1982). Increasing patient compliance with prescriptions. *Journal of the American Medical Association, 248,* 2874–2877.

Pelham, W., & Murphy, H. A. (1986). Attention deficit and conduct disorders. In M. Hersen (Ed.) *Pharmacological and behavioral treatments: An integrative approach.* New York: Wiley.

Pendelton, D. (1983). Doctor–patient communication: A review. In D. Pendelton & J. Hasler (Eds.), *Doctor–patient communication.* New York: Academic Press.

Pendelton, D., & Hasler, J. (1983). *Doctor–patient communication.* London: Academic Press.

Penry, J. K. (1978). Reliability of serum antiepileptic drug concentrations and partial management. In C. E. Pippenger, J. K. Penry, & H. Kutt (Eds.), *Antileptic drugs.* New York: Raven Press.

Peterson, C. M., Forhan, S. E., & Jones, R. L. (1980). Self-management: An approach to patients with insulin-dependent diabetes mellitis. *Diabetes Care, 3,* 82–87.

Peterson, D. (1968). *The clinical study of social behavior.* Englewood Cliffs, NJ: Prentice-Hall.

Pettegrew, L. S., & Turkat, I. D. (1986). How patients communicate about their illness. *Human Communication Research, 12,* 376–394.

Pfeiffer, E. (1980). Pharmacology of aging. In G. Lesnoff-Caravaghn (Ed.), *Health care of the elderly*. New York: Human Science Press.

Phillips, E. L. (1986). *Are theories of psychotherapy possible?* Paper presented at the Fifth National Conference on Cognitive Behavior Therapy, Clearwater Beach, Florida.

Pickert, J. W., & Elam, P. (1985). Readability and writing. *Diabetes Dateline, 6*, 1–3.

Pickering, G. (1978). Medicine on the brink: The dilemma of a learned profession. *Perspectives in Biology and Medicine, 37*, 551–560.

Pickering, G. (1979). Therapeutics: Art or science? *Journal of American Medical Association, 242*, 649–653.

Podell, R. N. (1975). *Physician's guide to compliance in hypertension*. Merck, Sharp, & Dohme.

Podell, R. N., & Gary, L. R. (1976). Compliance: A problem in medical management. *American Family Physician, 13*, 74–80.

Pomerleau, O. F., Adkins, D., & Pertschuk, M. (1978). Predictors of outcome and recidivism in smoking cessation treatment. *Addictive Behaviors, 3*, 65–70.

Porter, A. M. (1969). Drug defaulting in general practice. *British Medical Journal, 1*, 218–222.

Powell, B. J., Othmer, E., & Sinkhorn, C. (1977). Pharmacological aftercare of homogeneous groups of patients. *Hospital and Community Psychiatry, 28*, 125–127.

Powell, B. J., Penick, E. C., Likow, B. I., Rice, A. S., & McKnelly, W. (1986). Lithium compliance in alcoholic males: A six-month followup study. *Addictive Behaviors, 11*, 135–140.

Pratt, C., Wilson, W., Porter, C., Kingsley, L., & Leklem, J. (1983). Nutrition/diabetes education and peer support groups' effect on dietary modification in older diabetes. *Gerontologist, 23*, 201.

Primakoff, L., Epstein, N., & Covi, L. (1986). Homework compliance: An uncontrolled variable in cognitive therapy outcome research. *Behavior Therapy, 17*, 433–446.

Pyrczak, F., & Roth, D. H. (1976). The readability of directions in nonprescription drugs. *Journal of The American Pharmaceutical Association, 16*, 242–244.

Ramsey, J. A. (1982). Participants in noncompliance research. Compliant or noncompliant. *Medical Care, 20*, 615–622.

Rapoff, M. A., & Christophersen, E. R. (1982). Compliance of pediatric patients with medical regimens: A review and evaluation. In R. B. Stuart (Ed.), *Adherence, compliance and generalization in behavioral medicine*. New York: Brunner/Mazel.

Raven, B. H., & Haley, R. W. (1982). Social influence and compliance of hospital nurses with infection control policies. In J. R. Eiser (Ed.), *Social psychology and behavioral medicine*. New York: John Wiley.

Reader, G. G., Pratt, L., & Mudd, M. C. (1957). What patients expect from doctors. *Modern Hospital, 89,* 88–94.

Reed, H. B., & Janis, I. L. (1974). Effects of a new type of psychological treatment on smokers' resistance to warnings about health hazards. *Journal of Consulting and Clinical Psychology, 42,* 748.

Rees, D. W. (1985). Health beliefs and compliance with alcoholism treatment. *Journal of Studies on Alcohol, 46,* 517–524.

Renne, C. M., & Creer, T. L. (1976). Training children with asthma to use inhalation therapy equipment. *Journal of Applied Behavioral Analysis, 9,* 1–11.

Richardson, J. L. (1986). Perspectives on compliance with drug regimens among the elderly. *Journal of Compliance in Health Care, 1,* 33–46.

Rodin, J., & Janis, I. L. (1982). The social influence of physicians and other health care practitioners as change agents. In H. S. Friedman & M. R. DiMatteo (Eds.), *Interpersonal issues in health care.* New York: Academic Press.

Rogalski, C. J. (1984). Professional psychotherapy and its relationship to compliance in treatment. *International Journal of Addictions, 19,* 521–539.

Rogers, R. W. (1983). Cognitive and physiological processes in fear appeals and attitude change: A revised theory of protection motivation. In J. Cacioppo & R. Petty (Eds.), *Social psychophysiology.* New York: Guilford Press.

Rogers, R. W., & Mewborn, C. R. (1976). Fear appeals and attitude change: Effects of threats, noxiousness, probability of occurrence and the efficacy of coping responses. *Journal of Personality and Social Psychology, 34,* 54–61.

Rook, K.S. (1986). Encouraging preventive behavior for distant and proximal health threats: Effects of vivid versus abstract information. *Journal of Gerontology, 51,* 526–534.

Rosenberg, S. G. (1976). Patient education—an educator's view. In D. L. Sackett & R. B. Haynes (Eds.), *Compliance with therapeutic regimens.* Balitmore: Johns Hopkins University Press.

Rosenstock, I. M. (1974). Historical origins of the health belief model. *Health Education Monographs, 2,* 328.

Rosenstock, I. M. (1985). Understanding and enhancing patient compliance with diabetic regimens. *Diabetes Care, 8,* 610–616.

Rosenstock, I. M., & Kirscht, J. P. (1979). Why people seek health care. In G. C. Stone, F. Cohen, & N. E. Adler (Eds.), *Health psychology.* San Francisco: Jossey-Bass.

Rosenthal, T. L., & Downs, A. (1985). Cognitive aids in teaching and treating. *Advances in Behaviour Research and Therapy, 7,* 1–53.

Roter, D. (1977). Patient participation in the patient–provider interaction. *Health Education Monograph, 54,* 281–306.

Roth, H. P. (1979). Problems in conducting a study of the effects on patient compliance of teaching the rationale for antiacid therapy. In S. J. Cohen (Ed.), *New directions in patient compliance*. Lexington, MA: Lexington Books.

Rudd, P. (1979). In search of the gold standard for compliance measurement. *Archives of Internal Medicine, 139*, 627–628.

Sackett, D. L. (1976). Priorities and methods for future research. In D. L. Sackett & B. Haynes (Eds.), *Compliance with therapeutic regimens*. Baltimore: Johns Hopkins University Press.

Sackett, D. L. (1979a). A compliance practicum for the busy practitioner. In R. B. Haynes, D. W. Taylor, & D. L. Sackett (Eds.), *Compliance in health care*. Baltimore: Johns Hopkins University Press.

Sackett, D. L. (1979b). Future applications and hypotheses from old research. In S. J. Cohen (Ed.), *New directions in patient compliance*. Lexington, MA: Lexington Books.

Sackett, D. L., & Haynes, R. B. (Eds.). (1976). *Compliance with therapeutic regimens*. Baltimore: Johns Hopkins University Press.

Sackett, D. L., & Snow, J. C. (1979). The magnitude of compliance and noncompliance. In R. B Haynes, D. W. Taylor, & D. L. Sackett (Eds.), *Compliance in health care*. Baltimore: Johns Hopkins University Press.

Sackett, D. L., Haynes, R. B., Gibson, S., Hackett, D. C., Taylor, D. W., Roberts, R. S., & Johnson, R. (1975). Randomized clinical trials of strategies for improving medication compliance in primary hypertension. *Lancet, 1*, 1205–1207.

Salovey, P., Rudy, T. E., & Turk, D. C. (1986). *The effects of health salience and the structure and consistency of health-protective attitudes and behaviors*. Unpublished manuscript, University of Pittsburgh Medical School, Pittsburgh, PA.

Schachter, S. (1982). Recedivism and self-care of smoking and obesity. *American Psychologist, 37*, 436–444.

Schaefer, L. C., McCaul, K. D., & Glasgow, R. E. (1986). Supportive and nonsupportive family behaviors: Relationships to adherence and metabolic control in persons with Type I diabetes. *Diabetes Care, 9*, 179–185.

Schafer, L. C., Glasgow, R. E., & McCaul, K. D. (1982). Increasing the adherence of diabetic adolescents. *Journal of Behavioral Medicine, 5*, 353–362.

Schafer, L. C., Glasgow, E., McCaul, K. D., & Dreher, M. C. (1983). Adherence to IDDM regimens: Relationship to psychological variables and metabolic control. *Diabetes Care, 4*, 493–498.

Schmarak, K. L. (1971). Reduce your broken appointment rate: How a children and youth project reduced its broken appointment rate. *American Journal of Public Health, 61*, 2400–2404.

Schmidt, J. P. (1979). A behavioral approach to patient compliance. *Postgraduate Medicine, 65,* 39–42.

Schneider, J. A., O'Leary, A., & Bandura, A. (1985). *The development of a scale to assess self-efficacy in bulimics.* Unpublished manuscript, Stanford University, Stanford, California.

Schulman, B. A. (1979). Active patient orientation and outcomes in hypertensive treatment. *Medical Care, 17,* 267–280.

Seltzer, A., & Hoffman, B. F. (1980). Drug compliance of the psychiatric patient. *Canadian Family Physician, 26,* 725–727.

Seltzer, A., Roncari, I., & Garfinkel, P. (1980). Effect of patient education on medication compliance. *Canadian Journal of Psychiatry, 25,* 638–645.

Sergis-Deavenport, E., & Varni, J. W. (1982). Behavioral techniques in teaching hemophilia factor replacement procedures to families. *Pediatric Nursing, 8,* 416–419.

Sergis-Deavenport, E., & Varni, J. W. (1983). Behavioral assessment and management of adherence to factor replacement therapy in hemophilia. *Journal of Pediatric Psychology, 8,* 367–377.

Shakir, S. A., Volkmar, F. R., Bacon, S., & Pfefferbaum, A. (1979). Group psychotherapy as an adjunct to lithium maintenance. *American Journal of Psychiatry, 136,* 455–456.

Shapiro, A. R. (1960). A contribution to the history of the placebo effect. *Behavioral Science, 5,* 109–135.

Sharpe, J. R., & Mikeal, R. L. (1974). Patient compliance with prescription medical regimens. *Journal of American Pharmaceutical Association, 15,* 191–192.

Shelton, J. L., & Ackerman, J. M. (1974). *Homework in counseling and psychotherapy.* Springfield, IL: Charles C. Thomas.

Shelton, J. L., & Levy, R. L. (1981). *Behavioral assignments and treatment compliance: A handbook of clinical strategies.* Champaign, IL: Research Press.

Shepard, D. S., & Moseley, A. E. (1976). Mailed versus telephoned appointment reminders to reduce broken appointments in a hospital outpatient department. *Medical Care, 14,* 268–273.

Sheridan, A., & Smith, R. A. (1975). Student–family contracts. *Nursing Outlook, 23,* 114–117.

Sherwin, A. L., Robb, J. P., & Lechter, M. (1973). Improved control of epilepsy by monitoring plasma ethosuximide. *Archives of Neurology, 28,* 178–181.

Shou, M. (1980). *Lithium treatment of manic-depressive illness: a practical guide.* New York: S. Karger.

Skillern, P. G. (1977). A planned system of patient education. *Journal of American Medical Association, 238,* 878–879.

Skolnick, B. D., Eddy, J. M., & St. Pierre, R. W. (1984). Medication compliance and the aged: An educational challenge. *Educational Gerontology, 10,* 307–315.

Skoutakis, V. A., Acchiardo, S. R., Martinez, D. R., Lorisch, D., & Wood, G. C. (1978). Role effectiveness of the pharmacist in the treatment of hemodialysis patients. *American Journal of Hospital Pharmacy, 35,* 62–65.

Slimmer, L. W. (1986, personal communication). *Balance sheet procedure.* Unpublished manual. Elmhurst College, Deicke Center for Nursing Education, 190 Prospect, Elmhurst, IL 60126..

Slimmer, L. W., & Brown, R. T. (1985). Parents' decision-making process in medication administration for control of hyperactivity. *Journal of School Health, 55,* 221–225.

Smith, S., Rosen, D., & Trueworthy, R. (1979). A reliable method for evaluating drug compliance in children with cancer. *Cancer, 43,* 169–173.

Southam, M. A., & Dunbar, J. M. (1986). Facilitating patient compliance with medical interventions. In K. Holroyd & T. Creer (Eds.), *Self-management of chronic disease.* New York: Academic Press.

Soutter, R. B., & Kennedy, M. C. (1974). Patient compliance in drug trials: Dosage and methods. *Australian and New Zealand Journal of Medicine, 4,* 360–364.

Spevack, P. A. (1981). Maintenance of therapy gains: Strategies, problems and promise. *JSAS Catalog of Selected Documents in Psychology, 11,* 35 (Ms. No. 2255).

Spriet, A., Beiler, D., Dechorgnat, J., & Simon, P. (1980). Adherence of elderly patients to treatment with pentoxifylline. *Clinical Pharmacology Therapy, 27,* 1–8.

Steckel, S., & Swain, M. (1977). The use of written contracts to increase adherence. *Hospitals, 51,* 81–84.

Sternbach, R. (1974). *Pain patients: Traits and treatment.* New York: Academic Press.

Stewart, R. B., Cuff, L. E., & Leighton, E. D. (1972). Commentary: A review of medication errors and compliance in ambulatory patients. *Clinical Pharmacology Therapy, 13,* 463–468.

Stimson, G. V. (1974). Obeying doctor's orders: A view from the other side. *Social Science and Medicine, 8,* 97–104.

Stone, G. C. (1979). Patient compliance and the role of the expert. *Journal of Social Issues, 35,* 34–59.

Stoudemire, A., & Thompson, J. L. (1983). Medication noncompliance: Systematic approaches to evaluation and intervention. *General Hospital Psychiatry, 5,* 233–239.

Strecher, V. J., DeVellis, B. M., Becker, M. H., & Rosenstock, I. M. (1986). The role of self-efficacy in achieving health behavior change. *Health Education Quarterly, 13,* 73–81.

Stuart, R. B. (1982). *Adherence, compliance and generalization in behavioral medicine.* New York: Brunner/Mazel.

Stunkard, A. J. (1975). From explanation to action in psychosomatic medicine: The case of obesity. *Psychosomatic Medicine, 37,* 195–236.

Stunkard, A. J. (1979). Adherence to treatment for diabetes. In B. A. Hamburg, L. F. Lipsett, G. E Inoff, & A. C. Drash (Eds.), *Behavioral and psychological issues in diabetes*. Washington, DC: U.S. Department of Health and Human Services.

Stunkard, A. J., & Mahoney, M. J. (1976). Behavioral treatment of the eating disorders. In H. Leitenberg (Ed.), *Handbook of behavior modification and behavior therapy*. New York: Appleton-Century Crofts.

Sue, S. (1977). Community mental health services to minority groups. *American Psychologist, 32*, 616–624.

Sullivan, R. J., Jr., Estes, E. H., Stopford, W., & Lester, A. J. (1980). Adherence to explicit strategies for common medical conditions. *Medical Care, 18*, 388–399.

Sutton, S. R. (1982). Fear-arousing communications: A critical examination of theory and research. In J. R. Eiser (Ed.), *Social psychology and behavioral medicine*. New York: Wiley.

Svarstad, B. L. (1974). *The doctor–patient encounter: An observational study of communication and outcome*. Unpublished doctoral dissertation, University of Wisconsin, Department of Sociology, Madison, Wisconsin.

Svarstad, B. L. (1976). Physician–patient communication and patient conformity with medical advice. In D. Mechanic (Ed.), *The growth of bureaucratic medicine: An inquiry into the dynamics of patient behavior and the organization of medical care*. New York: Wiley.

Swain, M. (1978). *Experimental intervention to promote health among hypertensives*. Paper presented at the annual meeting of the American Psychological Association, Toronto, Canada.

Sweeney, J. A., Van Bulow, B., Shear, M. K., Freedman, R., & Plowe, C. (1984). Compliance and outcome of patients accompanied by relatives to evaluations. *Hospital and Community Psychiatry, 35*, 1037–1038.

Szasz, T. S., & Hollender, M. H. (1956). A contribution to the philosophy of medicine: The basic models of the doctor–patient relationship. *Archives of Internal Medicine, 97*, 585–592.

Taylor, C. B., Agras, W. S., Schneider, J. A., & Allen, R. A. (1983). Adherence to instructions to practice relaxation exercises. *Journal of Consulting and Clinical Psychology, 51*, 952–953.

Taylor, D. W. (1979). A test of the Health Belief Model in hypertension. In R. B. Haynes, D. W. Taylor, & D. L. Sackett (Eds.), *Compliance in health care*. Baltimore: Johns Hopkins University Press.

Taylor, S. E., & Thompson, S. C. (1982). Stalking the elusive "vividness" effect. *Psychological Review, 89*, 155–181.

Taylor, S. E., Lichtman, R. R., & Wood, J. V. (1984). Compliance with chemotherapy among breast cancer patients. *Health Psychology, 3*, 553–562.

Tebbi, C. K., Cummings, K. M., Zevon, M. A., Smith, L., Richards, M., & Mallon, J. (1986). Compliance of pediatric and adolescent cancer patients. *Cancer, 58*, 1179–1184.

Tierney, W. M., Hui, S. L., & McDonald, C. J. (1986). Delayed feedback of physician performance versus immediate reminders to perform preventive care: Effects on physician compliance. *Medical Care, 24,* 659–666.

Tracy, J. (1977). Impact of intake procedures upon client attrition in a community mental health center. *Journal of Consulting and Clinical Psychology, 45,* 192–196.

Trostle, J. A., Hauser, W. A., & Susser, I. S. (1983). The logic of noncompliance: Management of epilepsy from the patient's point of view. *Culture, Medicine, and Psychiatry, 7,* 35–56.

Turk, D. C., Sobel, H. J., Follick, M. J., & Youkilis, H. D. (1980). A sequential criterion analysis for assessing coping with chronic illness. *Journal of Human Stress, 6,* 35–40.

Turk, D. C., Meichenbaum, D., & Genest, M. (1983). *Pain and behavioral medicine: A cognitive-behavioral perspective.* New York: Guilford Press.

Turk, D. C., Salovey, P., & Litt, M. D. (1985). Adherence: A cognitive-behavioral perspective. In K. E. Gerber & A. M. Nehemkis (Eds.), *Compliance: The dilemma of the chronically ill.* New York: Springer.

Turk, D. C., Litt, M. D., Salovey, P., & Walker, J. (1985). Seeking urgent pediatric care: Factors contributing to frequency delay and appropriateness. *Health Psychology, 4,* 43–59.

Turk, D. C., Holzman, A. D., & Kerns, R. D. (1986). Chronic pain. In K. A. Holroyd & T. L. Creer (Eds.), *Self-management of chronic disease: Handbook of clinical interventions and research.* Orlando, FL: Academic Press.

Turk, D. C., Rudy, T. E., & Salovey, P. (In press). Implicit models of illness. *Journal of Behavioral Medicine, 9,* 453–474.

Turk, D. C., & Kerns, R. D. (1985). *Health, illness, and families: A life-span perspective.* New York: Wiley-Interscience.

Turk, D. C., & Rudy, T. E. (In press). Coping with chronic illness: The mediating role of cognitive appraisal. In S. McHugh & T. M. Vallis (Eds.), *Illness behavior: Issues in measurement, evaluation, and treatment.* New York: Plenum Press.

Turk, D. C., & Speers, M. A. (1984). Diabetes mellitus: Stress and adherence. In T. Burish & L. Bradley (Eds.), *Coping with chronic disease.* New York: Academic Press.

Turner, A. J., & Vernon, J. C. (1976). Prompts to increase attendance in a community mental health center. *Journal of Applied Behavior Analysis, 9,* 141–145.

Van Putten, I. (1974). Why do schizophrenic patients refuse to take their drugs? *Archives of General Psychiatry, 31,* 67–72.

Varni, J. W. (1983). *Clinical behavioral pediatrics: An interdisciplinary biobehavioral approach.* New York: Pergamon Press.

Varni, J. W., & Babani, L. (1986). Long-term adherence to health care regimens in pediatric chronic disorders. In N. A. Krasnegor, J. D. Arasteh, and M. F. Cataldo (Eds.), *Child health behavior: A behavioral pediatrics perspective.* New York: Wiley.

Varni, J. W., & Wallander, J. L. (1984). Adherence to health-related regimens in pediatric chronic disorders. *Clinical Psychology Review, 4,* 585–596.

Vetter, H., Ramsey, L. E., Luscher, T. F., Schrey, A., & Vetter, W. (1985). Symposium on compliance—improving strategies in hypertension. *Journal of Hypertension Supplement, 3,* 1–99.

Vincent, P. (1971). Factors influencing patient noncompliance: A theoretical approach. *Nursing Research, 20,* 509–516.

Waitzkin, H., & Stoeckle, J. D. (1976). Information control and the micropolitics of health care. *Social Science and Medicine, 10,* 263–276.

Wandless, I., & Davie, J. W. (1977). Can drug compliance in the elderly be improved? *British Medical Journal, 1,* 359–361.

Warren-Boulton, E., Auslander, W. F., Gettinger, J. W. (1982). Understanding diabetes routines: A professional training exercise. *Diabetes Care, 5,* 537–541.

Watkins, J. D., Roberts, D. E., Williams, T. F., Martin, D. A., & Coyle, I. V. (1967). Observation of medication errors made by diabetic patients in the home. *Diabetes, 16,* 882–885.

Watkins, J. D., Williams, T. F., Martin, D. A., Hogan, M. D., & Anderson, E. A. (1967). A study of diabetic patients at home. *American Journal of Public Health, 57,* 452–259.

Watts, F. N. (1979). Behavioral aspects of management of diabetes mellitis: Education, self-care and metabolic control. *Behaviour Research and Therapy, 18,* 171–180.

Watzlawick, P., Weakland, J., & Fisch, R. (1974). *Change: Principles of problem formation and problem resolution.* New York: W. W. Norton.

Weinberger, E., & Agras, W. S. (1984). *The weight reduction efficacy questionnaire.* Unpublished manuscript, Stanford University, Stanford, CA.

Weintraub, M. (1976). Intelligent noncompliance and capricious compliance. In L. Lasagna (Ed.), *Patient compliance.* Mt. Kisco, NY: Futura.

Weintraub, M. (1984). A different view of patient compliance in the elderly. In R. E. Vestal (Ed.), *Drug treatment in the elderly.* Sydney: Adis Health Science Press.

Wenerowicz, W. J. (1979). The use of behavior modification techniques for the treatment of hemodialysis patient non-compliance: A case study. *Journal of Dialysis, 3,* 41–50.

Wheeler, D. D., & Janis, I. L. (1980). *A practical guide for making decisions.* New York: Free Press.

Whitcher-Alagna, S. (1983). Receiving medical help: A psychosocial perspective on patient reactions. In A. Nadler, J. D. Fisher, & B. M. DePaulo (Eds.), *New directions in helping.* New York: Academic Press.

Williams, R. L., Maiman, L. A., & Broadbent, D. N. (1986). Educational strategies to improve compliance with an antibiotic regimen. *American Journal of Diseases of Childhood, 140,* 216–220.

Williamson, J. W. (1971). Evaluating quality of patient care: A strategy relating outcome and process assessment. *Journal of the American Medical Association, 218,* 564.

Wilson, D. P., & Endress, R. K. (1986). Compliance with blood glucose monitoring in children with Type 1 diabetes mellitus. *Journal of Pediatrics, 108,* 1022–1024.

Wilson, G. A., McDonald, C. J., & McCabe, G. P. (1982). The effect of immediate access to computerized medical record on physician test ordering: A controlled clinical trial in the emergency room. *American Journal of Public Health, 72,* 698–702.

Wilson, G. T., & Brownell, K. D. (1980). Behavior therapy for obesity: An evaluation of treatment outcome. *Advances in Behaviour Research and Therapy, 3,* 49–86.

Wilson, W., Ary, D. V., Biglan, A., Glasgow, R. E., Toobert, M. A., & Campbell, D. R. (1986). Psychosocial predictors of self-care behaviors (compliance) and glycemic control in non-insulin-dependent diabetes mellitus. *Diabetes Care, 9,* 614–622.

Winkel, L. M., & Thompson, C. (1977). Motivating people to be physically active: Self-persuasion vs. behavioral decision making. *Journal of Applied Social Psychology, 7,* 332–340.

Wing, R. L., Epstein, L. H., Nowalk, M. P., & Lamparski, D. M. (1986). Behavioral self-regulation in the treatment of patients with diabetes mellitus. *Psychological Bulletin, 99,* 78–89.

Wolkon, G. H. (1986). Patient compliance in mental health continuum of care. *Journal of Compliance in Health Care, 1,* 75–90.

Worthington, E. L., Jr. (1986). Client compliance with homework directives during counseling. *Journal of Counseling Psychology, 33,* 124–130.

Wynder, E. L., & Hoffman, D. (1979). Tobacco and health. *New England Journal of Medicine, 300,* 894–903.

Yates, A. J., & Thain, J. (1985). Self-efficacy as a predictor of relapse following voluntary cessation of smoking. *Addictive Behaviors, 10,* 291–298.

Youngren, D. E. (1981). Improving patient compliance with self-medication teaching program. *Nursing, 11,* 60–61.

Ziesat, H. A. (1978). Behavior modification in the treatment of hypertension. *International Journal of Psychiatry in Medicine, 8,* 257–265.

Zifferblatt, S. M. (1975). Increasing patient compliance through the applied analysis of behavior. *Preventive Medicine, 4,* 173–182.

Zisook, S., & Gammon, E. (1981). Medical compliance. *International Journal of Psychiatry, 10,* 291–303.

Zola, I. K. (1981). Structural constraints on the doctor–patient relationship: The case of non-compliance. In L. Eisenberg & A. Kleinman (Eds.), *The relevance of social science for medicine.* New York: D. Reidel.

Author Index

Subject Index